Creating Infographics with Adobe Illustrator: Volume 2

2D and 3D Graphics

Jennifer Harder

Apress®

Creating Infographics with Adobe Illustrator: Volume 2: 2D and 3D Graphics

Jennifer Harder
Delta, BC, Canada

ISBN-13 (pbk): 979-8-8688-0040-5   ISBN-13 (electronic): 979-8-8688-0041-2
https://doi.org/10.1007/979-8-8688-0041-2

Copyright © 2024 by Jennifer Harder

Managing Director, Apress Media LLC: Welmoed Spahr
Acquisitions Editor: Spandana Chatterjee
Development Editor: James Markham
Editorial Assistant: Jessica Vakili

Cover designed by eStudioCalamar

Cover image designed by Freepik (www.freepik.com)

Distributed to the book trade worldwide by Springer Science+Business Media New York, 1 New York Plaza, Suite 4600, New York, NY 10004-1562, USA. Phone 1-800-SPRINGER, fax (201) 348-4505, e-mail orders-ny@ springer-sbm.com, or visit www.springeronline.com. Apress Media, LLC is a California LLC and the sole member (owner) is Springer Science + Business Media Finance Inc (SSBM Finance Inc). SSBM Finance Inc is a **Delaware** corporation.

For information on translations, please e-mail booktranslations@springernature.com; for reprint, paperback, or audio rights, please e-mail bookpermissions@springernature.com.

Apress titles may be purchased in bulk for academic, corporate, or promotional use. eBook versions and licenses are also available for most titles. For more information, reference our Print and eBook Bulk Sales web page at http://www.apress.com/bulk-sales.

Any source code or other supplementary material referenced by the author in this book is available to readers on GitHub. For more detailed information, please visit https://www.apress.com/gp/services/source-code.

Paper in this product is recyclable

Table of Contents

About the Author

Jennifer Harder has worked in the graphic design industry for over 15 years. She has a degree in graphic communications and is currently teaching Acrobat and Adobe Creative Cloud courses at Langara College. She is also the author of several Apress books and related videos.

About the Technical Reviewer

Sourabh Mishra is an entrepreneur, developer, speaker, author, corporate trainer, and animator. He is a Microsoft guy; he is very passionate about Microsoft technologies and a true .NET warrior. Sourabh started his career when he was just 15 years old. He has loved computers since childhood. His programming experience includes C/C++, ASP.NET, C#, VB.NET, WCF, SQL Server, Entity Framework, MVC, Web API, Azure, jQuery, Highcharts, and Angular. He is also an expert in computer graphics. Sourabh is the author of the book *Practical Highcharts with Angular* published by Apress. Sourabh has been awarded a Most Valuable Professional (MVP) status. He has the zeal to learn new technologies, sharing his knowledge on several online community forums.

He is a founder of "IECE Digital" and "Sourabh Mishra Notes," an online knowledge-sharing platform where one can learn new technologies very easily and comfortably.

Acknowledgments

For their patience and advice, I would like to thank the following people, for without them I could never have written this book:

- My parents, for encouraging me to read large computer textbooks that would one day inspire me to write my own books.

- My dad, for reviewing the first draft before I sent a proposal.

- My program coordinator, Raymond Chow, at Langara College, who gave me the chance to teach evening courses and allowed me to find new and creative ways to teach software.

- My various freelance clients whose projects, while working on them, helped me research and learn more about various topics.

At Apress, I would like to thank Spandana Chatterjee and Mark Powers for showing me how to lay out a professional textbook and pointing out that even when you think you've written it all, there's still more to write. Also, thanks to the technical reviewer for providing encouraging comments. And thanks to the rest of the Apress team for being involved in the printing of this book and making my dream a reality again. I am truly grateful and blessed.

Introduction

Welcome to the book *Creating Infographics with Adobe Illustrator: Volume 2*. This book is the second of a three-volume set.

What This Book Is About

In the previous book, we looked at the history and explored the basics of infographic creation.

In this book, you will be building on the knowledge you have acquired and then look at how to work with Illustrator's graphing tools as well as exploring two-dimensional and three-dimensional effects that can be applied to graphs and infographic illustrations. We will also explore the Image Trace panel and its features as well as look at an overview of the Perspective tools and related resources.

This book is divided into six chapters in which we will explore how to enhance your infographic creation. Much of what you learn in this book can also be applied to logo creation. If you are a beginner to the idea of infographics, make sure to review Volume 1 before moving on to the more complex ideas of this book like 3D or general page layout with text which we will explore in this volume and Scalable Vector Graphics (SVG) interactivity in Volume 3. As you work along in this book on projects, if you are a student, make sure to consult with your instructor about their thoughts on infographics as well as work with your fellow classmates to discover what makes an ideal infographic. They may have different thoughts on this topic than myself that will be insightful as well.

Here is a brief overview of the chapters in this volume:

- Chapter 1: Graphs and charts are an important part of 2D infographic creation, though if they only have solid colors, you may feel that they are unengaging to the audience. However, graphs have historically been a part of our lives for hundreds of years. This chapter will help you understand how to use Illustrator's graphing tools as well as how to add data.

- Chapter 2: In this chapter, we will continue to look at how to use Illustrator's graphing tools and use some additional graphing features that will make the information and graph stand out when you edit the design further. This will include looking at the Pattern Options panel as well as recoloring and working with Symbols.

- Chapter 3: In this chapter, we will continue to work with Illustrator for the manipulation of graphs from another application and also see how to retrace and alter graphics using the updated Image Trace panel and then review some additional graph ideas.

- Chapter 4: This chapter will explore various 2D effects that you can add to your infographics and text to enhance your design layout.

- Chapter 5: While 2D infographics and charts in Illustrator are great, we can also add a 3D effect to graphics to make them more engaging to the audience. 3D has been a part of Illustrator for many years; however, with the new 3D and Materials panel, we can adjust shadows, light, and symbols to make the infographic appear more realistic.

- Chapter 6: Based on what you have learned about graphs and 3D, this project focuses on how to turn your graphic into a more engaging 3D layout. We look at how to do this with multiple 3D objects overlayed onto a graph. Later, in the chapter, we look at some additional 3D ideas. Finally, we look at the basics of the Perspective Grid and its related tools for infographic creation.

Note: The data in this book that we will be using for the infographic design is purely fictitious and is subject to change. It is not meant to reflect any actual data, only act as a placeholder to display the graphic. For your own projects, you will want to have accurate and up-to-date data if you are going to present your infographic to the public.

- Volume 3 will focus on SVG interactivity and how it can enhance your infographic. This book also gives some additional ideas on infographics and 3D as well as additional thoughts on how to work with your client on your infographic project and what applications to explore next that are part of the Creative Cloud.

Adobe Illustrator

Adobe Illustrator is one of the many drawing applications that is part of the collection of the Adobe Creative Cloud when you have a subscription with the company. Refer to Figure 1.

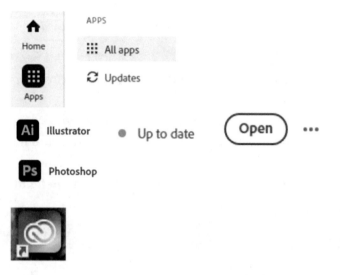

Figure 1. *Creative Cloud Desktop console with some applications and icon shortcut*

Note In this volume, it is assumed you have already downloaded and installed the Creative Cloud Desktop as well as the applications of Photoshop and Illustrator. For more details on how to do this, refer back to Volume 1 and these next sections to review those steps.

The topics in this book do not cover Adobe Illustrator for the iPad.

While some people like working with a single software like Photoshop, I prefer Creative Cloud because it offers you access to many applications including the web application as well as other applications in my plan which included Adobe Color that we saw in Volume 1. Refer to Figure 2.

Figure 2. *Link to Adobe Color online application via the Creative Cloud*

If you have purchased and downloaded the Creative Cloud Desktop console from Adobe, you will want to Install Illustrator along with Photoshop and InDesign on your desktop computer. You can refer to the section "System Requirements" if you need to first check whether your device can handle these applications. Refer to Figure 3.

Figure 3. *Desktop application icons for Photoshop, Illustrator, and InDesign that you can install*

System Requirements

If you are unsure if your computer meets the following requirements for running the latest version of Adobe Illustrator (Version 27.9) on your Windows or macOS desktop computers, then please consult the following links:

https://helpx.adobe.com/download-install/kb/operating-system-guidelines.html

https://helpx.adobe.com/creative-cloud/system-requirements.html

https://helpx.adobe.com/illustrator/system-requirements.html

With the Creative Cloud Desktop console visible, the installation steps are similar for all Adobe applications on your computer. I will, in the next section, "Install and Open Application Steps," give a brief overview of how to load and open your Illustrator application.

In this volume, you should have by now installed Photoshop and Illustrator. We will be using Illustrator mostly throughout this book, but Photoshop will be mentioned in this book as well and later in Volume 3.

Notice that when you download Photoshop, at the same time this will cause Camera Raw and possibly Bridge to download as well. That's OK. Though not required for this book, Camera Raw is a useful tool for color correction of photos and Bridge is great for keeping your images and photos organized. InDesign is a great layout application that can be used for incorporating graphics to create your final publication. Both Bridge and InDesign will be mentioned again in Volume 3. Refer to Figures 3 and 4.

Figure 4. *Adobe application icons Camera Raw and Bridge*

At this point, if you have not used any other applications before such as Animate, which comes with Media Encoder or Dreamweaver, you can wait on downloading them until Volume 3 as they are not required for this book, and I will merely be showing how these applications could be used later to incorporate your original infographics for additional interactivity. Refer to Figure 5.

Figure 5. *Adobe application icons Animate, Media Encoder, and Dreamweaver*

Note   Though not required for this book, for myself and my personal workflow, I also Install Acrobat Pro, as this application can assist you in your graphics workflow for PDF file creation after completing your work in InDesign. In addition, if you are doing a lot of video work, then you may also want to later install Premiere Pro, After Effects, and Audition for video and audio work. Though none of these are required for the book, they will be mentioned again in Volume 3. Refer to Figure 6.

Acrobat Premiere Pro After Effects Au Audition

Figure 6. *Adobe application icons Acrobat Pro, Premiere Pro, After Effects, and Audition*

Install and Open Application Steps

If you have not already installed Photoshop or Illustrator on your computer, as mentioned in Volume 1, then do so now from the Creative Cloud console. Refer to Apps ➤ All apps ➤ Desktop tabs. Click the Install button beside each application one at a time. Refer to Figure 7.

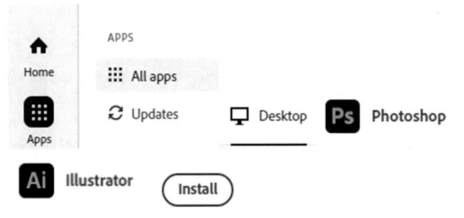

Figure 7. *Use the Adobe Creative apps Desktop area to install Photoshop and Illustrator*

The installation may take several minutes. You will then receive a notification once the installation is complete, and then from time to time, the Creative Cloud will send automatic updates to you as well as bug fixes. Some installations may require a computer restart. In the installed area, Photoshop and Illustrator will appear up to date. Then, to open, for example, Illustrator, just click the Open button on the same line. Refer to Figure 8.

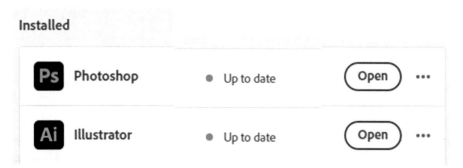

Figure 8. *Open these installed applications using the button*

The Illustrator application will then open after a minute, and then you will be presented with a desktop interface. We will look at this area throughout the book. But for now, if you want to close the application, then choose from the above menu File > Exit or Ctrl/CMD+Q, and Illustrator will close. Refer to Figure 9.

Figure 9. *Use Illustrator's File menu to exit Illustrator*

These are the same steps you can use with the Photoshop application, and then to close, use File ➤ Exit.

Additional Resources

While not required for this book, if you are interested in other related topics that I have written on Adobe applications, after you have read the three volumes on the topic of infographics, you might also want to view one of the following:

- *Graphics and Multimedia for the Web with Adobe Creative Cloud: Navigating the Adobe Software Landscape*

- *Accurate Layer Selections Using Photoshop's Selection Tools: Use Photoshop and Illustrator to Refine Your Artwork*

- *Perspective Warps and Distorts with Adobe Tools: Volume 1: Putting a New Twist on Photoshop*

- *Perspective Warps and Distorts with Adobe Tools: Volume 2: Putting a New Twist on Illustrator*

- *Data Merge and Styles for Adobe InDesign CC 2018: Creating Custom Documents for Mailouts and Presentation Packages*: While this is an older book, you could certainly use it to incorporate some of your graphic designs in future layout projects that involve mass mail-outs.

Also, for the most up-to-date information, make sure to use Adobe online help links which can be found at

- https://helpx.adobe.com/photoshop/using/whats-new.html
- https://helpx.adobe.com/illustrator/using/whats-new.html
- https://helpx.adobe.com/photoshop/user-guide.html
- https://helpx.adobe.com/illustrator/user-guide.html
- https://helpx.adobe.com/photoshop/tutorials.html
- https://helpx.adobe.com/illustrator/tutorials.html

I will be referring to these links throughout the book if you need additional information on a specific tool or panel. However, the focus of the book will be mostly on Illustrator, and it is assumed that you have some experience already with Photoshop.

You can also find these links in the Creative Cloud Desktop console when you hover over them in the installed area and click the icon. Refer to Figure 10.

Figure 10. *Adobe Creative Cloud and Help menu links to additional resources*

Or you can access similar areas in the Illustrator Help drop-down menu or the Discover panel that can be accessed via a magnifying glass icon when a file is open. The same settings are available in Photoshop as well, which are helpful for speeding up your workflow. Refer to Figure 11.

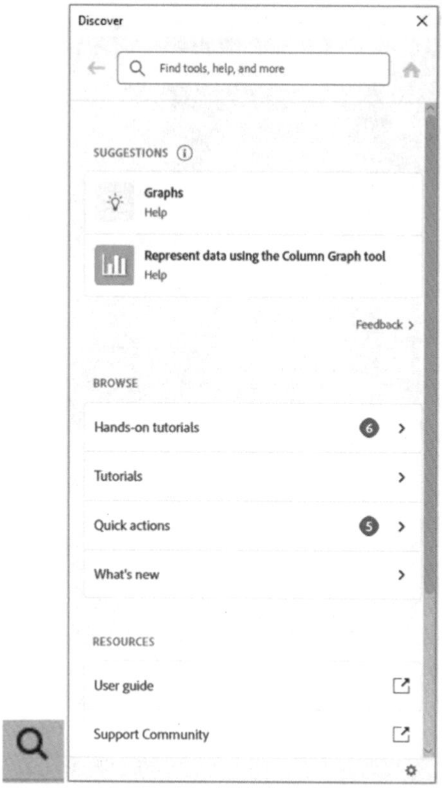

Figure 11. *Adobe Illustrator application icon and Discover panel*

Now that you are a bit more familiar with how to install and open Photoshop and Illustrator and have worked with them in Volume 1, let's continue our journey into infographic creation.

For this book, you can find the following project files for each chapter at this link: `http://github.com/apress/illustrator-basics`

CHAPTER 1

Illustrator's Graphing Tools: Creating a 2D Infographic – Part 1

In this chapter, you will be working with Illustrator graphing and drawing tools to create an infographic.

Graphing tools have been in Adobe Illustrator since 1993, yet I often, in the past, overlooked them because I did not fully understand their graphic potential and how I could later modify them to appear more infographic-like, with color, text, and design. This chapter focuses on the nine graph tools and how you can use them. In later Chapters 2 and 3, we will look at other Illustrator tools such as the Patterns panel and Image Trace panel to create unique graphic creations.

Note This chapter does contain projects that can be found in the Volume 2 Chapter 1 folder.

Some Early History Review

Earlier in Volume 1, we looked at some of the individuals who were influential in the creation of the graphs in the late 1700s and early 1800s. Playfair is believed to have been one of the first people to have created many of the graphs (originally called charts) that we use today, which include the column/bar graph, line, and area, as well as the pie.

However, out of all of them, the pie chart was the last, in 1801, to be used on a regular basis, but this did not happen until the work of Florence Nightingale 50+ years later and then Minard in 1858. Yet the pie chart has always remained controversial to some.

© Jennifer Harder 2024
J. Harder, *Creating Infographics with Adobe Illustrator: Volume 2*,
https://doi.org/10.1007/979-8-8688-0041-2_1

Edward Tufte, an American statistician and professor emeritus of political science, statistics, and computer science at Yale University, has written on topics of informational design and data visualization. He has made an interesting comment on the pie chart/graph in 1983: "The only thing worse than a pie chart is several of them."

Yet could this not be said to a certain degree about any chart or infographic if the data does not mesh together with the presented graphic?

In this chapter, we will next look at when to use the correct graph for the data you collect. Let's first begin by collecting the data in Microsoft Excel.

Collecting Data to be Graphed Using Microsoft Excel

Microsoft Excel is a good place to organize your data into tables once you have collected it. As we will see shortly, Illustrator has a similar simplified Graph Data table/window area layout for working with your charts, but more often, you will find it easier to work and move your data around in Excel and then apply it to your graph in Illustrator later on, via import or copy and paste. Also, you can save your Excel file as a backup for other projects when you need to edit the data again.

For practice in Microsoft Excel, let's first look at a few ways that you could layout your data. This will later determine how it will appear in Illustrator. You can view my Excel Data_Graph.xlsx if you would like to follow along.

Open up Microsoft Excel and create from the home page a new blank workbook to enter your data into the table cells. Refer to Figure 1-1.

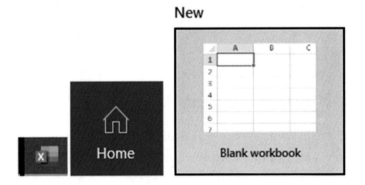

Figure 1-1. *Microsoft Excel icon and Home page icon and blank workbook selection*

Whatever your topic is you are working on, if you are just entering numbers, you may have a layout that looks something like this. It might be the start of a column graph. Refer to Figure 1-2.

	A	B	C
1	100	30	70
2	30	40	90
3	40	56	75
4			
5			

Figure 1-2. *Entering some data into a new Excel blank workbook*

However, if you plan to have data set labels with a legend, then you need to add them now.

To move your data to accommodate that, click in the first upper left cell A1 and then in whatever the lower right cell is, in this case, C3, and holding on to the right edge of the selection when the four arrows appear, drag the cells down one row and right one column. Refer to Figure 1-3.

	A	B	C	D
1	100	30	70	
2	30	40	90	
3	40	56	75	
4				
5				

	A	B	C	D
1	100	30	70	
2	30	40	90	
3	40	56	75	
4				
5				
6				

	A	B	C	D
1				
2		100	30	70
3		30	40	90
4		40	56	75

Figure 1-3. *Moving the data in Excel so that there is room for column headers and legends*

Now you can begin to add some headers to the rows and columns; however, make sure to keep cell A1 blank. At the moment, the text on the left will be below the data (column) in the graph, while the data on the top will be in the legend. Refer to Figure 1-4.

◢	A	B	C	D	E
1		"2021"	"2022"	"2023"	
2	January	100	30	70	
3	February	30	40	90	
4	March	40	56	75	
5					
6					

Figure 1-4. *Leave the A1 cell empty and add the text data into the correct cells*

Note If my labels are years rather than data numbers, I put them within straight quotes. We will look at this in more detail later in regard to organization and formatting for each chart/graph, but you could also, if doing a span of years, write 2022–2023 in the cell, and that would be OK. Note that the above orientation of labels will cause the date to be in the legend and the months to be below the column in the graph.

If the data is reversed, for example, the months are in the first top row, they would be in the legend and the dates below the column in the graph, which I will show you later in the chapters, as well as how to transpose your rows/columns if you discover you made a mistake in the ordering. Refer to Figure 1-5.

	January	February	March
"2021"	100	30	40
"2022"	30	40	56
"2023"	70	90	75

Figure 1-5. *While in Excel you may want to reorder your data if you need to display it a certain way in the graphic in Illustrator*

According to Adobe, the data should only contain decimal points, not commas, or the data will not be plotted. For example, you can enter 7007.2 but not 7,007.2.

Once you have completed typing in your data, then File ➤ Save first as a (.xlsx) file in your project folder. You can always use this file to copy and paste directly into Illustrator as you will see shortly. Refer to Figure 1-6.

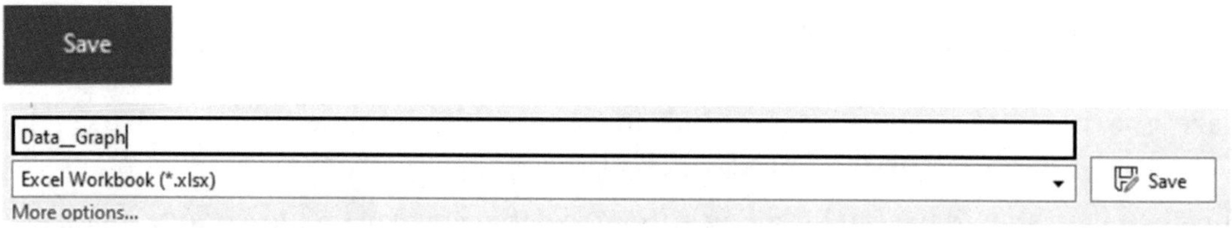

Figure 1-6. *After you complete your data, make sure to save your Excel workbook*

However, if you plan to import the data, then afterward File ➤ Save As in the following Text (Tab delimited) (*.txt) format which you can access from the drop-down list of options. If you open the file in a program like Notepad, you will see that the data is separated by tabs and the data in each row is separated by a paragraph return. Do not edit this file or remove any extra quotes that may appear. Refer to Figure 1-7.

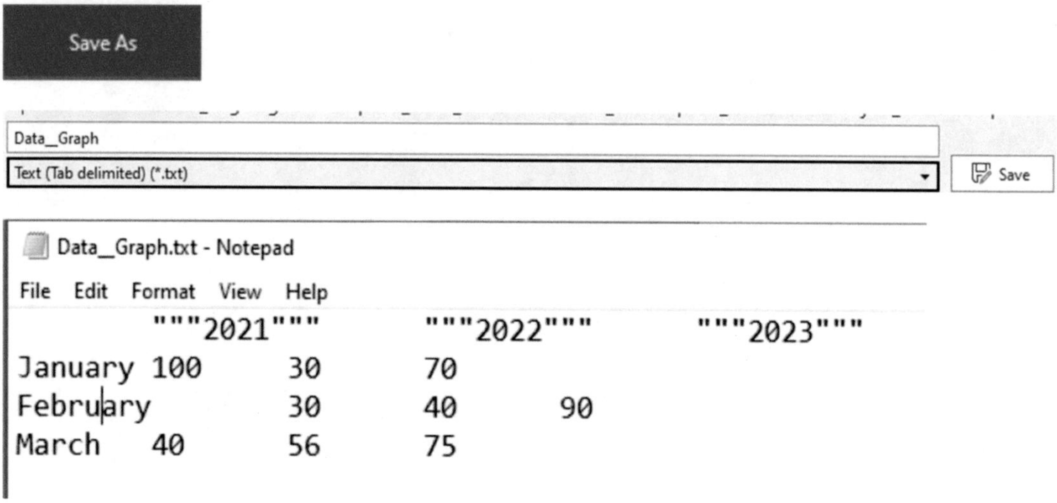

Figure 1-7. *If you plan to export your data to Illustrator, then you need to save as a Text (Tab delimited) (*.txt) file and how it appears when Notepad is open*

You can close your .txt file and remember if you want to make updates, always work from the .xlsx file and then save it as a new (Tab delimited) (.txt) file from the original if you need the file for import.

For now, you can close the (.txt) file but leave your (.xlsx) file open as we will look at it again later in the chapter.

Creating Your Illustrator Graph

Make sure that you have Illustrator Open, and, as you did in Volume 1 Chapter 4, use File ➤ New to create a new blank document letter (8.5×11 inches) CMYK color document. The document should have at least one artboard so that you can create a graph. Later, as described in that chapter and Volume 1 Chapter 5, "Working with Artboards and Saving Files," you can create more artboards or expand the current artboard as you practice creating more graphs as you go along. This section is just about practicing, for the moment. Refer to Figure 1-8.

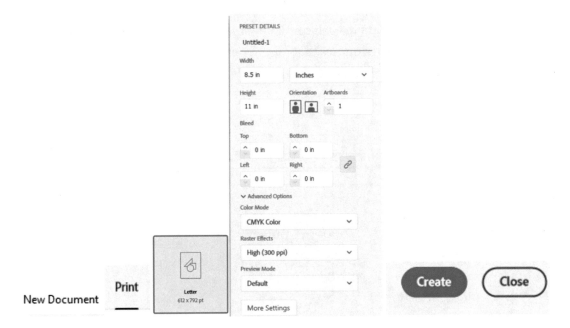

Figure 1-8. *Always practice with a new document as you learn about graphs*

Click Create and then make sure that your View ➤ Rulers ➤ Show Rulers are active. Refer to Figure 1-9.

Figure 1-9. *Illustrator Rulers are on in the new document*

Graphing Tools and Their Options

Now we will look at the nine graphing tool options in Illustrator: Column Graph Tool (J), Stacked Column Graph, Bar Graph, Stacked Bar Graph, Line Graph, Area Graph, Scatter Graph, Pie Graph, and Radar Graph. Refer to Figure 1-10.

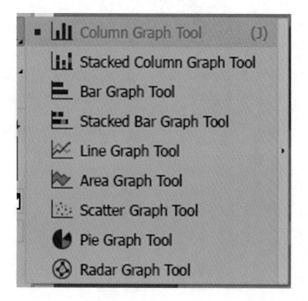

Figure 1-10. *Illustrator's graphing tools in the Toolbars panel*

To begin, we will start with the Column Graph Tool, but you can begin with any graph that you like and change it later. Double-click the graph tool in the Toolbars panel to reveal its options, or from the menu, choose Object ➤ Graph ➤ Type. This dialog box is what we will look at in more detail in a moment. But I will just point out that here you can easily switch to another graph by choosing a different type of icon if the current one does not suit your needs. Refer to Figure 1-11.

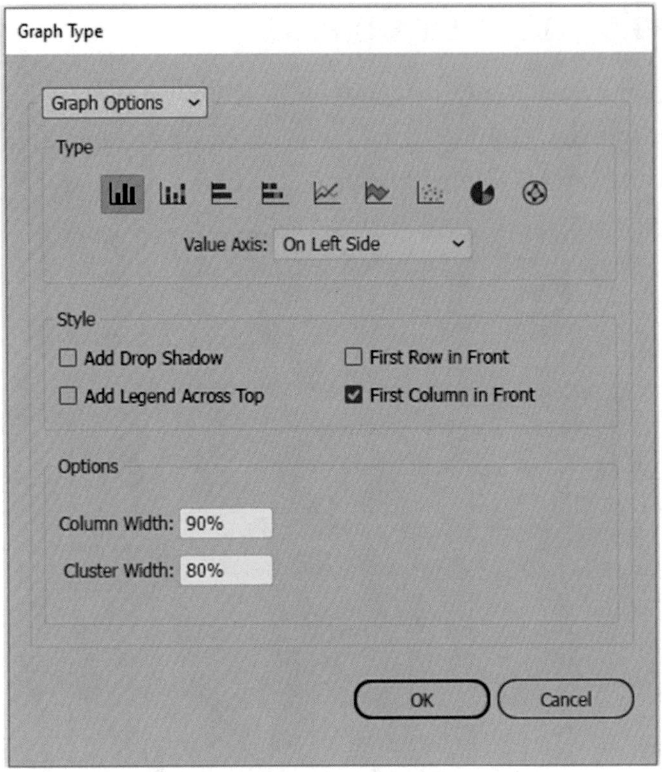

Figure 1-11. *Graph Type dialog box*

For the moment, click Cancel to exit this area. And now we will discuss these graph types one at a time.

Column

Also known as a bar or bar chart outside of Illustrator. In this case, it is called column because they rise vertically upward with positive numbers or lower downward if negative numbers are input. They are great for comparison of values of quantity and averages across a specific category, in this case, a duration of time.

They can be clustered into groups. Each item is a different color in clusters, and it is often, to the side, explained with a legend. Refer to Figure 1-12.

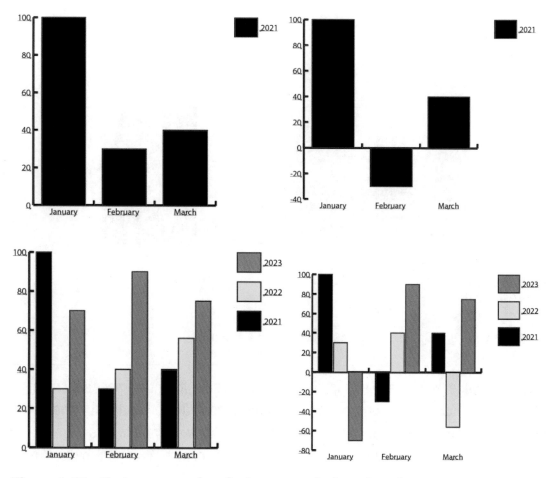

Figure 1-12. *Various examples of column graphs based on data*

They look good in a 3D shape and can be appear as boxes of cubes when extruded, as I will show later in Chapter 6 when we work on a project.

The actual subject of these graphs is currently ambiguous. Later with your type tools, as mentioned in Volume 1 Chapter 8, you would need to create your own heading so that we would know exactly what this was about such as "Annual Sales" for a specific product. I will look at adding type in more detail in this volume in Chapter 2.

To create your first graph, begin by selecting the Column Graph Tool and click the center of the artboard. The Graph dialog box will appear, and like basic shapes, you can use this area to set the width and height as well as constrain width and height proportions when the link is enabled. This step is the same for all graphs. Refer to Figure 1-13.

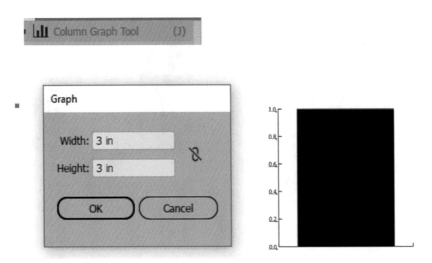

Figure 1-13. *Click the artboard and use the graph tool to create your first blank graph*

Once you click OK, the graph appears on the artboard.

Note Another way to add a graph is to drag diagonally from the upper left corner from where you want the graph to appear, downward to the lower right to where you want the graph to stop, Shift+Drag when you want the graph to be square, and Alt/Option+Drag when you want to drag from the center. You can also use Shift+Alt/Option+Drag as well.

In either method of starting the graph, note that this width and height dimension does not include the graph's legend or labels as they will take up additional space. Later, once the graph is completed, you can always scale and size your graph which we will look at later in Chapter 2. That is why you are practicing on a blank artboard first rather than incorporating it with other elements.

After adding your graph to the artboard, you will be presented with a default Column graph on the artboard, and in this example, one column has been started for you. You will alter this data in a moment using the Graph Data table window (Object ➤ Graph ➤ Data) which also appears beside the graph. Refer to Figure 1-14.

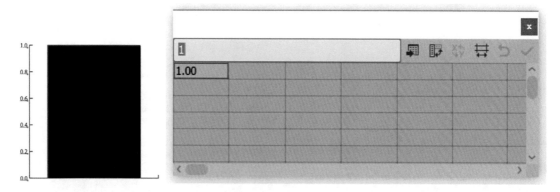

Figure 1-14. *Use the Graph Data window to enter you data*

Graph data as we will see in a moment needs to be entered and arranged in a specific order, and this can vary from graph to graph. In this example, we are focusing on arranging it for a column. The window will stay open as long as you are using a graphing tool, but you can also use your Selection tool if you need to move the graph around. However, if you use another tool, like the Pen tool, while the window is open, it will go blank but remain open. Choose the Selection tool again if you need to see the graph data in the window.

Let's look at the icons within the Graph Data window.

Graph Data Window Overview

In the Graph Data window, the first item from left to right is the entry text box. In this location, you can enter your text header or number data. Depending on what lower cell is selected, this is where that data will be entered. You can click a new cell and then use the entry text box to enter new data into that cell and then press the Tab key to move across the row to another cell or the Enter/Return key to move to a new cell in the column. Or you can use the Arrow keys on your keyboard to navigate the cells. Refer to Figure 1-15.

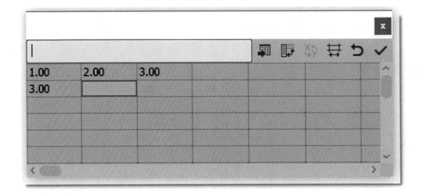

Figure 1-15. *You can use the Graph Data window to enter new data into each cell from the upper entry text box*

The first icon that looks like a list with a right-pointing arrow is the Import data button. Click the cell in the upper left and then click this import button icon, locate the (.txt) file, and click Open, and you will be able to import data that you created in Excel as a Text (.txt) file, and it will override the original data. Refer to earlier notes on settings from Excel if data does not import correctly. Click Cancel if you choose not to import. Refer to Figure 1-16.

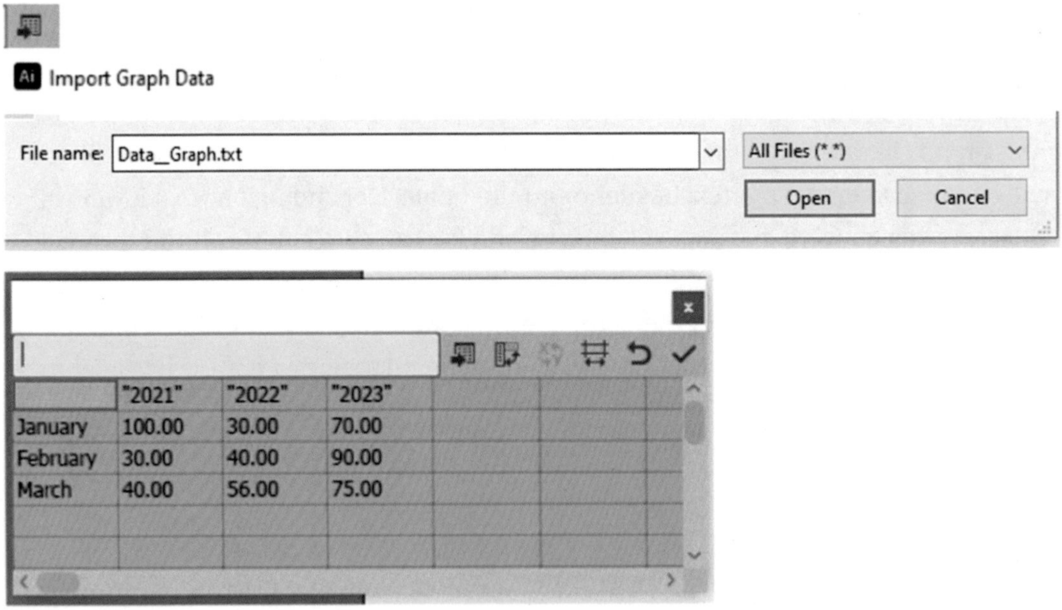

Figure 1-16. *Locate a (*.txt) file and then import the data the data into the Graph Data window*

Or, if you click Open and realize you made a mistake, you can use Ctrl/CMD+Z to undo the override of data.

You can continue to modify the imported data at this point. However, it will not be the same as the original Excel file. I will show you later how you can update if required.

The second icon that contains a double-headed arrow is the Transpose row/column. If you discover that the rows and columns are in the wrong order and you want to reorder them, click this Transpose button, and it will switch the columns and rows. Refer to Figure 1-17.

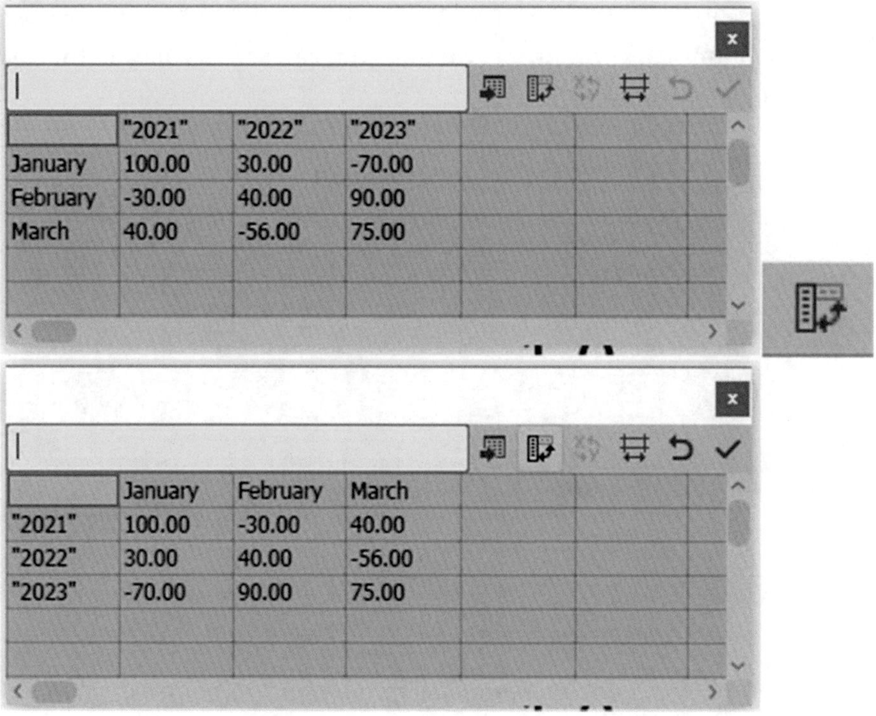

Figure 1-17. *Transpose the row/column data in the Graph Data window*

Click that icon again if you need to switch back; at this point the graph will not be altered until the check icon is clicked, which we'll do shortly.

The third icon which is currently grayed out because it is not available for column graphs is the Switch x/y; this allows you to switch the x and y axis of the graphs. Not all graphs will have this option, only scatter graphs; refer to the section "Scatter Graph" for more details. Refer to Figure 1-18.

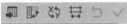

Figure 1-18. *Certain graphs like scatter will allow you to switch the x/y axis in the Graph Data window*

The fourth icon is the cell style. This allows you to adjust the number of decimal digits and column width digits within the Graph Data window. By default, it is set to decimal digits 2 and column width digits 7. The range is (0–10) for decimal and (0–20) for width. The following is set to decimal 3 and width 8. This will not affect the width of columns in the graph itself and is referred to later in this chapter under the section "Applying Graph Options" to know how to do that. You can set this back to the default settings for now. Refer to Figure 1-19.

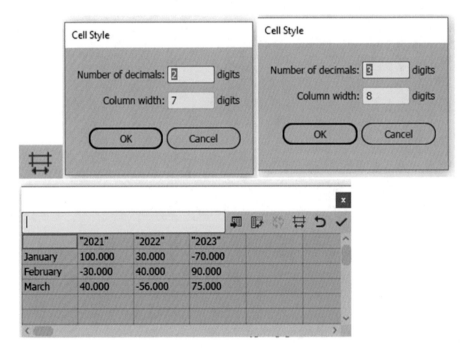

Figure 1-19. *Adjust the cell size in the Graph Data window and number of decimals using the Cell Style dialog box*

Note   When you change number of decimals and column width, if you have more than one graph active, this can cause the graphs/charts to group together. So keep these numbers the same for all graphs on the page while working.

These columns themselves can be manually adjusted. If you position your mouse pointer at the right edge of the column, it will change to double arrows and then drag on the edge until the column is the width you require. Narrow columns will hide some numbers. Use the next icon in the list if you need to reset the columns back to the original cell style. Refer to Figure 1-20.

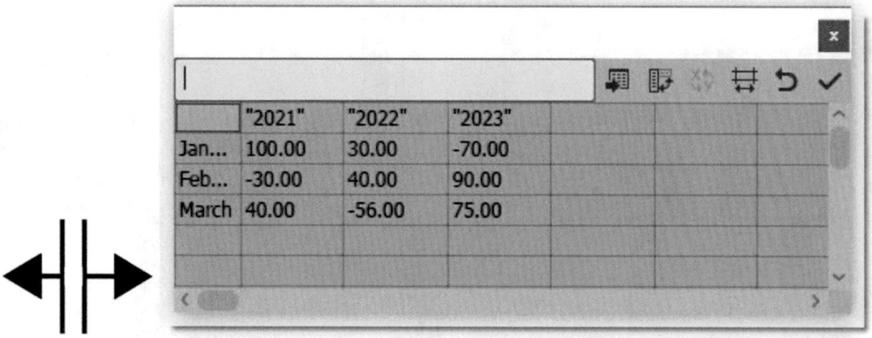

Figure 1-20. *You can manually adjust the width for each column in the Graph Data window by dragging on the columns*

The fifth icon, backward arrow, is when you need to revert a step in the changes that you made in the graph data adjustments and is much like Edit ➤ Undo, but for the graph. Likewise, as mentioned earlier, you can use the key command Ctrl/CMD+Z as well. Refer to Figure 1-21.

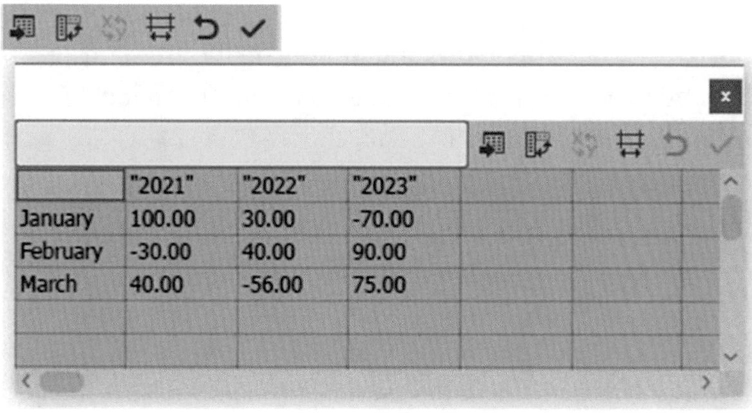

Figure 1-21. *Reset the columns or data in the Graph Data window with the backward arrow*

Once the change is made, it will disable until you make another change.

The sixth check icon is the Apply. Once you have entered or edited your data, click the check to update your graph. Refer to Figure 1-22.

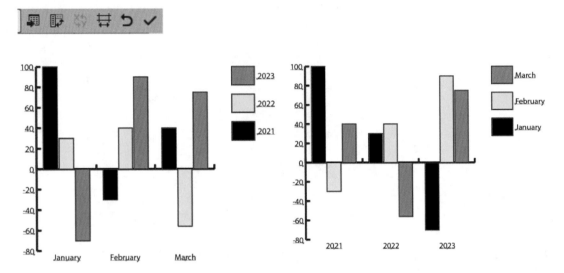

Figure 1-22. *Click the check in the Graph Data window when you want to apply the data to the graph*

If you switch to the Transpose row/column icon, click the check to update your graph. Refer to Figure 1-22.

After you have finished working with the Graph Data window, you can close it by clicking on the red X in the upper right of the window. If you have not saved your data, you may get an alert, click Yes. This allows you to work on the artboard again, File ➤ Save the graph and file, and move the graph around with the Selection tool. If you need to enter this area again, then from the main menu, choose Object ➤ Graph ➤ Data. Refer to Figure 1-23.

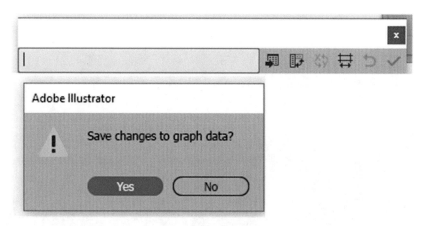

Figure 1-23. *Click the red (X) to close in the Graph Data window and alert message*

Use the lower and right siders on the window when you want to navigate around and view larger amounts of data. Refer to Figure 1-21.

Note   Another way to enter your data if you do not want to use the Import data button is to simply from the Excel file (.xlsx) Shift+click select and copy (Ctrl/CMD+C) the cells in the worksheet you want to use for your Graph Data window, and then in Illustrator, Shift+click the cells that you want to enter the new data into and then Edit ➤ Paste (Ctrl/CMD+V) them into the Graph Data window and click the Apply icon check to update. Refer to Figures 1-24 and 1-25.

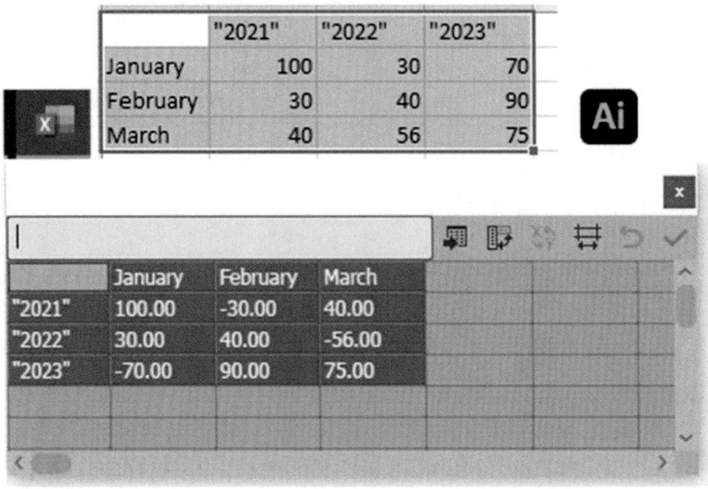

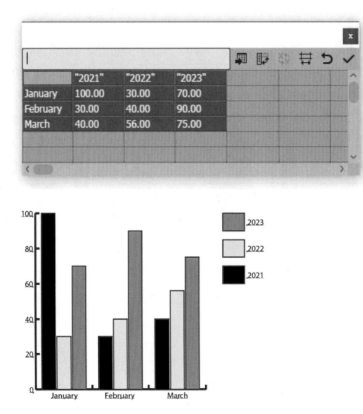

Figure 1-24. *Copy data from Excel workbook and select the area in Illustrator's Graph Data window that you want to paste the text into*

Figure 1-25. *Paste the new data into the Graph Data window and then click the check to update the data*

Data can be copied (Ctrl/CMD+C) and pasted (Ctrl/CMD+V) from another cell while in the window, and if you need to remove information from a selected cell, click the delete button. Or highlight the text in the data entry window and press Backspace/Delete.

Likewise, you can copy and paste numbers back into Excel if you have made some changes in Illustrator.

Adding of Graph Labels and Data Sets

Whether you entered the data in the field via Excel or typed it in yourself, you may want to edit the data by adding some graph labels or organizing your data sets. As you can see in the earlier examples, this was already done. However, you may want to do this if you just created it in Illustrator and currently no labels are added. Refer to Figure 1-26.

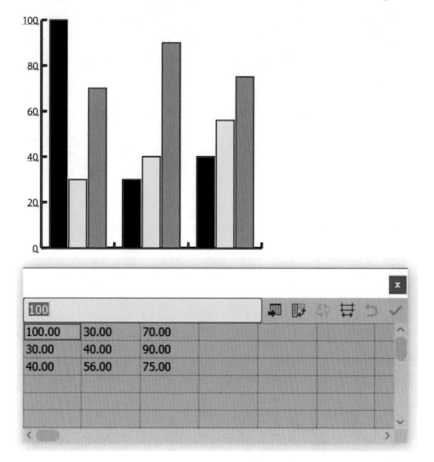

Figure 1-26. *The chart contains no labels or legends or categories*

Labels can be in the form of words or numbers that can be used to describe either your sets of data for comparison or categories that you want to compare them against. Without them, you will have no labels in the graph.

Besides the current column graph, here are some tips for how the labels should appear. These settings can later be applied to other graphs such as the stack column, bar stacked bar, line, area, and radar graphs:

- When you create Labels for both the column and legend at the same time, always leave the upper left cell blank if you want to generate a legend. Otherwise, no legend or category will appear together. Refer to Figure 1-30.

- For the column headings or data set labels, enter a word in the top row, and these labels will appear on the legend. If you don't want a legend, then do not enter these data set labels. If all labels are across the top, only a legend is generated with no category. So, in this case, we want to leave the left column in the Graph Data window blank for now. Refer to Figures 1-27 and 1-28.

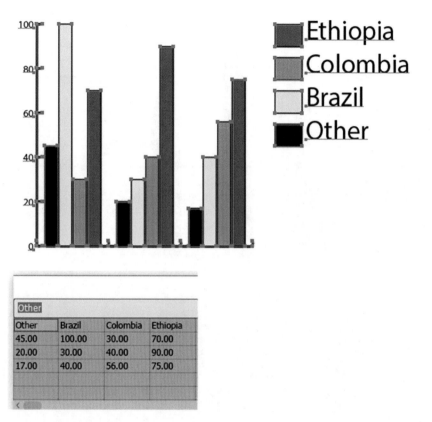

Figure 1-27. *When you enter text into the upper header of the Graph Data window, this creates legend*

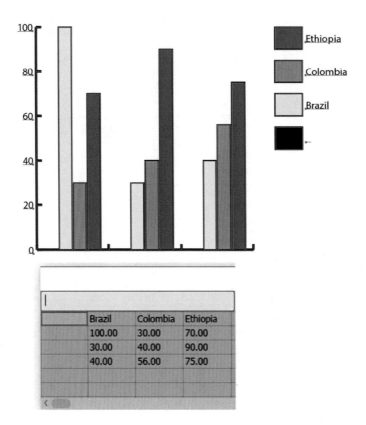

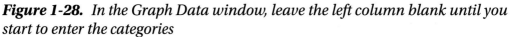

Figure 1-28. *In the Graph Data window, leave the left column blank until you start to enter the categories*

Now you would

- For the category, use the left column below the blank cell to enter the categories. Categories can be number units of time duration which may be the day, the month, or the year. These labels, depending upon the type of graph chosen, will appear along the horizontal or vertical axis. Refer to Figures 1-28 and 1-29.

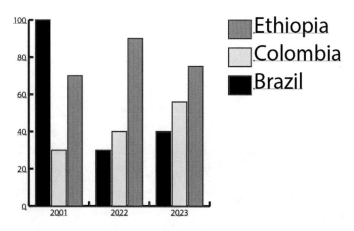

Figure 1-29. *Adding of categories to a graph*

The exception is the radar graph which we will look at later. In that case, each label will result in a separate axis.

- So that Illustrator does not confuse numbers (values) and year labels when a label is all numbers such as 2022, make sure to add straight quotations around it like this "2022". Refer to Figure 1-30.

	Brazil	Colombia	Ethiopia	
"2001"	100.00	30.00	70.00	
"2022"	30.00	40.00	90.00	
"2023"	40.00	56.00	75.00	

Figure 1-30. *Add straight quotes so that in the Graph Data window, Illustrator does not confuse the labels for the category with actual data*

- In some situations, you may want to have line breaks in your label so that it does not flow all onto one line. To space the words in the cell, you would then use the vertical bar key (|) to separate the lines. You could type it in the cell Sales |in| 2021, and it would produce this on the graph when you click the Apply check. Refer to Figure 1-31.

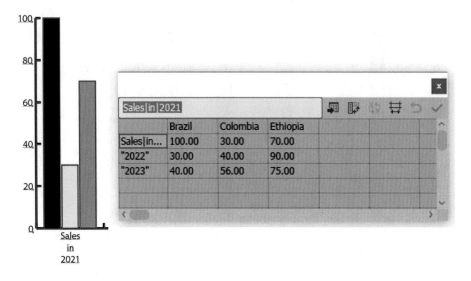

Figure 1-31. *Using the Graph Data window, you can add category labels with more than one line*

Remember   In the case of data sets for the column graph, you can combine positive and negative numbers; positive numbers above and negative numbers below. The height of the column and numbers on the left side of the graph Value Axis will adjust as new data is added to the graph. Refer to Figure 1-32.

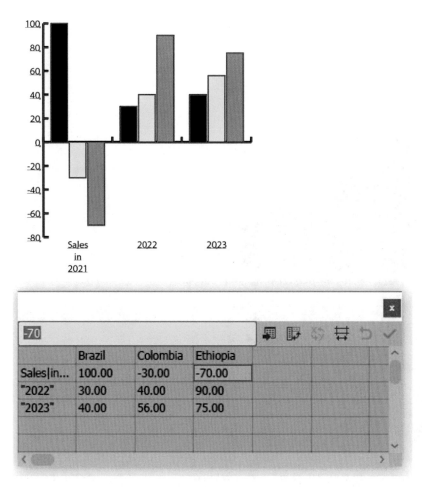

Figure 1-32. *Column graphs can have positive and negative numbers which can be entered into the Graph Data window and confirmed with a check*

Example: Coffee Production

Here you can see the beginning of a nonclustered graph that could represent the results of coffee production for a set year. We will explore how to adjust the colors from the default black for this graph later in Chapter 2 and then make it appear more 3D-like later in Chapter 6. Refer to Figure 1-33.

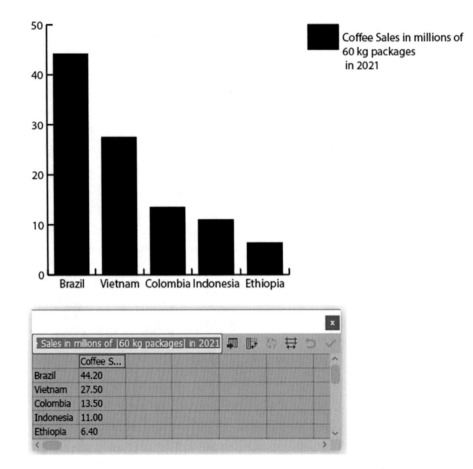

Figure 1-33. *Create a noncluster column graph when you do not want a lot of data using the Graph Data window*

Stacked Column

Similar to the column graph. However, a stacked column graph will display more data in each column, often as a type of composite range. The range is used for comparison of a few variables, either relative or absolute, over time. Rather than one item, they deal with a collection of related things that change within the group. They represent the combined result. Like the column graph, it can accept positive (above) and negative numbers (below). But you cannot have both kinds of values at the same time in one stacked column. The category column must be either all positive or all negative values. Each item is a different color and is often explained with a legend adjacent to the graph.

The height of the column and numbers on the left side of the graph will adjust as new data is added to the graph. Refer to Figure 1-34.

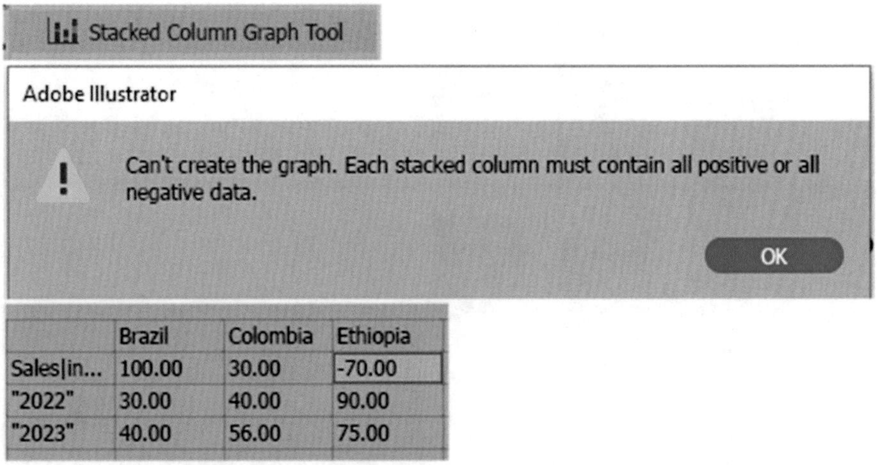

	Brazil	Colombia	Ethiopia
Sales|in...	100.00	30.00	-70.00
"2022"	30.00	40.00	90.00
"2023"	40.00	56.00	75.00

Figure 1-34. Stacked Column Graph Tool: Stacked column graphs will give a warning if you try to add both positive and negative numbers to a Category column using the Graph Data window, and the graph will not generate or update

For more details on how to add the graph to your artboard and edit the labels, refer to the section "Column Graph" earlier in the chapter.

Example of a Clustered Stacked Column Graph

Here is how information could appear in a clustered stacked graph. Refer to Figure 1-35.

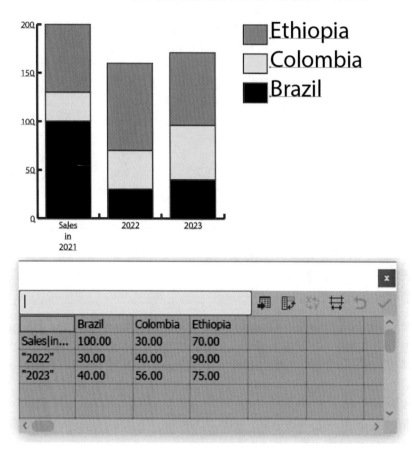

Figure 1-35. *Stacked column graphs can be set up the same as a column graph using the Graph Data window*

Likewise, if you needed to see how those sales were for each country collectively by years, you could transpose the row and columns with the second icon to see a different result. Refer to Figure 1-36.

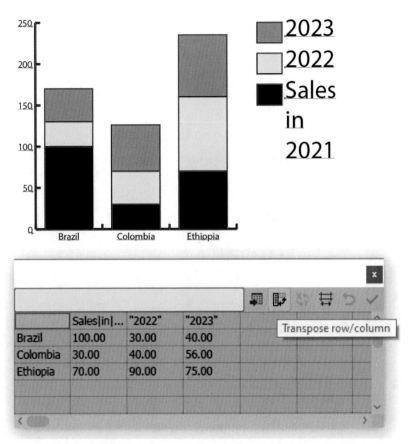

Figure 1-36. *Transpose row/column in the Graph Data window when you want to view your data differently for the stacked column graph*

Bar Graph

Similar to a column. In this case, because they are a bar, they move horizontally right with positive number values or horizontally left if negative number values are input. They are great for comparison of things and for visually greater and lesser quantities and averages for specific items or a category over a duration of time. They can be clustered. Each item is a different color and is often explained with a legend adjacent to the graph. The length of the column and numbers on the lower side of the graph (Value Axis) will adjust as new data is added to the graph. Refer to Figure 1-37.

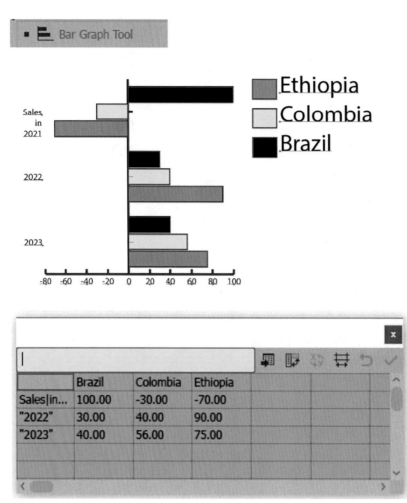

Figure 1-37. *Bar Graph Tool: The Bar Graph data can be set up the same as a column graph using the Graph Data window for a cluster*

They look good in a 3D shape and can be appear as boxes or cubes when extruded, which we will look at later when editing a graph in Chapter 6.

For more details on how to add the graph to your artboard and edit the labels, refer to the section "Column Graph" earlier in this chapter. As with the column graph, the data can be transposed from row to column. Refer to Figure 1-38.

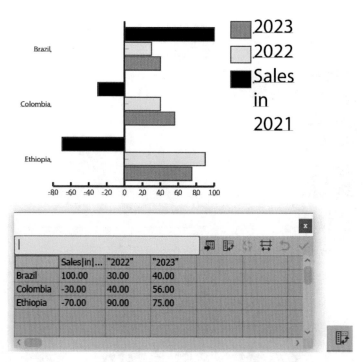

Figure 1-38. *Transpose row/column in the Graph Data window when you want to view your data differently for the bar graph*

Example: Coffee Production

Here is an example of the same coffee production graph, now in a bar graph orientation. Refer to Figure 1-39.

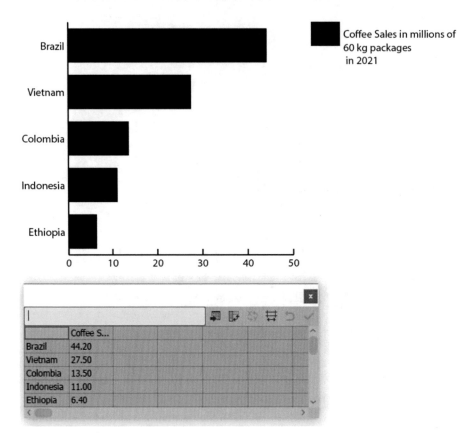

Figure 1-39. *Create a noncluster bar graph when you do not want a lot of data using the Graph Data window*

Stacked Bar Graph

Similar to the bar graph. However, a stacked bar graph will display more data in each row, often as a type of composite range. The range is used for comparison of a few variables, either relative or absolute, over time. Rather than one item, they deal with a collection of related things that change within the group. Like the bar graph, it can accept positive (right) and negative (left) numbers. But you cannot have both kinds of values at the same time in one category column. They must be either all positive or all negative values. Each item is a different color and is often explained with a legend adjacent to the graph. Refer to Figure 1-40.

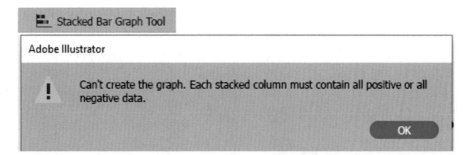

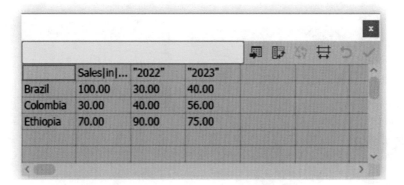

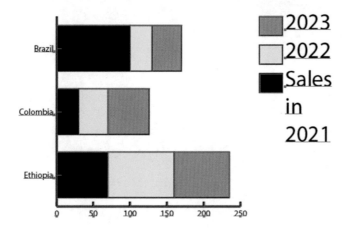

Figure 1-40. *Stacked Bar Graph Tool: Stacked column graphs will give a warning if you try to add both positive and negative numbers using the Graph Data window for one category and the graph will not generate or update. Positive data was entered in the Graph Data window to generate the graph*

The length of the bar and numbers on the lower side (Value Axis) of the graph will adjust as new data is added to the graph.

For more details on how to add the graph to your artboard and edit the labels, refer to the section "Column Graph" earlier in this chapter.

Example of a Clustered Stacked Bar Graph

Here is how information could appear in a clustered stacked bar graph with the data transposed for row/column. Refer to Figure 1-41.

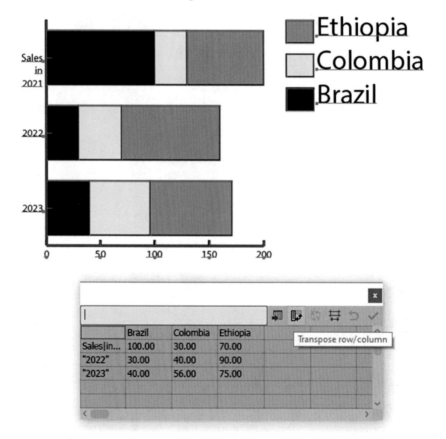

Figure 1-41. *Transpose row/column in the Graph Data window when you want to view your data differently for the stacked bar graph*

Note   In the case of bar or column graphs, you may prefer one or the other depending upon the area you have for your layout.

Line Graph

Probably one of the oldest types of graphing charts going back to the 1700s.

The line graph or curve chart is good for showing a continuous change of trends over time as the values go up or down. The points of data are called "markers" connected by straight line segments. You can show one item or compare several as they increase or decrease over time. You can use positive and negative input numbers to input data. This is good for when you want to review cost increase or decrease. Each line is a different color and is often explained with a legend adjacent to the graph.

They have an x axis (horizontal) and a y axis (vertical). Usually, the x axis has numbers or dates for the time period (category), and the y axis has numbers for what is being measured (value) such as an increase or decrease in income when looking at finance or speed of an object. Refer to Figure 1-42.

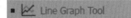

Figure 1-42. *Line Graph Tool*

For more details on how to add the graph to your artboard and edit the labels, refer to the section "Column Graph" earlier in this chapter.

Each column of data will correspond to one line in the line graph. Negative and positive values can be added and will then fall below or rise above the 0 baseline.

Example: Fossil Fuel Usage Over Time

Here we can see how positive and negative numbers appear for a certain country over time. Refer to Figure 1-43.

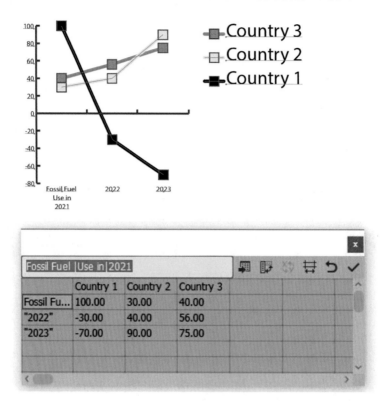

Figure 1-43. *Line graphs can have positive and negative numbers which can be entered into the Graph Data window and confirmed with a check icon*

Here is the same example again, now with the data transposed for row and column. But presenting the data this way would be confusing. Refer to Figure 1-44.

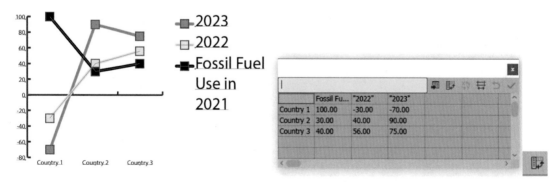

Figure 1-44. *Transpose row/column in the Graph Data window when you want to view your data differently for the line chart*

Note   You would still have to determine, for your project, what the values represent and add some supplementary text near the graph with the Type tool which you will look at more in Chapter 2.

Area Graph

This type of chart was also created around the same line as the line graph in the later 1700s.

The area graph has some similarities to the Line Graph Tool and again is good for continuous changes over time as the values go up and down. But all number values must be either negative or positive when input for each category. There cannot be negative and positive values in the same chart category or you will get an error. They share some similarities to stacked columns and bar charts in that the data is overlayed or shaded in below. It can help in visualizing a connectedness within a collective. Each area is a different color and is often explained with a legend adjacent to the graph. Refer to Figure 1-45.

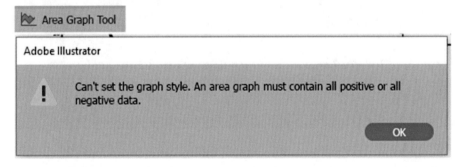

Figure 1-45. *Area Graph Tool: Stacked column graphs will give a warning if you try to add both positive and negative numbers for a single category using the Graph Data window and the graph will not generate or update*

For more details on how to add the graph to your artboard and edit the labels, refer to the section "Column Graph" earlier in this chapter.

Example: Fossil Fuel Usage Over Time

Here is an example of the same data using the area graph over time. Refer to Figure 1-46.

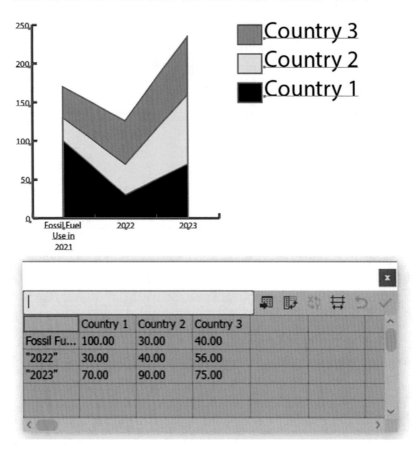

Figure 1-46. *Positive data entered into an area graph using the Graph Data window*

Note   Each row of data entered will correspond to a filled area on the graph. Area graphs will add each column value to the previous column's total. This causes the area graph and the line graph to appear different even if they contain the same data. Depending on how you want the data to display, this is something to consider. Refer to Figures 1-46 and 1-47.

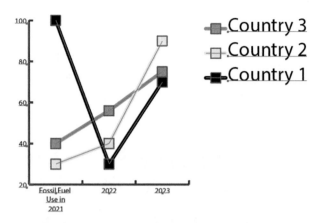

Figure 1-47. *Same data was used to create a line graph instead of an area graph*

As well, if you transpose the row and column, this can be confusing depending on the kind of the data presented. Refer to Figure 1-48.

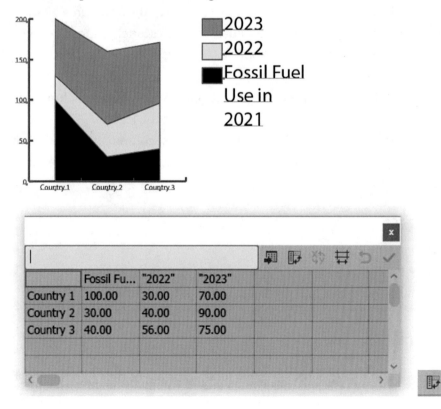

Figure 1-48. *Data in this area graph is a harder to interpret because the data was transposed*

Scatter Graph

Often used with line charts and shows the relationship between two sets of values. The "markers" or data point appear to be scattered all over the graph randomly. However, with a few connected lines, this can bring some order to the confusion so that we can see what the trend is among the scattered markers. Refer to Figure 1-49.

Figure 1-49. *Scatter Graph Tool*

Each area marker and line is a different color and is often explained with a legend adjacent to the graph.

For more details on how to add the graph to your artboard and edit the labels, refer to the section "Column Graph" earlier in the chapter.

A scatter graph, as you will discover, is not the same as the other previously mentioned graphs as both axes measure values, but only scatter graphs allow you to switch the x and y axes. There is also no option for categories, so you must set up your data set labels a bit differently.

You must enter data set labels in every other cell, starting with the leftmost cell along the top row of the cell worksheet. These labels appear in the legend.

When you enter the y axis, place this value in the first column and the x axis in the second column of that set; they can have data set headers as well but in the second row. Refer to Figure 1-50.

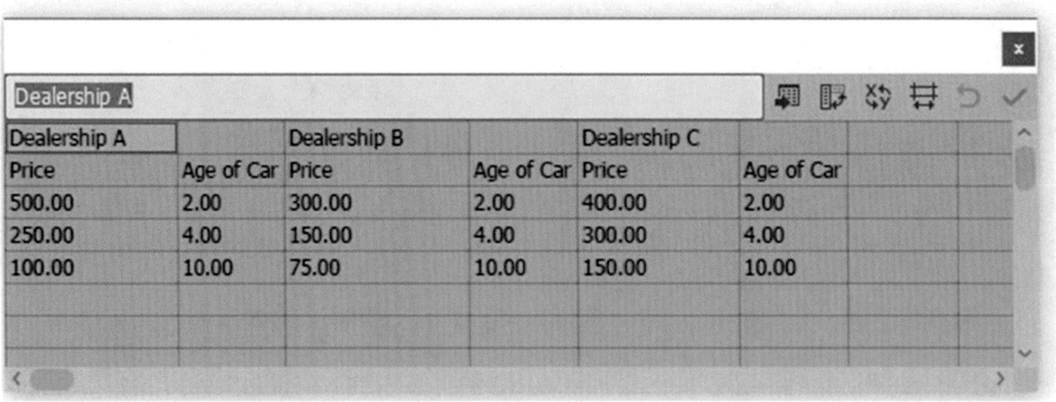

Dealership A		Dealership B		Dealership C			
Price	Age of Car	Price	Age of Car	Price	Age of Car		
500.00	2.00	300.00	2.00	400.00	2.00		
250.00	4.00	150.00	4.00	300.00	4.00		
100.00	10.00	75.00	10.00	150.00	10.00		

Figure 1-50. *Care must be taken to get your data correct in the Graph Data window when creating a scatter graph*

Note   Always check your options before starting this type of graph. You can use my file Scatter_Graph.xlsx if you need some data to practice with.

Refer to the section "Applying Graph Options" if you need to disable the connected data points and make it appear more scattered without the lines. Refer to Figure 1-51.

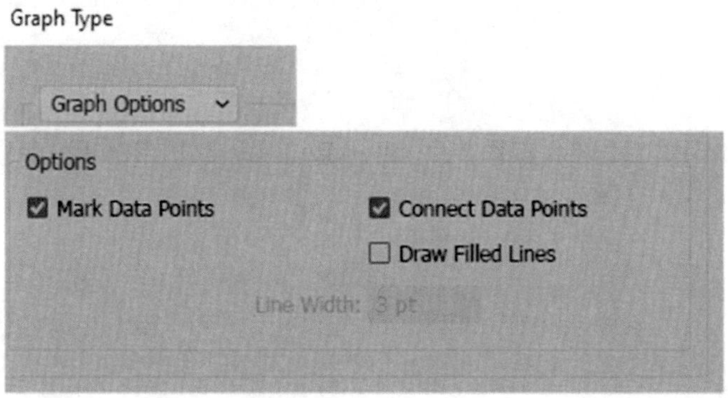

Graph Type

Graph Options   ⌄

Options
☑ Mark Data Points   ☑ Connect Data Points
                           ☐ Draw Filled Lines

Line Width: 3 pt

Figure 1-51. *Check your Graph Options for the scatter graph if you want to ensure the data point are connected or not*

Example: Car dealership Age of Car and Price

Here we can see the result of the scatter graph after adding the data. Note that you would have to add some supplemental text to explain the axis of age of car and price. Refer to Figure 1-52.

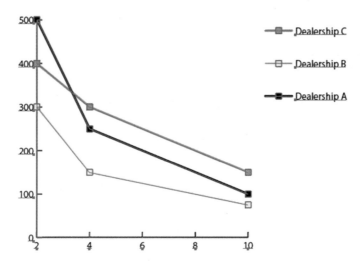

Figure 1-52. *Scatter graph generated from Graph Data window*

The same data can have its rows and columns transposed. Refer to Figure 1-53.

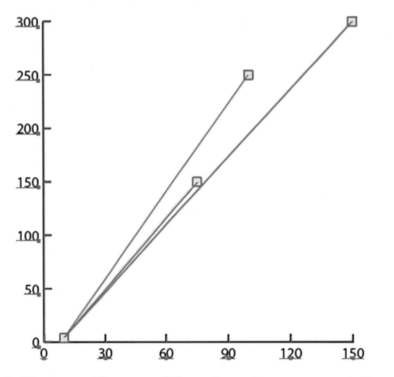

Figure 1-53. *Data will appear differently on the scatter graph if you transpose the row/column in the Graph Data window*

You can also switch the x/y axes. Though keep in mind that if you do this too many times, the data can become confusing and jumbled, so always keep a backup copy in your Excel workbook file when you can't figure out how to revert to the original values layout. Refer to Figure 1-54.

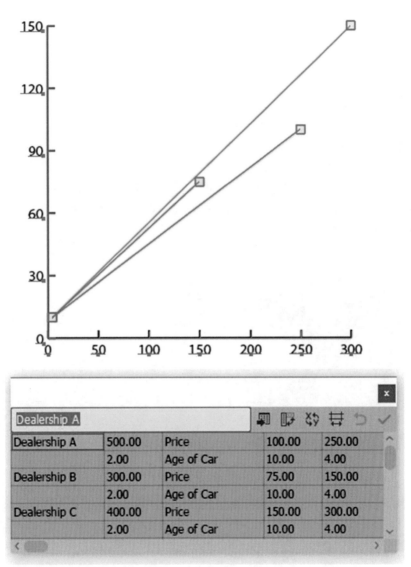

Figure 1-54. *Data will appear differently on the scatter graph if you transpose the x and y coordinates in the Graph Data window and starts to jumbled when switched too many times*

Pie Graph

The pie or circle chart is often used to address percentages or to look at a whole collection of items or parts as they add up to 100% and see what share they have in a piece of the pie. As mentioned, it was created in 1801 but took some decades to become popular. It is often good for visualizing such questions as what percent of the population "does" a specific thing, which could include speaking a certain language, what they believe, or how they vote. Refer to Figure 1-55.

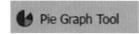

Figure 1-55. *Pie Graph Tool*

However, it could also represent how much space something takes up in volume compared to other things, for example, which moons are larger around a certain planet compared to others. Refer to Figure 1-56.

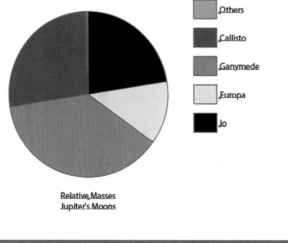

	Io	Europa	Ganymede	Callisto	Others	
Relative Masses...	22.721	12.210	37.696	27.370	0.003	

Figure 1-56. *Create a single pie graph and enter data using the Graph Data window*

Amount is determined by arc length of each item.

The pie graph also has some similar ways to organize its data sets, like the column graph, and you can refer to that section for more details. However, each row of data in the worksheet will generate a separate graph.

As before, you create a data set label and then enter the category labels if you want to generate graph names and a legend. Refer to Figure 1-57.

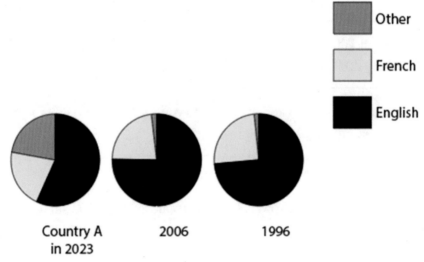

Figure 1-57. Create a multiple pie graphs and enter data using the Graph Data window

When you want to create a single pie graph, enter the values for only one row of data. Each of the Pie charts can have positive or negative values but not both at the same time.

When you want to create multiple pie graphs, plot several rows of data in either all positive or all negative values. Multiple pie graphs may appear larger or smaller as the size is proportional to the total of each graph's collective data.

Remember, however, they are best with minimal amounts of data. Very small amounts may become too thin, as we saw with the moon/planet example when "Other" moons only resulted in 0.003% of the total even if they were clumped together under one wedge. Also, while color does help, too many colors or similar colors may become overwhelming.

However, depending on the situation, a bar or column graph may prove to be more visually accurate when numbers are not going to add up to 100%. Refer to those previous sections for more information.

It can often appear more dynamic when rendered in 3D, along with additional graphics which we will review in Chapters 5 and 6. However, it can also be later adapted to appear donut-shaped without a center and information can be placed there instead. Refer to the section "Selecting and Editing Parts of a Graph" in Chapter 2 for more information.

Tip   Remember you can use your rectangular grid tool to create a simple waffle chart for adding up to 100% as you saw in Volume 1.

For more details on how to add the graph to your artboard and edit the labels, refer to the section "Column Graph" earlier in this chapter.

Example: Languages Spoken in a Country

When the data is transposed to row/column, you can see large and small pie graphs if we go according to language data rather than year. Refer to Figure 1-58.

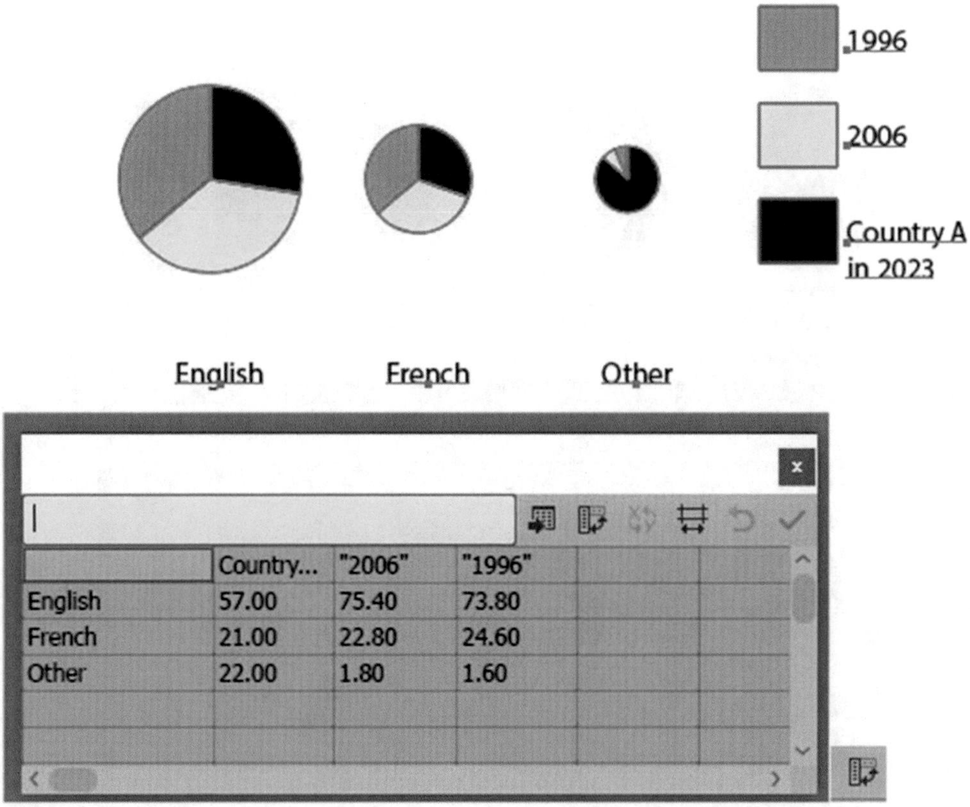

Figure 1-58. *Transpose the row and column when you want to see the data differently for the pie chart*

This may be confusing and does not explain much about what is happening.

A better use of larger and smaller pie charts would be to show perhaps by population growth of various language speakers over the years. Refer to Figure 1-59.

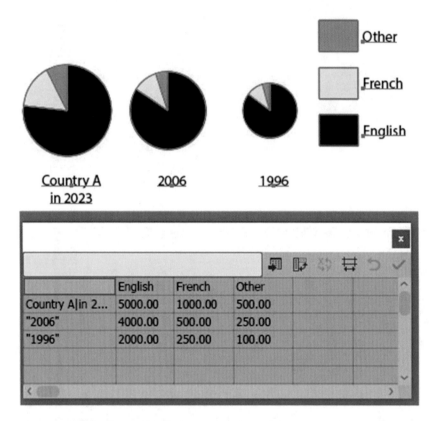

Figure 1-59. *Changing how the data is displayed by entering new numbers in the Graph Data window for a pie chart may make the data easier to understand*

Radar Graph

While similar to a pie chart, the radar graph does have some differences. It resembles very much a spider's web and looks similar to the polar grid tool. Though not used as much as the other graphing tools, it can be useful for showing the connectives of data, as well as the strength and the weakness of the similar or different trends. Only by stacking the data points over top can you fully see this. Refer to Figure 1-60.

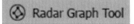

Figure 1-60. *Radar Graph Tool*

Each segment is a different color and is often explained with a legend adjacent to the graph.

Each number is plotted on the axis and is connected to others in the same axis to create the Web. Like the column graph, you can have both positive and negative numbers. As numbers are added, the graph will expand. The legend will appear in an outline form.

For more details on how to add the graph to your artboard and edit the labels, refer to the section "Column Graph" earlier in this chapter.

Example: Mineral Resources Mined at Various Mine Sites

There might be a way to show how much gold was mined at four mine sites over the years. Refer to Figure 1-61.

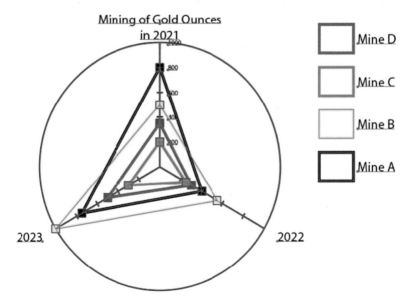

Figure 1-61. *Use the Data Graph window to enter the data into the radar graph*

When the rows and columns are transposed, you can see the information based on mine rather than year. Refer to Figure 1-62.

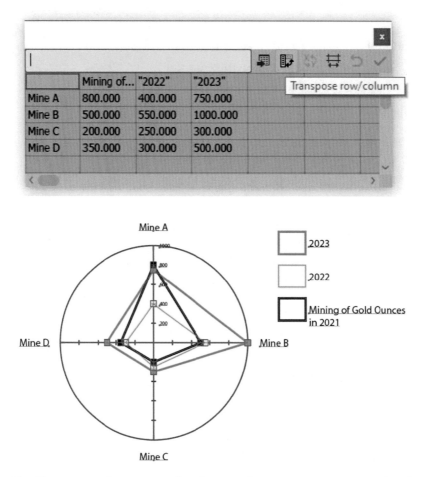

Figure 1-62. *Transpose the row and column when you want to see the data differently for the radar graph*

Graphs Can Be Combined

In some cases, you may want to display two graphs together, such as the bar/column and line graph, and they need to appear as part of the same data set. This is a last step in organizing your data because if you decide afterward to transpose your rows and columns, now you may lose the combined graph and its new settings.

All graph types can be combined except for the scatter graph which must always be used separately.

Let's suppose you started with a column graph. To begin, decide which part or parts of the legend you want to change to a new graph type. Let's change the graph type for Store C and Store D to a line graph. Refer to Figure 1-63.

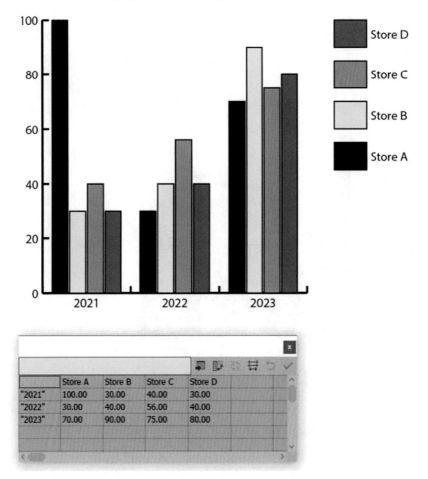

Figure 1-63. *Review the graph and the Data Graph window to decide what data you want to be another data graph type*

To do that, click the rectangle icon in the legend you want to change with the Group Selection tool. First click Store C. Refer to Figure 1-64

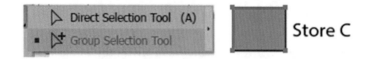

Figure 1-64. *Use the Group Selection tool to select the legend rectangle and click it twice*

Don't move the Group Selection pointer from the legend icon, but now click one more time on the Store C rectangle. All of those columns that relate are now selected for Store C. Refer to Figure 1-65.

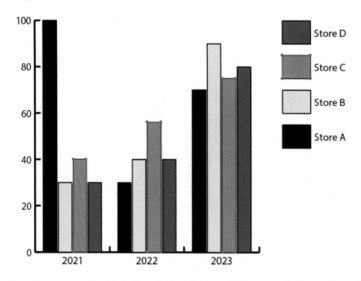

Figure 1-65. *On the second click, both the legend bar and the related column are selected*

Now, with the Group Selection tool, Shift+click the rectangle in the legend for Store D and then just click again the Store D rectangle once more to select all those related columns. It should now look something like this. Refer to Figure 1-66.

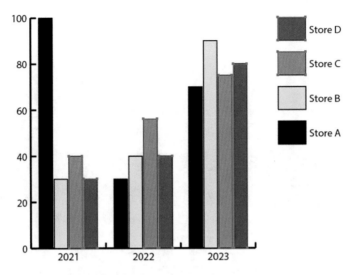

Figure 1-66. *Shift+click another legend rectangle and click again when you want to select its related column*

Now choose Object ➤ Graph ➤ Type or double-click the graph tool in the Toolbars panel to bring up the Graph Type dialog box. Refer to Figure 1-67.

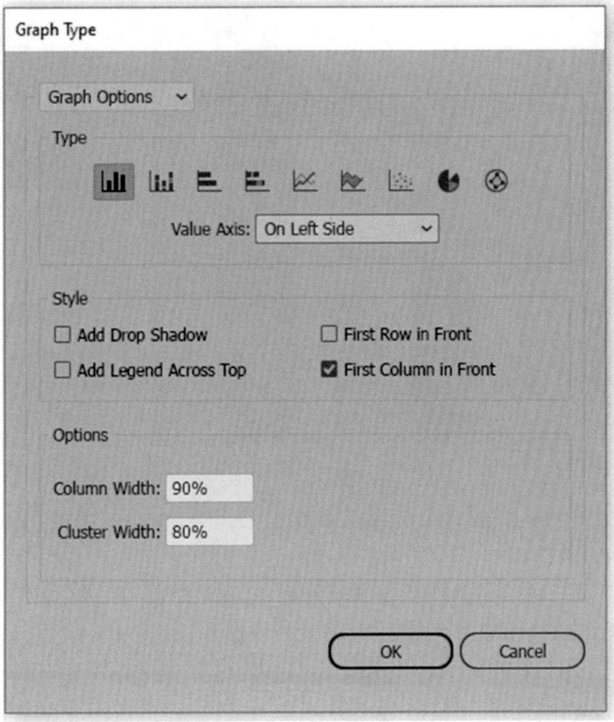

Figure 1-67. *Graph Type dialog box*

Select the new graph type that you want to use, such as line, and click OK, and then the new graph is combined. Refer to Figure 1-68.

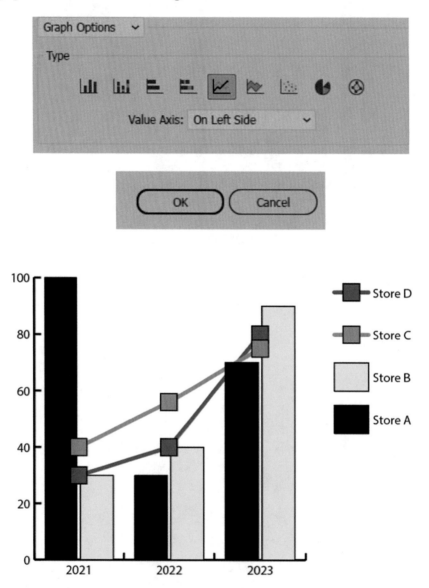

Figure 1-68. *Graph Type dialog box with the new Type settings, and now two types of graphs are combined*

To modify this further when a graph uses more than one graph type, you may want one set of data Value Axis on the Left Axis and the other on the Right Axis so that it's easier to visualize. We will look at how to set the Value Axis setting in a moment.

However, I will just point out that you should always, when creating the initial column graph, set the Value Axis to "On Both Sides" first. Then you can make part of your graph a line graph as you just saw and set the value axis again if required. If you do this, Value Axis changes to the bar graph after you add the line graph to add a second side, it may reset back to all columns, and you must add the line graph again. Refer to Figure 1-69.

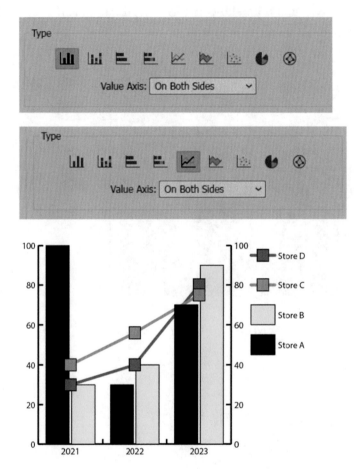

Figure 1-69. *Always make sure you set your Graph Type Value Axis kind first in the Graph Type dialog box before you create any combined graph types*

In this case, each Value Axis measures the left and right data.

Likewise, if you use a stacked column with other graph types, be sure to use the same Value Axis for all data sets that are represented by a stacked column graph.

Also, remember that stacked column, stacked bar, and stacked area graphs can either accept positive or negative numbers but not both at the same time in a category, while other graphs can. So, this may lead to an error message as you try to convert part of the chart to another type.

As you will see in the next section, some sets of data default to left, while on others, you may prefer right column heights or maybe you want to incorporate a pie graph that has no Value Axis. However, if not balanced correctly, the data can become misleading, confusing, or even overlap. Refer to Figure 1-70.

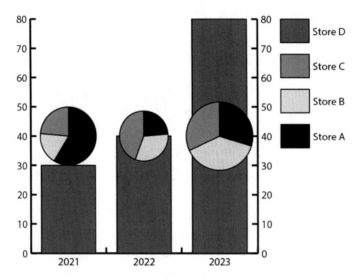

Figure 1-70. *Some types of graph combinations can be confusing if not correctly combined or explained*

Adjusting and Editing Your Graph

While, as you saw earlier in Volume 1, there are some basic modifications that you can make to your simple shapes, edits such as adjust colors, blends, or opacity and alter the type face and type style as well as you can move rotate, reflect, shear, and scale another path or parts of a path. The same is true for graphs and charts. I will show this in more detail in a moment and later in Chapter 2. However, I will first just show some of the Graph Type editing options you can encounter for various graphs while that graph is selected with the Selection Tool. To review them from the menu, choose Object ➤ Graph ➤ Type to review the dialog box.

Applying Graph Options

Let's look at the following Graph Options; these can be found when Graph Options is selected in the Graph Type dialog box. Refer to Figure 1-71.

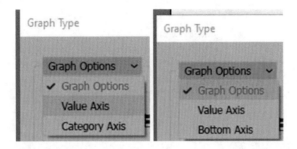

Figure 1-71. *Graph Type dialog box options for viewing Graph Options and axis settings using the list to change settings*

Value Axis, Category Axis, and Bottom Axis, as they relate to a specific graph type, can also be found in this list, and we will look at that shortly. For now, look at the Graph Options setting in the drop-down. Refer to Figure 1-71

Graph Options

Under Type, we have seen there are nine types of graphs, and you can switch between graph types from here. In this area, you can also change the Value Axis for column, stacked column, bar, stacked bar, line, area, and scatter. Pie has no Value Axis options, and for radar, the Value Axis by default is on all sides. The Value Axis is the graph's unit of measurement. Refer to Figure 1-72.

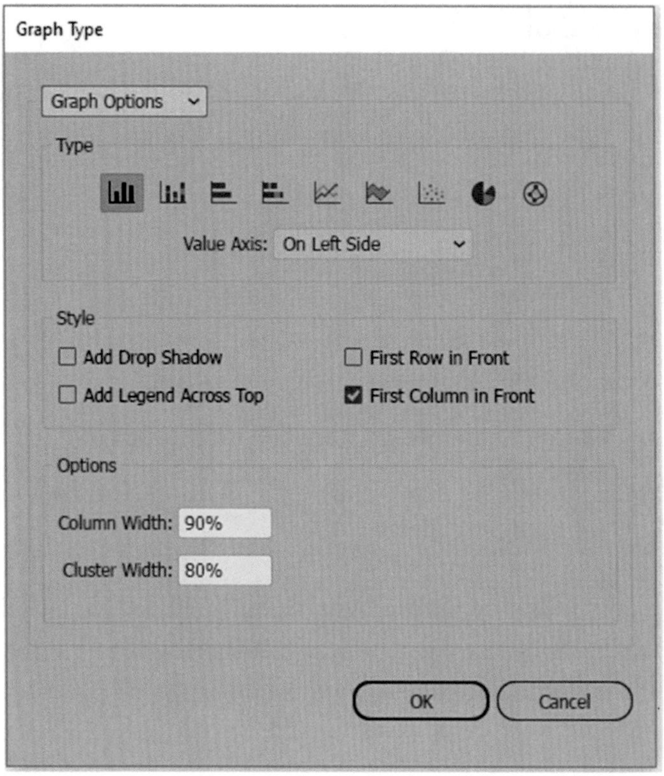

Figure 1-72. *Graph Type dialog box with Graph Option settings*

From the Value Axis drop-down list, you can choose

- Options for column, stacked column, line, and area are available for the Left Side, Right Side, and Both Sides. Left is generally the default. Refer to Figure 1-73.

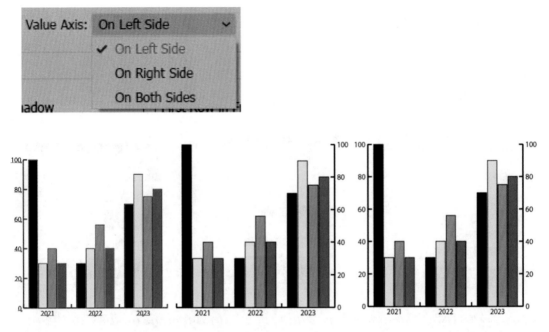

Figure 1-73. *Using the Graph Type dialog box, you can set the options for the Value Axis to left, right, or both sides for a column graph*

- Options for bar and stacked bar are Top Side, Bottom Side, and Both Sides. Bottom is generally the default. Refer to Figure 1-74.

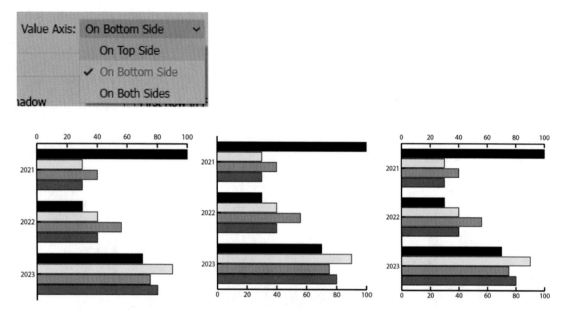

Figure 1-74. *Using the Graph Type dialog box, you can set the options for the Value Axis to Top, Bottom, or Both Sides for a bar graph*

- Options for scatter is On Left Side or Both Sides. Left is generally the default. Refer to Figure 1-75.

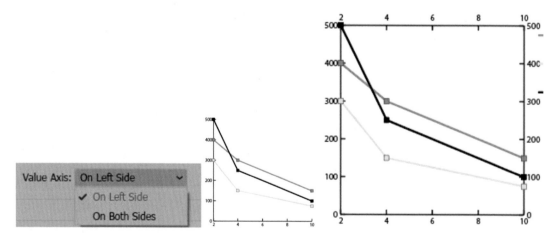

Figure 1-75. *Using the Graph Type dialog box, you can set the options for the Value Axis to Left or Both Sides for a scatter graph*

- No Value Axis options as mentioned earlier will be presented for the pie or radar graph though the radar will have Value Axis present on the graph and it is On All Sides. Refer to Figure 1-76.

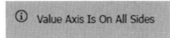

Figure 1-76. *Radar graphs default to Value Axis Is On All Sides*

Style

Style, in the Graph Options, allows for some basic styling to be added to the graph, and the four options are the same for all graphs. Refer to Figure 1-77.

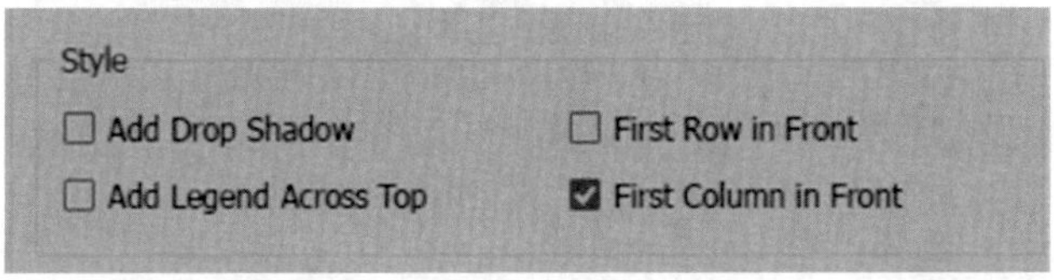

Figure 1-77. *Using the Graph Type dialog box, you can set the style options for a graph*

- Add Drop Shadow: Rather than use the Effects menu to apply a drop shadow, you can enable this check box; by default, it is unchecked. Note This type of drop shadow is actually another solid box behind the bar or circle behind the pie and not a true Drop Shadow effect. This effect will not work for combined graphs. Refer to Figure 1-78.

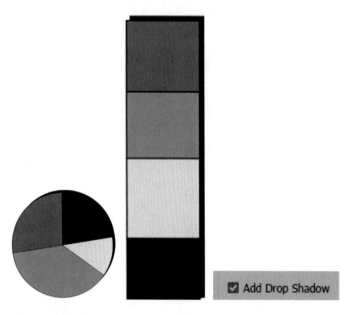

Figure 1-78. *Add a drop shadow to a graph*

- Add Legend Across Top: By default, when unchecked, the legend appears on the right side of the graph. However, when the setting is checked, it appears along the top of the chart. Refer to Figure 1-79.

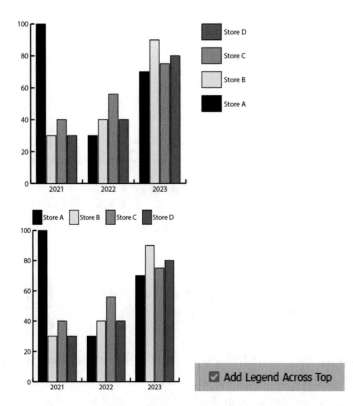

Figure 1-79. *Default legend and right or Add Legend Across Top of the graph*

- First Row in Front: When working with column and bar graphs, this controls how the clusters (categories) of data in a graph overlap when the cluster width is above 100%. This is more apparent when you work with nonclustered items that have had their column width increased. The first row in this example would be the top one.

See options for settings for Column and Cluster Width. Refer to Figure 1-80.

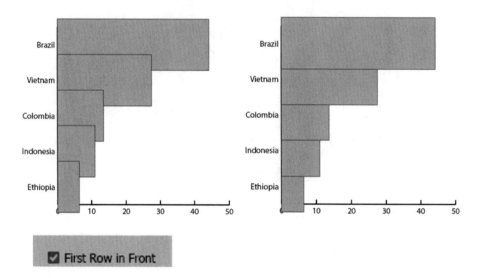

☑ First Row in Front

Figure 1-80. *When graph width overlaps you, let the last row overlap or you can make the first row in front as seen in the right graph*

- First Column in Front: Checked by default, this is used by column, stacked column, bar, stacked bar, and line graphs that correspond to the first column of data in the Graph Data window on top. For stacked columns and stacked bars, this setting determines which column appears on top if it has a column or bar width that is more than 100%. See options for settings for Column and Cluster Width. Refer to Figure 1-81.

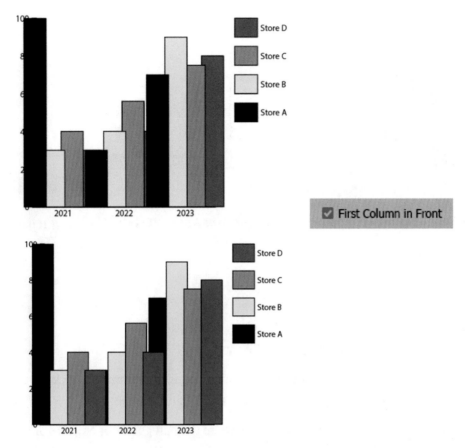

Figure 1-81. *By default, the first column in a wide cluster will overlap when the check is enabled, but if you disabled the setting, the last column will overlap instead*

Note   Adobe recommends that you always select style "First Column in Front" for area graphs as some areas may not appear correctly if this option is left unselected and will disappear. Refer to Figure 1-82.

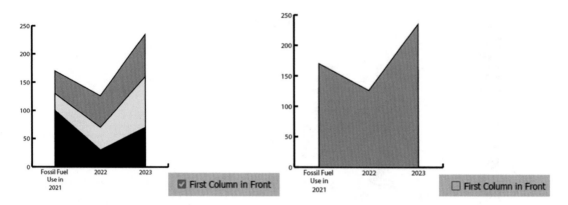

Figure 1-82. *Do not disabled the First Column in Front style when you work with an area graph*

Options

Depending on the graph, options will vary.

For column and stacked column, the following options are available:

- Column Width: Adjust the spacing between each column or stacked column. The range is 1%–1000% and the default is 90%.

- Cluster Width: Adjust the space between the categories or clusters of data (1%–1000%). The default is 80%. Refer to Figure 1-83.

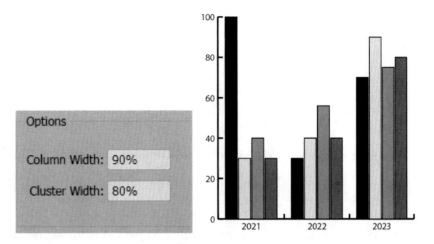

Figure 1-83. *Graph Type, Graph Options dialog box for Column Width and Cluster Width and how the graph appears at default settings*

Setting the column width and cluster with too high a percent will cause crowding. While too low may spread the data too far apart. Refer to Figures 1-84 and 1-85.

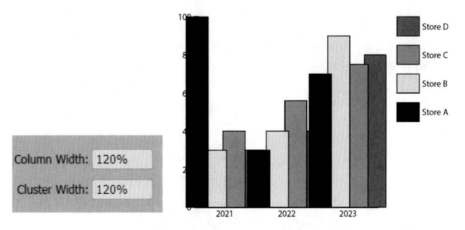

Figure 1-84. *Graph Type, Graph Options dialog box for Column Width and Cluster Width higher than 100% and how the graph appears*

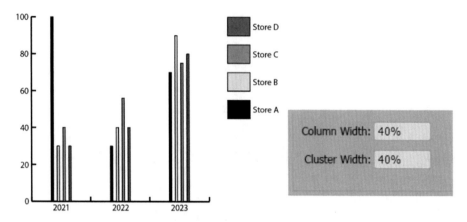

Figure 1-85. *Graph Type, Graph Options dialog box for Column Width and Cluster Width lower than 100% and how the graph appears*

For bar and stacked bar, the following options are available:

- Bar Width: This is the same as column width, only horizontal; adjust the spacing between each bar or stacked bar. The range is 1%–1000% and the default is 90%.

- Cluster Width: Adjust the space between the categories or clusters of data (1%–1000%). The default is 80%. Refer to Figure 1-86.

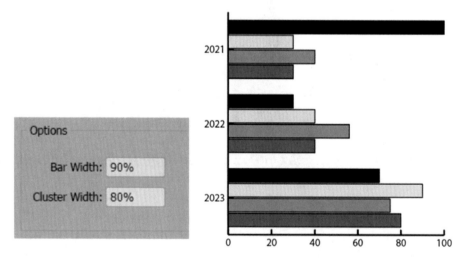

Figure 1-86. *Graph Type, Graph Options dialog box for Bar Width and Cluster Width lower than 100% at default and how the graph appears*

Note   For Cluster width values above 100%, this can cause bars or columns in a cluster to overlap, while values lower than 100% cause spaces between the bars or columns in the cluster. Exactly 100% causes the bars to touch each other. If you are not sure what settings to use, stick with the default values or make the percentages slightly lower to avoid crowding of too many bars or columns.

For line, radar, and partially for scatter, the following options are available when you need to alter the lines and various data points. Refer to Figure 1-87.

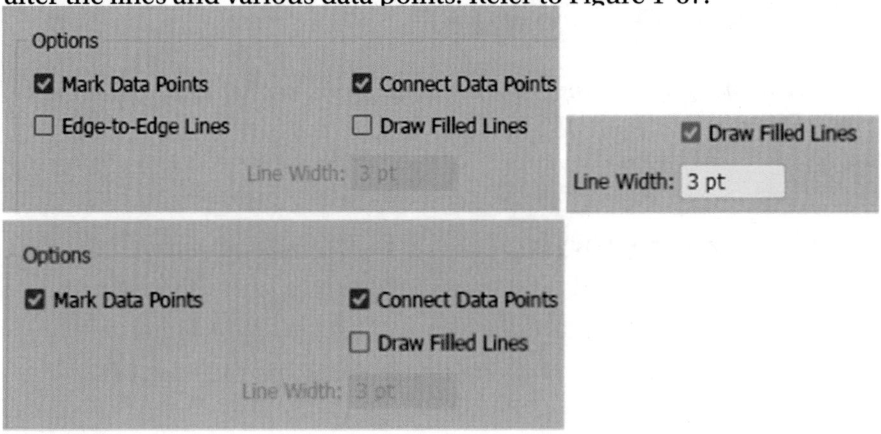

Figure 1-87. *Graph Type, Graph Options dialog box for line, radar, and scatter charts*

- Mark Data Points: When the check box is enabled, it will place square markers at each point but no connection lines, that is a separate setting. See Connect Data Points. Refer to Figure 1-88.

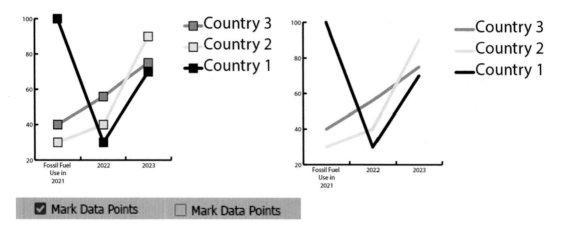

Figure 1-88. *Graph Type, Graph Options dialog box set Mark Data Points when you want them to appear or disable when you do not want them to appear on the line graph*

- Edge-to-Edge Lines (Only for Line and Radar Graphs): When the check box is enabled, it draws lines that extend across the whole graph along the horizontal (x) axis, moving left to right. Otherwise, there a margin of space between the value axis and the edge of the graph. Refer to Figure 1-89.

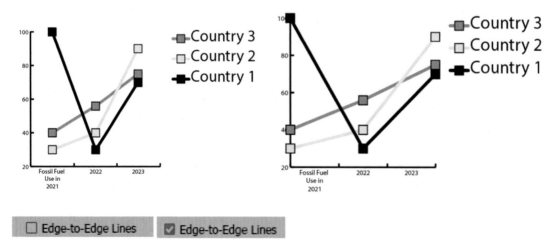

Figure 1-89. *Graph Type, Graph Options dialog box: Disable Edge-to-Edge Lines when you want space after the Value Axis or enable when you want them to touch the Value Axis on the line graph*

- Connect Data Points: When the check box is enabled, it draws lines that make it easier to see relationships between data points. We can see how this would affect line and scatter graphs in a similar way. Refer to Figure 1-90.

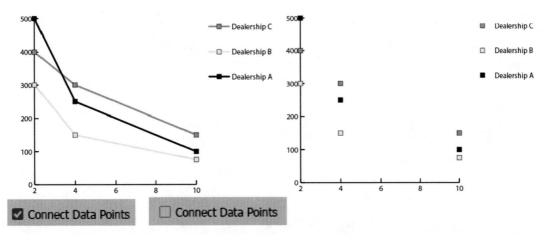

Figure 1-90. *Graph Type, Graph Options dialog box set Connect Data Points when you want the lines to appear on the graph and disabled when you only want to see the points/markers*

- Draw Filled Lines: When the check box is enabled, this creates a wider line. You then have access to the line width (0–100pt) setting, and you can enter a new width value higher than 3pt (points). Refer to Figure 1-91.

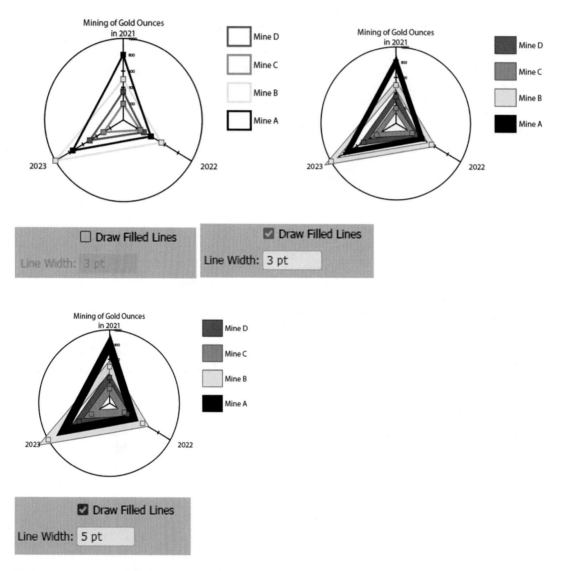

Figure 1-91. *Graph Type, Graph Options dialog box on radar graphs you can enable Draw Filled Lines and adjust the thickness of the line width*

Area graphs have no options. Refer to Figure 1-92.

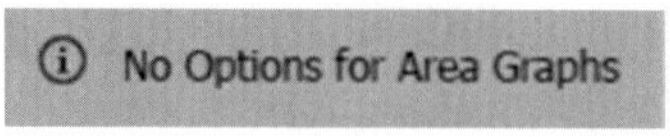

ⓘ No Options for Area Graphs

Figure 1-92. *This message for Graph Type dialog box Options will appear when you select the Area Graph Type*

For pie charts, the following options are available for adjusting and sorting selected pie graphs. Refer to Figure 1-93.

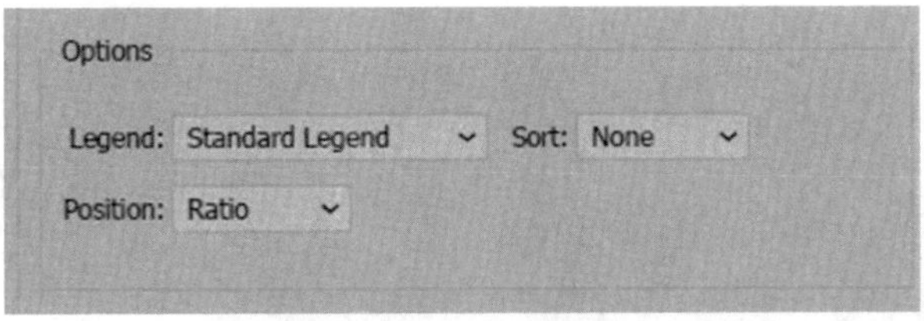

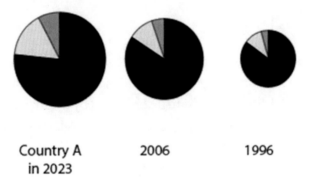

Figure 1-93. *Graph Type, Graph Options dialog box for the pie graph*

Legend

- No Legend: This removes the legend. Refer to Figure 1-94.

Figure 1-94. *Pie graphs appear without a legend*

- Standard Legend: Creates the default legend on the right, outside the graphs. This is ideal for when you need to combine your pie chart with another graph such as a column or bar. Refer to Figure 1-95.

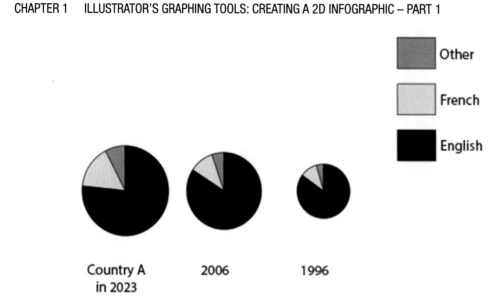

Figure 1-95. *Pie graphs appear with a legend*

- Legend in Wedges: The labels are placed inside of the related wedges. Note that at first, the text will appear quite small, and you will have to alter this size later on using your Control panel and Type tool options. Later, if you find any of the text to be obscured by a dark background, you can outside of the dialog box use the Group Selection tool to select the part of the legend and wedge and choose a new color from the Color or Swatches panel. We will look at the type later when we change the formatting of the text in Chapter 2. Refer to Figure 1-96.

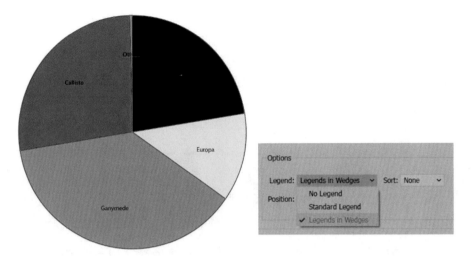

Figure 1-96. *Pie graph appears with the Legends in Wedges based on setting in dialog box, but it's currently difficult to read*

When you have multiple charts of a similar size, you can sort

- All: Sorts the wedges of the selected pie graph from the largest to the smallest in a clockwise direction, starting from the top of the pie. Refer to Figure 1-97.

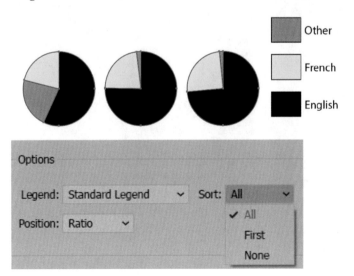

Figure 1-97. *Graph Type, Graph Options dialog box to sort the wedges in the pie chart by All*

- First: The wedges of the selected pie graph are sorted so that the largest value found in the first graph is placed in the first wedge and then the rest will sort from largest to smallest. Multiple graphs will then follow the order of the first graph. The legend will also adjust. Refer to Figure 1-98.

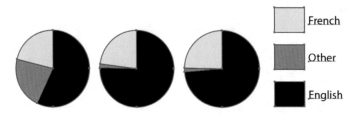

Figure 1-98. *Graph Type, Graph Options dialog box to sort the wedges in the pie chart by First*

- None: Sort the wedges of the selected pie graphs in the order in which you entered the values, clockwise from the top of graphs for all. Refer to Figure 1-99.

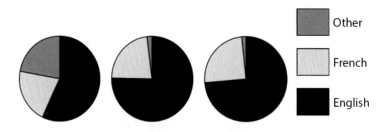

Figure 1-99. *Graph Type, Graph Options dialog box to sort the wedges in the pie chart by None*

- Position: For the display of multiple pie charts of same and different sizes.

- Ratio: Graphs are sized proportionately. Refer to Figure 1-100.

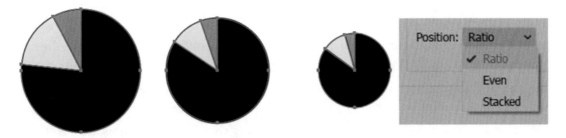

Figure 1-100. *Graph Type, Graph Options dialog box to position the pies in the pie chart by ratio*

- Even: All graphs are the same diameter. Refer to Figure 1-101.

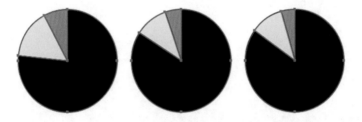

Figure 1-101. *Graph Type, Graph Options dialog box to Position the pies in the pie chart by Even*

- Stacked: Graphs are stacked on top of each other, and each graph is sized proportionately, so all are visible. Refer to Figure 1-102.

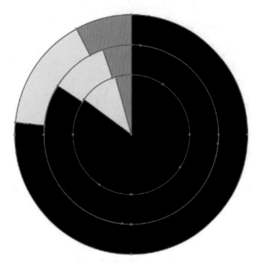

Figure 1-102. *Graph Type, Graph Options dialog box to position the pies in the pie chart in a stack*

Value Axis (Left Axis, Right Axis, Bottom Axis, Top Axis)

The next section in the drop-down list is the Value Axis or unit of measurement for the graph, and this is the same for all charts except pie. The Value Axis, as we saw earlier, controls the data numbers that may appear on the left, right, top, bottom, or on two sides (both), depending on the graph. If you have, in the Graph Options area, selected on Both Sides depending on the graph, then rather than seeing the word "Value Axis," you will see Right Axis and Left Axis or Top Axis and Bottom Axis in the drop-down list, but the options will still be the same. Refer to Figures 1-103 and 1-104.

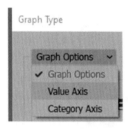

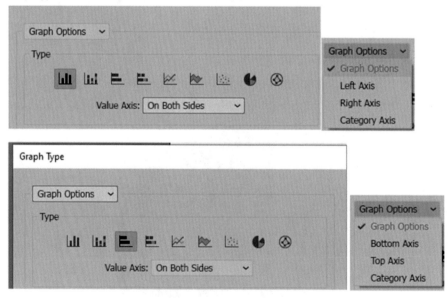

Figure 1-103. *Graph Type Options will be different if the graph type and Value Axis is altered in the dialog box to both sides*

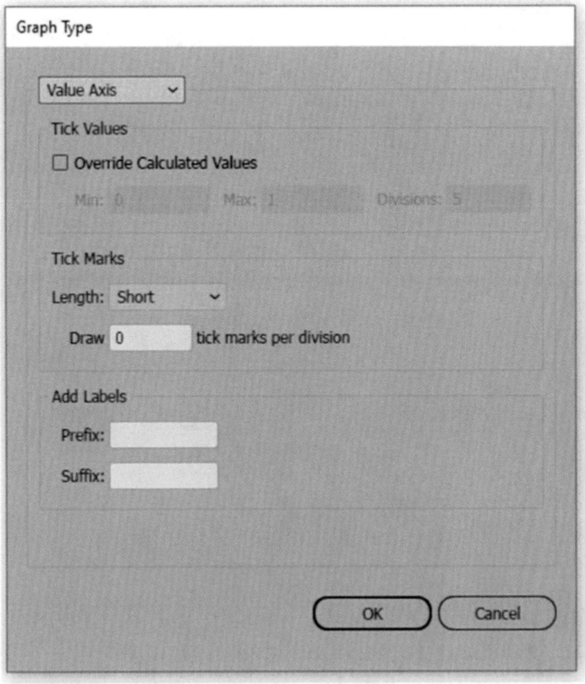

Figure 1-104. *Graph Type dialog box Value Axis options*

The following settings for Value Axis are

- Tick Values: Override Calculated Values, by default this check box is unchecked, and you can accept the default values of Min: 0, Max:1, and Divisions: 5. The Min or Max will change as the graph increases in data. When checked, wherever your Value Axis is located (left, right, top, bottom) on the graph, you can now set new minimum, maximum, and number of divisions between the labels. Later, I set the Divisions to 10 instead of 5. Refer to Figure 1-105.

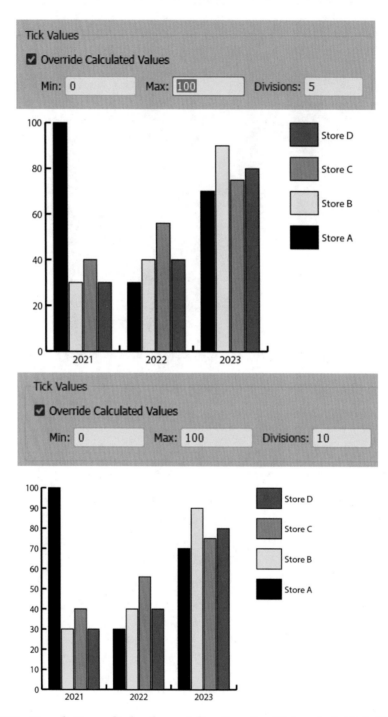

Figure 1-105. *Graph Type dialog box: Adjusting the Value Axis Tick Values will alter the graph*

- Tick Marks: This area determines the length of each tick mark (None, Short, Full Width). Refer to Figure 1-106.

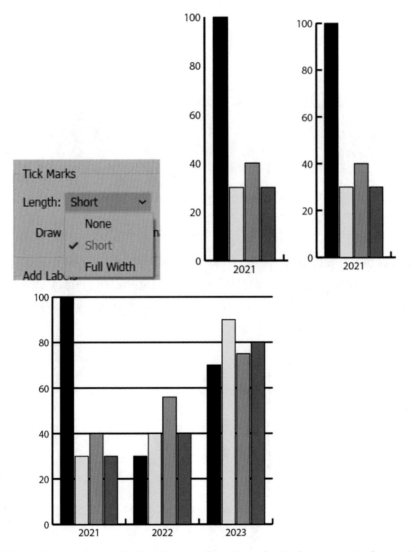

Figure 1-106. *Graph Type dialog box: Adjusting the Value Axis Tick Marks will alter the graph*

For Draw number Tick Marks per division, you can change the number when set to Length: Short or Full Width. If set to None, they will not appear. Refer to Figure 1-107.

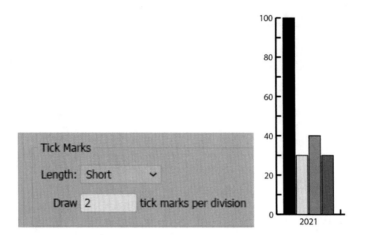

Figure 1-107. *Graph Type dialog box: Adjusting the Value Axis Draw number of Tick Marks will alter the graph*

- Add Labels: Prefix and Suffix. This is useful when you need to add a currency symbol to the start (Prefix) or end (Suffix) of your number. Here I will try it with a $, but you can use noncurrency symbols as well. Refer to Figure 1-108.

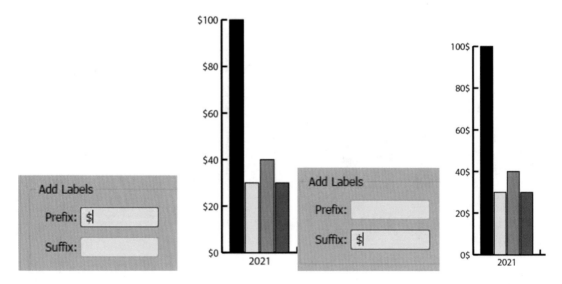

Figure 1-108. *Graph Type dialog box: Adjusting the Value Axis Labels for Prefix or Suffix will add extra symbols to the Value Axis on the graph*

Combined Graph with Different Axis

As mentioned earlier, graphs can be combined when a graph has two value axes (left/right or top/bottom). You can, outside the Graph Type dialog, use the Selection tool and choose Object ➤ Graph ➤ Type and then from the drop-down list, choose Value Axis on Both Sides. Then in this example, under the Right axis and Left axis, you want to assign the change in settings too both and click OK to exit the menu to commit. Note that currently both axes will have the same Value Axis setting regardless of which side you set first. Refer to Figures 1-109 and 1-110.

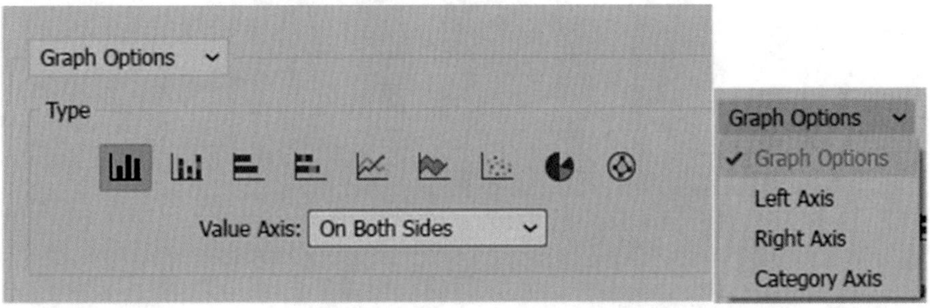

Figure 1-109. *Set your Graph Options to Both Sides before you edit the Left and Right Value Axis*

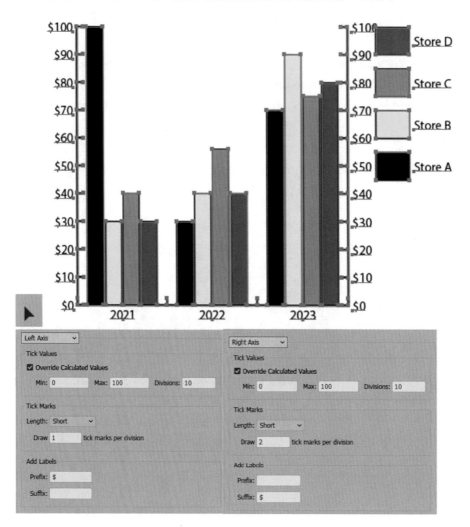

Figure 1-110. *Use the Graph Type dialog box to alter the Left and Right Axis*

After you click OK to exit, then you would again use your Group Selection tool and click the legend of the data set you want to assign to the axis. Then click again and all columns in the group are selected. As well, you can Shift+click another rectangle and click again the same rectangle to select those columns as well.

Go to Object ➤ Graph ➤ Type and this time select that line graph which should be on the Value Axis of the right side. Refer to Figure 1-111.

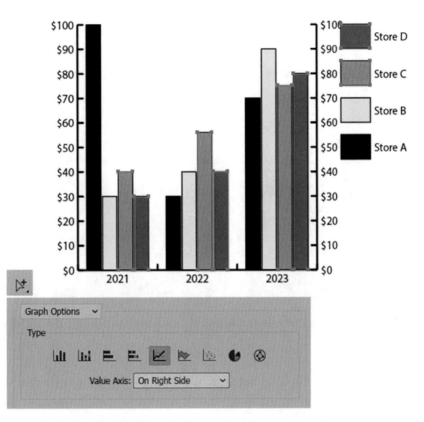

Figure 1-111. *Use the Group Selection tool when you want to create a combined graph and set a new graph type*

Click OK and now those setting that you set for the Right Axis earlier will be applied. Refer to Figure 1-112.

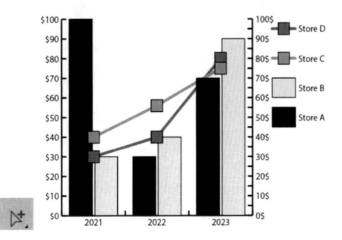

Figure 1-112. *Combined graph will have two slightly different Value Axis settings*

Here we can see how a combined graph could have two slightly altered Value Axis.

Note   You will have to reset your graph back to a column again first if you want to access the Left and Right Axis, as only Value Axis will be available for the whole graph. Refer to Figure 1-113.

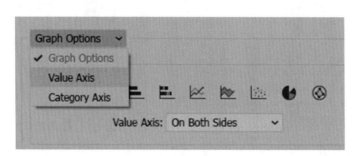

Figure 1-113. *Once the graphs are combined, only the Value Axis setting and not Left and Right are available*

Now we will continue to view the settings in the Graph Type dialog box.

Bottom Axis

In the drop-down list, this option is only available for the bar, stacked bar, and scatter graph. For the scatter graph, whether you chose the option of left or both for the Value Axis, you can also set the same settings for the Bottom Axis, as you saw for Value Axis for Tick Values, Tick Marks, and Labels. This will also affect the Top Axis as well if the settings of Value Axis on Both Sides are chosen. Here on the Bottom Axis, I add the suffix of "year" with a space so that the upper and lower numbers made more sense. Refer to Figures 1-114 and 1-115.

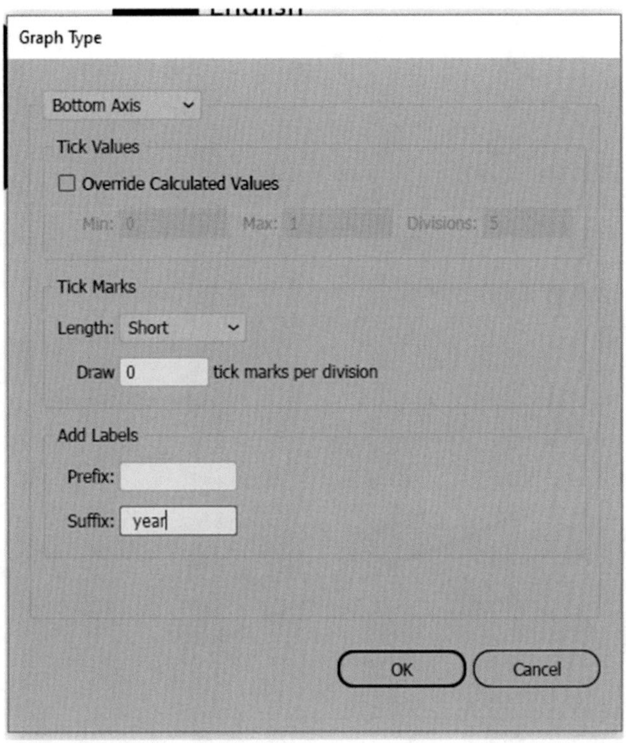

Figure 1-114. *Graph Type dialog box for Bottom Axis is available for scatter graphs*

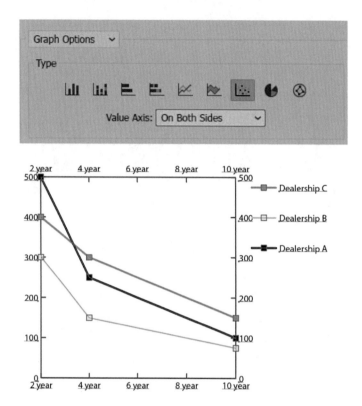

Figure 1-115. *Scatter graph with Suffix added to both sides using the Graph Type dialog box to set the Bottom Axis and Graph Options to a Value Axis on Both Sides*

You could then add a prefix to your Value Axis to show a $ sign for price. Refer to Figure 1-116.

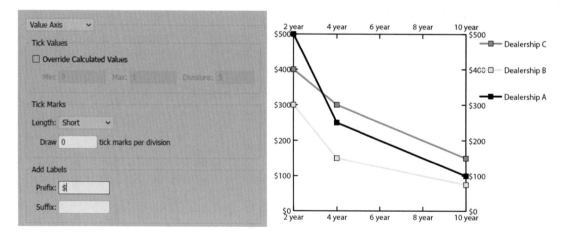

Figure 1-116. *Scatter graph with Prefix added to both sides using the Graph Type dialog box to set the Value Axis and Graph Options to a Value Axis on Both Sides*

Category Axis

This section in the drop-down list is available for column, stacked column, bar, stack bar, line, and area. It defines the categories of data for the graph. Refer to Figure 1-117.

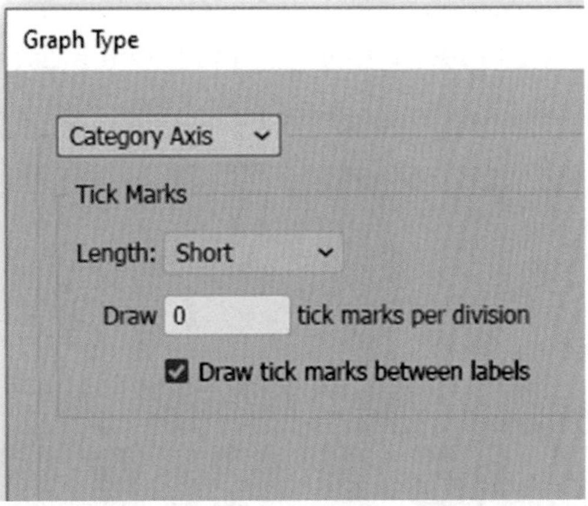

Figure 1-117. *Graph Type Dialog box Category Axis options*

Here you can set the Tick Marks with the various settings for

- Length: None, Short, or Full Width as you did for the Value Axis. Refer to Figure 1-118.

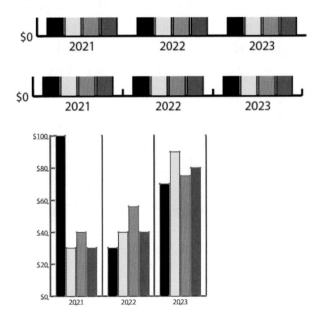

Figure 1-118. *Set the Tick Marks Length to None, Short, or Long for the graph*

Tip   When both the Value Axis and Category Axis Lengths are set to Full Width, then you would have a grid.

- Draw #Tick Marks per Division: You can add additional divisions, but they may be difficult to see if there are many columns present. Refer to Figure 1-119.

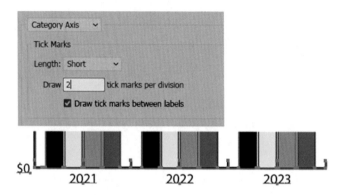

Figure 1-119. Set the Draw number of Tick Marks per division for the Category Axis

- Draw Number Tick Marks Between Labels: Will allow you to draw tick marks between labels on either side of the label or columns and over the labels and columns when disabled. You will still have the division marks, but the ones between will disappear, and the division may be hidden as well, if not, set to Length: Full Width. Keep this setting enabled. Refer to Figures 1-119 and 1-120.

Figure 1-120. Setting enabled for Draw tick marks between labels removed

Once you are done with this dialog box, you can click OK to commit changes or Cancel to exit. Figure 1-121.

Figure 1-121. *Click OK to exit the dialog box after making changes to the settings or Cancel to exit*

Make sure that you File ➤ Save any of your work at this point.

To review similar examples up to this point, File ➤ Open and refer to my files graphs1.ai and graphs2.ai where I have placed some examples of the graphs we have explored so far.

Summary

In this chapter, we reviewed the following topics of the early history of the graph, as well as how to collect the data before you apply it to a graph type in Illustrator. As we reviewed the types of graphs, you learned how to alter the data and some of the appearance for each one.

In the next chapter, you will look at how to alter your graph further working with color, patterns, and type as well as altering the symbols and designs to suit your needs for your graph.

CHAPTER 2

Illustrator's Graphing Tools: Creating a 2D Infographic – Part 2

In this chapter, you will continue to work with Illustrator graphing and drawing tools to create an infographic.

This chapter continues to focus on the nine graph tools and how you can use them, along with other Illustrator tools such as adding color, altering type, working with Pattern Options panel, and using symbols to create designs for your graph. Later in Chapter 3, we'll work with the Image Trace panel to create unique graphic creations. On your own, for practice in this chapter, you can continue to use the files that you created earlier or create a File ➤ New document and practice on a fresh artboard.

Note This chapter does contain projects that can be found in the Volume 2 Chapter 2 folder. Some of the texts on Patterns Topics in this chapter have been adapted and updated from my earlier books *Accurate Layer Selections Using Photoshop's Selection Tools* and *Perspective Warps and Distorts with Adobe Tools: Volume 2*.

© Jennifer Harder 2024
J. Harder, *Creating Infographics with Adobe Illustrator: Volume 2*,
https://doi.org/10.1007/979-8-8688-0041-2_2

Selecting and Editing Parts of a Graph

As mentioned earlier, a graph can be selected as a whole using the Selection tool. All elements of graph and legend must be kept as part of the group in order to update the data.

You can see this is a graph because, in the Control panel, the word Graph appears. Refer to Figure 2-1.

Figure 2-1. *Graph identifier in the Control panel and Selection tool for moving a graph*

The Selection tool allows you to move the graph around on the page to a new location. You can also use Alt/Option+Drag when you need to make a copy of the graph. Or press the Delete/Backspace key to delete the graph once the Graph Data window is closed.

However, you need to use other tools as seen in Volume 1 Chapter 6 to make adjustments as the bounding box handles for this grouped graph will not be available for the Selection tool as with other basic shapes and paths.

Tools you can use after you have selected your graph with the Selection tool are

- Scale Tool: Hold down the Shift key while scaling, or use Object ➤ Transform ➤ Scale to access the dialog box to scale proportionally or make a copy so that you don't distort the original graph. Using the dialog box is usually the best option for an accurate uniform scale. Refer to Figure 2-2.

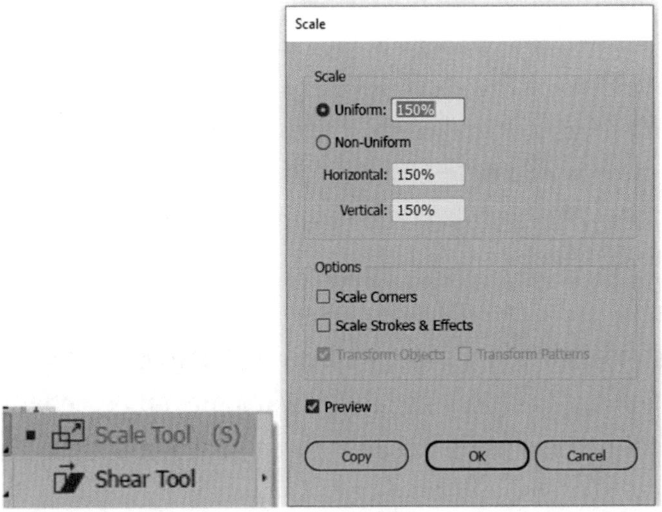

Figure 2-2. *Use the Scale Tool and Scale dialog box when you want to scale a graph or a copy*

- Rotate Tool: Or use Object ➤ Transform ➤ Rotate. Rotation may be required if in the surrounding layout you need place the graph at 90 or -90 degrees on its side. Refer to Figure 2-3.

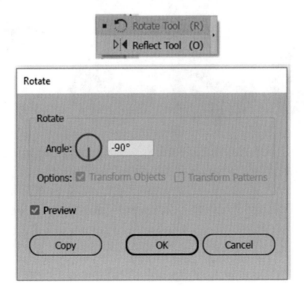

Figure 2-3. *Use the Rotate Tool and Rotate dialog box when you want to scale a graph or a copy*

- Likewise, you can use your other Object ➤ Transform commands and related tools that you saw in Volume 1 to do such things as shear or reflect. However, keep in mind that while you can use tools of reflect and shear, that in order to make the data appear accurate, you, in most cases, would want to avoid doing this when working with graphs. However, if the chart was meant to be abstract or part of a design, that might be acceptable.

Remember   Elements that are meant to be a part of a group can be selected with the Group Selection tool to select subgroups within the graph and Shift+click on other groups and then click again to select those subgroups. Or marquee drag to select around several paths. Refer to Figure 2-4.

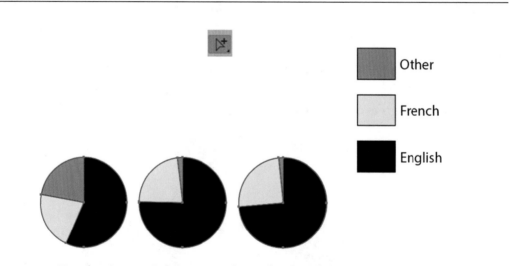

Figure 2-4. *Use the Group Selection tool to select wedges or parts of the graph together (marquee select) or when you click multiple times*

Then, like the Selection tool, use the Group Selection tool to move selected parts of the design if you find that elements are blocking part of the graph or are too far away. Refer to Figure 2-5.

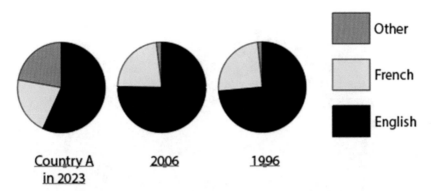

Figure 2-5. *Use the Group Selection tool to select a similar category or legend type and move it into place*

Likewise, you can use your Direct Selection tool to select individual paths as well. However, do not delete selected parts of your path, or you may destroy the original graph.

Tip   To create a doughnut pie chart, use your Ellipse tool to cover part of the graph. Alt/Option+Shift+Drag over the graph to center the ellipse as you create it, and then use your Control panel to set a white fill and black stroke. Make sure to also with the Selection tool Shift+click and select the ellipse with the graph if you plan to copy/paste it into another document. Refer to Figure 2-6.

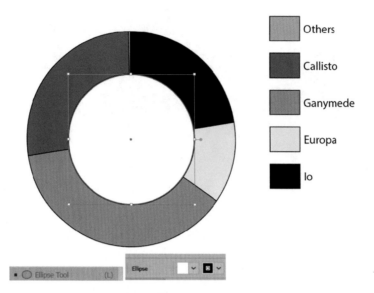

Figure 2-6. *Use the Ellipse tool to cover areas of the graph when you want to make your pie graph look like a doughnut graph instead and color the Ellipse with the Control panel by selecting Swatches*

Within the doughnut hole, you could add some text as well.

Note   If you want to make a graph into several regular grouped paths, you cannot use Object ➤ Expand. You must use Object ➤ Ungroup. Doing so, you will lose the ability to edit and change your data, so always keep a backup copy. If you do want to ungroup the graph, click the Yes button if a warning message appears. Otherwise click No.

Change the Formatting of the Text in Your Graph

In some situations, you may want to change the formatting of your text overall as you may not like the current default font. You can do that quickly and easily using either the Control panel or the Properties panel. First, I will show you how to do that with text, and then in a later section, we will focus on colors.

When you select your graph with the Selection tool, look at the Control panel. Refer to Figure 2-7.

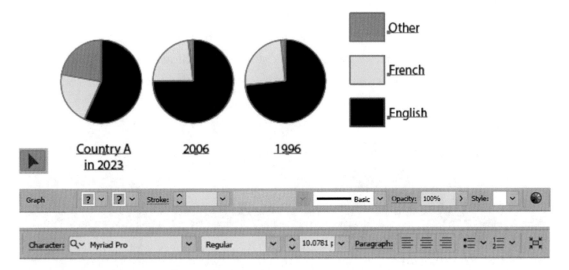

Figure 2-7. *Select your graph with the Selection tool when you want to make global text changes to your graph*

Look at the Character section. To keep your type all consistent and the same font size, then select a new font family, style, and point size. Refer to Figure 2-8.

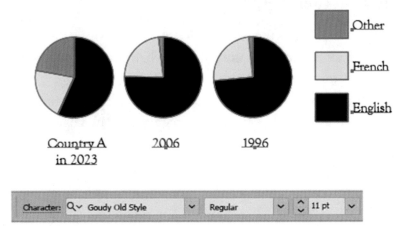

Figure 2-8. *Use the Control panel to set a new font family, style, and size for all the text*

Or use the Direct Selection tool and change the individual font sizes or colors if you need to, one at a time. But keep in mind that in order for the layout not to be confusing, such as two different type styles with the style no longer matching with the legend, it is better to keep the font family consistent and only adjust the style, size, or color. Refer to Figure 2-9.

Figure 2-9. *Use the Direct Selection tool to change individual text lines one at a time using the Control panel Character styles from regular to bold and the font size from 11pt to 12pt*

We will look at color adjustments shortly.

Create a Title for Your Graph

Likewise, if you need to enhance the graph with a title, then use your Type tool as you did in Volume 1 Chapter 8. Click once the artboard when you want to type out a new line of text at a point while the text is highlighted.

Then, while your text is highlighted, use the Control panel, as mentioned in Volume 1, to change your type settings for character and paragraph. Then use your Selection tool to move the title to where you want it on or around your graph. Refer to Figure 2-10.

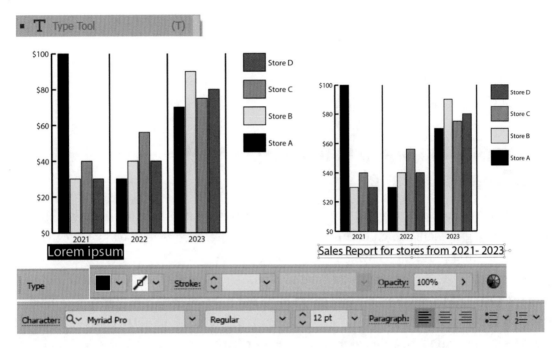

Figure 2-10. *Use the Type tool to create a separate title at a point that gives more detail about the graph and then edit it with your Type tool*

Because this text is not part of the graph, you can continue to make color (Fill and Stroke), character, and paragraph adjustments to it separately. Make sure that you, with the Selection tool Shift+click it with the graph if you want to copy/paste it into another document. Refer to Figure 2-10.

At this point, re-entering and modifying data is easily done in the Object ➤ Graph ➤ Data. However, as you make more creative adjustments to your design, it can be a bit more difficult to update if you still need the Graph Data window. After you close the window, it is important to complete and File ➤ Save your data at this point. Refer to Figure 2-11.

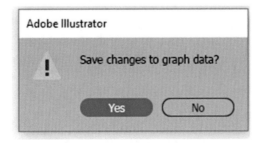

Figure 2-11. *Make sure to save your graph changes if prompted by an alert message*

Later in this chapter, we will look at how to customize the column and marker designs. These kinds of customizations should always be the last step in your graph design.

Now we will explore other creative ways to modify your graphs so that they do not just appear in the default grayscale but in color.

Recoloring the Graph Using the Control and Properties Panel

As you have noticed throughout the chapter, as you build your graph, the default colors are often in a grayscale, which is not very interesting. There are several ways you can go about recoloring your graphs, which I will show you now.

The first way, if, for example, you have a column or bar chart that is not clustered, is to use the Direct Selection tool and select each bar path one at a time. Once you have selected one, you can then use your Control panel or Properties panel to color each of the bars in the graph a new fill color. Refer to Figure 2-12.

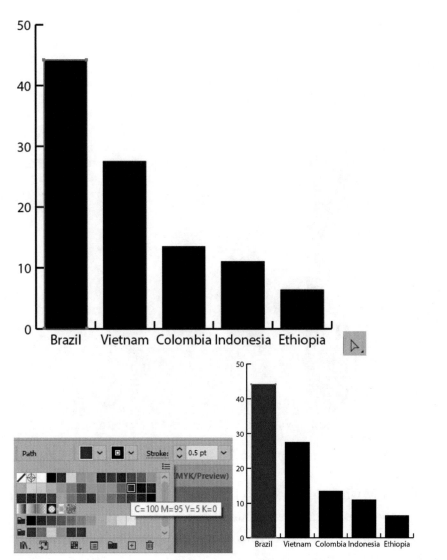

Figure 2-12. *With nonclustered graphs without a legend, you can select each bar with the Direct Selection tool and color it using the Swatches in the Control panels*

This is a good method in situations where a legend might not be necessary for the graph. However, you would still want to, with your Type tool, add a title so that you would know what the topic of the graph was. Refer to Figure 2-13.

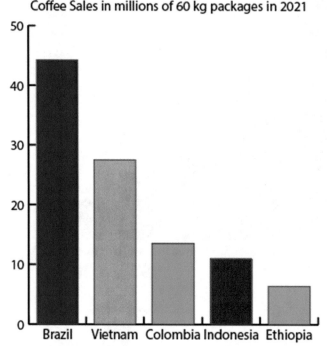

Figure 2-13. *Nonclustered column graph with different colored columns*

The second way, when dealing with clusters of bars or columns, would be to use the Group Selection tool to click select part of your graph's legend rectangle, as you did earlier when you combined two types of graphs. Then click again to select both the rectangle and the column or bar and then use the Control panel and recolor the columns' fills again with brighter colors. Note that I will leave the stroke in black because it gives a nice outline. But you can always adjust the stroke weight from the Control panel if you feel it is too thin at 0.5pt. Refer to Figures 2-14 and 2-15.

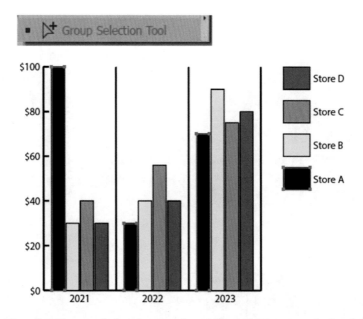

Figure 2-14. *Use the Group Selection tool to select the rectangle in the legend and then click again to select related columns*

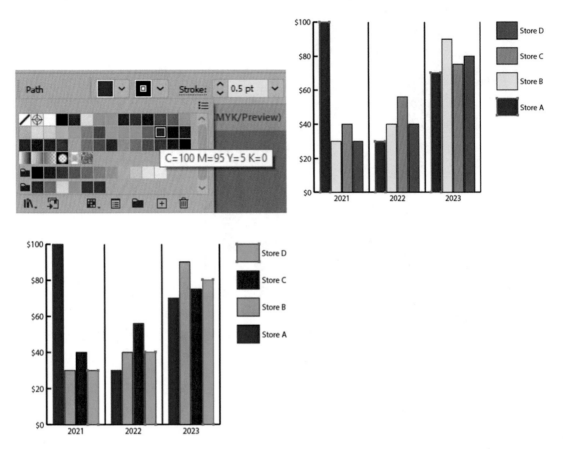

Figure 2-15. *Use the Control panel to color selected legends rectangles and the related columns*

In other situations, once you have assigned colors to the graph, you can then use your recolor icon which is found in the Control panel and in the Quick Actions of the Properties panel. I find this method best to use after you have changed the black bar or column to a new color because if you change the black fill using the Recolor panel, it will also affect the stroke of the graph.

When you want to do an overall color change, use the Selection tool and then click the Recolor Artwork icon in the Control panel or button in the Properties panel under Quick Actions. Refer to Figure 2-16.

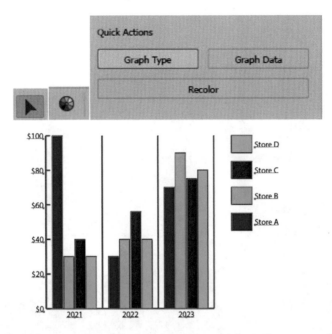

Figure 2-16. *Select the graph with the Selection tool and use Recolor Artwork from the Control panel or Properties panel to do a mass recolor on your graph*

As you saw in Volume 1 with shapes and paths even if grouped, you can use this panel to recolor areas quickly by changing the colors in the Assign Swatches and moving them around on the color wheel. You can double-click the swatch to access the Color Picker or use your Color Library drop-down, limit colors, or use the Color Theme Picker to select surrounding colors. Refer to Figure 2-17.

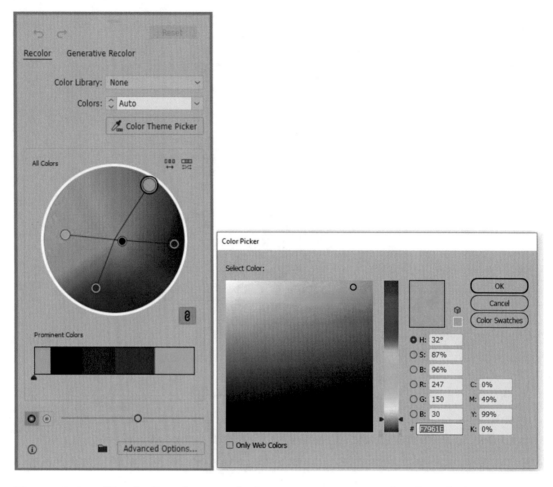

Figure 2-17. *Use the Recolor panel when you want to recolor the whole graph at once and double-click the swatch stop to access the color for a custom color*

You can also use the Advanced Options if you need to access the color harmonies. Here we can see how I have moved the colors and how the graph colors are now altered. In this case, I unlinked the harmony colors so that the swatches could move independently. Refer to Figure 2-18.

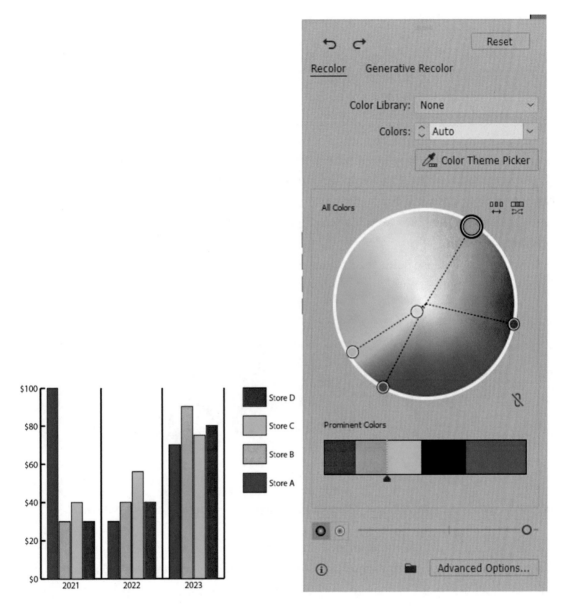

Figure 2-18. *Adjust the Recolor settings and unlink swatches in the Recolor panel for greater freedom of color choice, and the graph will update*

Note   If you like a certain color theme, then make sure to save it. Use the folder to save all prominent colors to the Swatches panel. Refer to Figure 2-19.

Figure 2-19. *Save the Prominent Colors that you create from Recolor in the Swatches panel as a color group*

Or save copies of the graph (Alt/Option+Drag) with the Selection tool so that you have several variations to compare.

You can click the blank area of the artboard, for now, to close the Recolor panel and deselect the graph.

You can apply these color techniques to the other graphs including the pie graph. Refer to Figure 2-20.

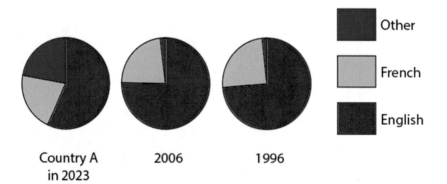

Figure 2-20. *You can recolor any graph type quickly including the pie chart*

However, with pie graphs, if legends are in the wedges, as we saw earlier in Chapter 1 in the section "Applying Graph Options," you may want to use the Direct Selection tool afterward to change some text, using the Control panel, to a white fill font, adjust the font family, the font style to bold, and increase the size of the text. Refer to Figure 2-21.

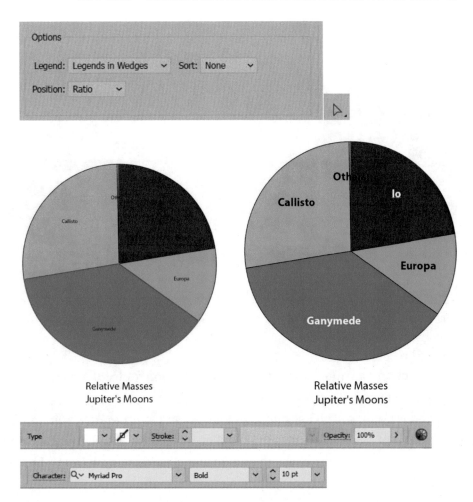

Figure 2-21. *On pie charts with Legends in Wedges, you may have to use the Direct Selection tool to move color, enlarge font, and alter style of some type that is difficult to read using the Control panel*

In other situations, use Direct Selection tool to move the text outside of the wedge. This may be better visually, and then you can with your Line Segment tool, especially for smaller wedges, point to the wedge. Use the Line Segment tool to direct a stroke at the wedge so that the audience can see what it represents clearly and add an arrowhead to the stroke as well using the Stroke panel. Refer to Figure 2-22.

Others
Io
Callisto
Europa
Ganymede
Relative Masses
Jupiter's Moons
Line Segment Tool (\)
Stroke
Weight: 1 pt
Cap:
Corner:
Limit: 10
Align Stroke:
Dashed Line
dash gap dash gap dash gap
Arrowheads:
Scale: 100% 100%
Align:
Profile: Uniform

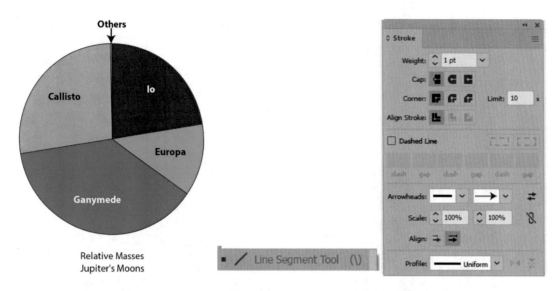

***Figure 2-22.** When wedges are too small to fit part of the legend, move it out of the wedge and then use the Line Segment tool and Stroke Panel to add an arrow for clarification*

With the Selection tool, make sure to, using the Selection tool Shift+click the line with the graph if you need to move them together.

You can, at this point, still go back into your Object ➤ Graph ➤ Data and update the Labels text if you want to add percentages as well on a separate line. Remember to use your vertical bar key (|). Click the check to update and close the Graph Data window. Refer to Figure 2-23.

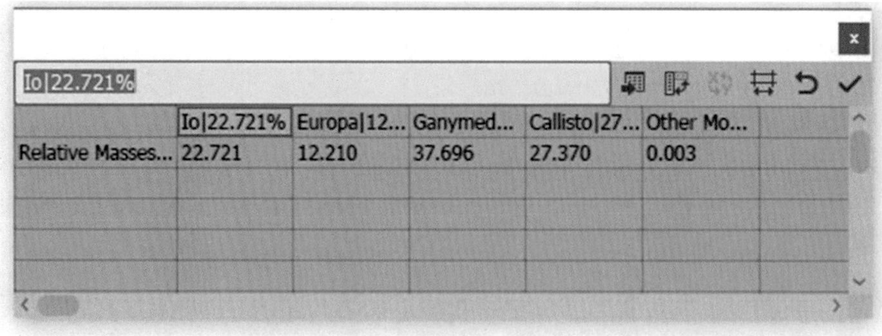

Io|22.721%
Io|22.721%
Europa|12...
Ganymed...
Callisto|27...
Other Mo...
Relative Masses...
22.721
12.210
37.696
27.370
0.003

***Figure 2-23.** Return to your Graph Data window if you need to update some of the headers for the legends, and click the check to commit the change*

However, keep in mind that when you add more text to the labels, the font size may alter, and then you have to use the Direct Selection tool for selection and movement and your Control panel to increase your font size again. Refer to Figure 2-24.

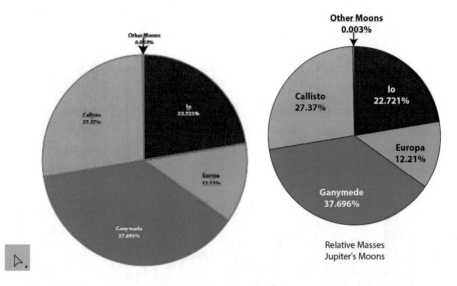

Figure 2-24. *If the texts decrease in size after the data updates, make sure to select each text line with the Direct Selection tool and update using the Control panel*

Note   If you add more data to your chart, you will need to color that bar, column, or wedge along with its data in the legend using one of the methods just mentioned. That is why it is best to complete the graph layout before recoloring.

Using your Group Selection tool and the Control panel, you can continue to edit the following on select legends and paths:

- Apply gradient or pattern swatches and adjust stroke weight, variable width profile, brush definitions, opacity/transparency, with varying blend modes, and graphic styles which could have other effects (fx) like 3D as we will see later in Chapters 5 and 6. Refer to Figure 2-25.

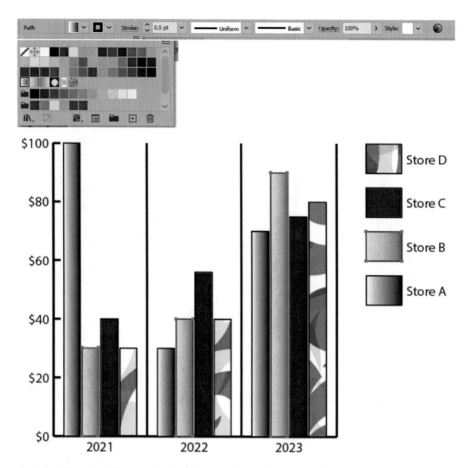

Figure 2-25. *Use the Group Selection tool and Control panel to apply gradients and patterns to a graph not just solid colors*

Note   Once graphs are painted with gradients, this might cause unexpected results. The best practice is to only apply the gradient when the graph is complete. If you encounter an issue, try using the Direct Selection tool or Group Selection tool to select gradient-painted areas. Choose a solid color from the Control panel temporarily, while you edit the data and apply it, save the data, close the Graph Data window, and then apply the gradient again to the fill using your Control panel.

For the graphs, we have just talked about you can refer to the following file graphs3.ai and review some of examples I have created.

Add a Custom Pattern to Part of a Graph

As mentioned, patterns are stored in the Swatches panel. However, you can even add a custom pattern to a graph's legend and related column, bar, or wedge. I will show you how to add a simple custom pattern background that you can later modify on your own. Let's take a moment to look at how the Swatches and Pattern Options panel can be used to create a simple background repeating pattern.

To begin, you need to create some artwork on your artboard that you want to be the repeating pattern. It should fit with the theme on your graph and not be overly distracting or busy. It can also contain items that have opacity/transparency. It also should be something you don't mind if part of the pattern is chopped off on the sides or top because each bar, column, or wedge may be a different size or height.

In this case, I created some ellipses with my Ellipse tool that could represent a colorful type of candy or cookie with a white icing center. I then Object ➤ Group each colorful shape and then used my Direct Selection tool and Swatches panel to color each of the cookies and some I left the same color. Currently, there are seven cookies arranged in kind of a hexagon pattern. When working with repeating patterns, it is best to arrange them in groupings like squares, triangles, or hexagons so that they will fit together seamlessly with few gaps. However, as you will see in a moment, you can continue to edit and correct patterns while in pattern editing mode if you don't get it quite right on the artboard. Refer to Figure 2-26.

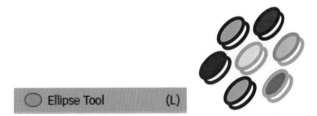

Figure 2-26. *Create your own simple pattern for a graph design*

Once you have completed your design, save your file. In my case, you can use the one in this file graphs4_start.ai for practice. It already has a few graphs with which to practice.

Use the Selection tool to marquee around the entire pattern, and then, while selected, drag it into the Swatches panel and release your mouse, and it will appear with the other patterns. Refer to Figure 2-27.

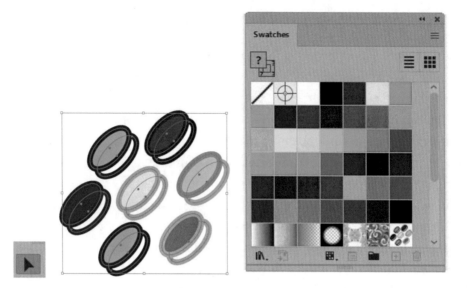

Figure 2-27. *Use the Selection tool to marquee your starting pattern and drag it into the Swatches panel*

Then use from the menu Select ➤ Deselect to deselect all artwork on your artboard. If you do not do this, you may add the pattern to the original artwork by mistake.

Now double-click the pattern swatch in the Patterns panel, and you will have entered pattern editing mode, which you will know, as you will see a surrounding, repeating preview around the current pattern. The Pattern Options panel should be visible as well. Refer to Figure 2-28.

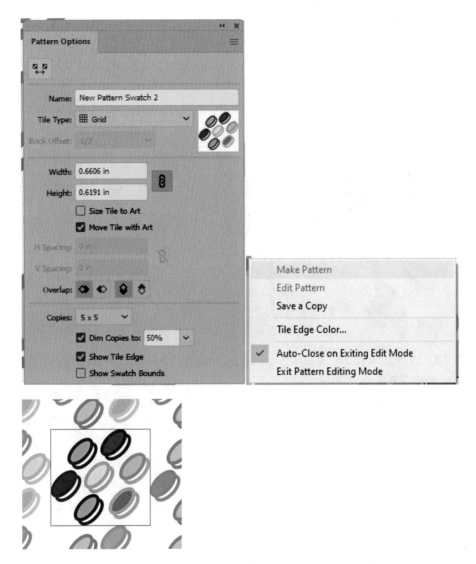

Figure 2-28. *In pattern editing mode, you have access to the Pattern Options panel*

While I will not be going into detail on all possible Pattern Options, I will just point out a few steps, tips, and settings in the panel that you can adjust so that you can edit your repeating pattern.

To begin, you may notice that your repeating pattern has a few large gaps. Refer to Figure 2-28. Use the Selection tool to Alt/Option+Drag out a few more cookies, making the pattern appear more seamless. You can also rearrange the cookies so that they don't overlap and touch one another. With the Selection tool, you can Shift+click each cookie, and while holding down the Shift key, drag inward to scale the cookies to a smaller size. Refer to Figure 2-29.

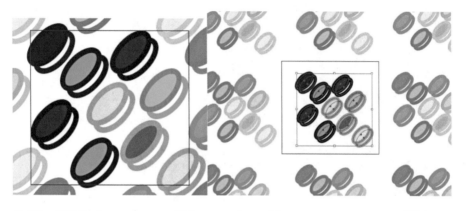

Figure 2-29. *While in pattern editing mode, add to your pattern to fill in gap area or scale the pattern to make it smaller*

This would add some surrounding gaps again, but you can use the Pattern Options panel to adjust this.

For some patterns, you may want to add a solid background which you can do with your Rectangle tool and place behind (Object ➤ Arrange ➤ Send to Back), to add a fill that covers the blue square tile area, but no stroke using the Control panel. Currently, the gaps between the cookies are transparent.

While in pattern editing mode, you can set the following for your pattern in the Pattern Options panel:

- Pattern Tile Tool: Resize and adjust your pattern area when this icon is enabled. Use the bounding box handles to scale the tile. It can go into the cookie area if you need a closer fit, and then click the button again to disable the setting. Refer to Figure 2-30.

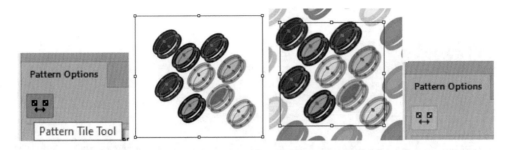

Figure 2-30. *Use the Pattern Options panel Pattern Tile tool to scale the tile surrounding the pattern*

- Name: Give your pattern a new name rather than keep the default name of New Pattern Swatch 1, 2, or however many patterns you have recently created. I will call mine "Colorful Cookies." Refer to Figure 2-31.

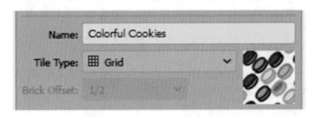

Figure 2-31. *Use the Pattern Options panel to name your pattern swatch*

- Tile Types: This area allows you to choose five different Tile Types. The default is Grid which in my case works best and leaves the least amount of gaps. But for your pattern, Brick by Row, Brick by Column, Hex by Column, or Hex by Row may work better. Take a moment to experiment with these options. Refer to Figure 2-32.

Figure 2-32. *Use the Pattern Options panel to set a new Tile Type Configuration*

- Brick Offset: If you are using the Tile Type of Brick by Row or Brick by Column, then you can set a Brick Offset by ¼, ⅓ , ½, and so on. Depending on your pattern, some offsets may improve the spacing and gaps. A setting of ½ is the default. Take a moment to test these settings. Refer to Figure 2-33.

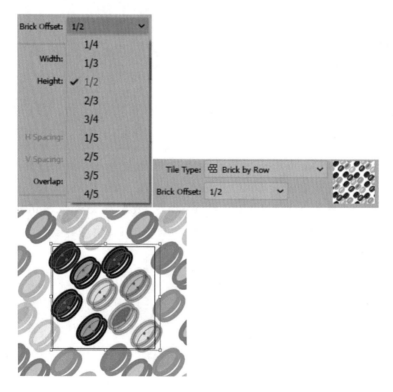

Figure 2-33. *Use the Pattern Options panel to set a new Brick Offset for the Tile Type*

For now, if you are using my pattern, set your Tile Type back to Grid as we look at the rest of the Pattern Options settings:

- Width and Height: It is seen here in inches, and if you set your artboard rulers to that increment, it describes the current width and height of the tile pattern area. If I scale my entire selected pattern in the red bounding box or move a part of it, these settings will not change unless I either go back to my Pattern Tile tool icon and enable it or type in a new width and height. Currently, the link icon is enabled to maintain width and height proportions of the tile. Refer to Figure 2-34.

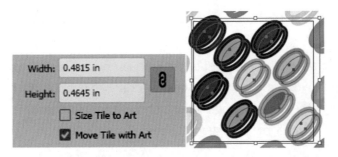

Figure 2-34. *Use the Pattern Options panel to adjust the patterns width and height tile area*

You can click the link icon to unlink it and set the width and height to new numbers, and then click the link again to lock the new ratio. Refer to Figure 2-35.

Figure 2-35. *In the Pattern Options panel, you can link or link the scaling of the tile*

- Size Tile to Art: Enable this setting when you want the tile to size to the current artwork. This may add more or less spacing around the current artwork. Refer to Figure 2-36.

Figure 2-36. *In Pattern Options panel, select the Size Tile to Art option*

- Move Tile with Art: This is set by default; as you move the current selected artwork, the tile moves or expands with it, and if you uncheck it, the tile will move separately or remain stationary while the selected artwork is dragged. Refer to Figure 2-36.

- H Spacing and V Spacing: Horizontal (H) and Vertical (V) Spacing can be adjusted when Size Tile to Art is enabled. By default, it is set to 0 in. The link icon maintains spacing ratios, but it can be unlinked so that you can create custom spacing. Use your up and down Arrow keys on your keyboard to adjust the spacing, or type in a number in this example in inches. In this example negative numbers have compressed the cookies together, so they overlap. Refer to Figure 2-37.

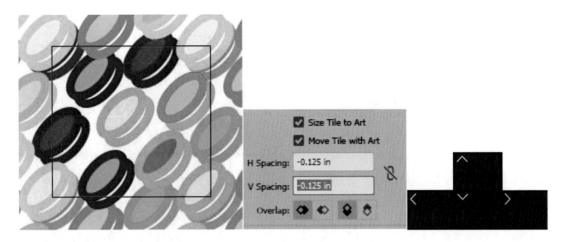

Figure 2-37. *In the Pattern Options panel, when the Size Tile to Art is selected, adjust the H and V Spacing*

- Overlap: When the items in the pattern overlap, you can set different settings using the overlap button icons: Left in Front, Right in Front, Top in Front, and Bottom in Front. By default, it is set to Left and Top in Front, but click the buttons and see how it affects your pattern. Refer to Figure 2-38.

Figure 2-38. *In Pattern Options panel, adjust the Overlap settings*

At this point, if you do not like crowding, uncheck the Size Tile to Art button, and with the link unlinked, set your width and height back to 0.45 inches. Your setting may be slightly different than mine depending on how you scaled the pattern earlier. Refer to Figure 2-39.

Figure 2-39. *In Pattern Options panel, uncheck Size Tile to Art and continue to adjust width and height spacing*

The last section in the Pattern Options panels does not affect the pattern and is just used to display how the pattern may preview. Refer to Figure 2-40.

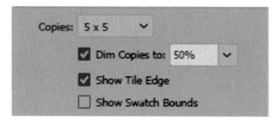

Figure 2-40. *In Pattern Options panel, set the preview of how pattern copies are displayed*

- Copies: How many surrounding copies of the preview will show? You can set 5×5 or 3×3 or another option from the list.

- Dim Copies to 50%: When this check box is enabled, your preview of the surrounding copies shows at 50%, but you can set a lower or higher percentage from the list (0%–100%). When disabled, it shows at 100%.

- Show Tile Edge: If you need to temporarily hide the blue tile edge, click this check box to disable. By default, it is enabled.

- Show Swatch Bounds: This is unchecked by default. When checked, objects outside of these bounds are not repeated. It appears as a thin dotted blue line in pattern editing mode.

Once you have set the pattern the way you want it, then you want to save your work and exit this area. Refer to Figure 2-41.

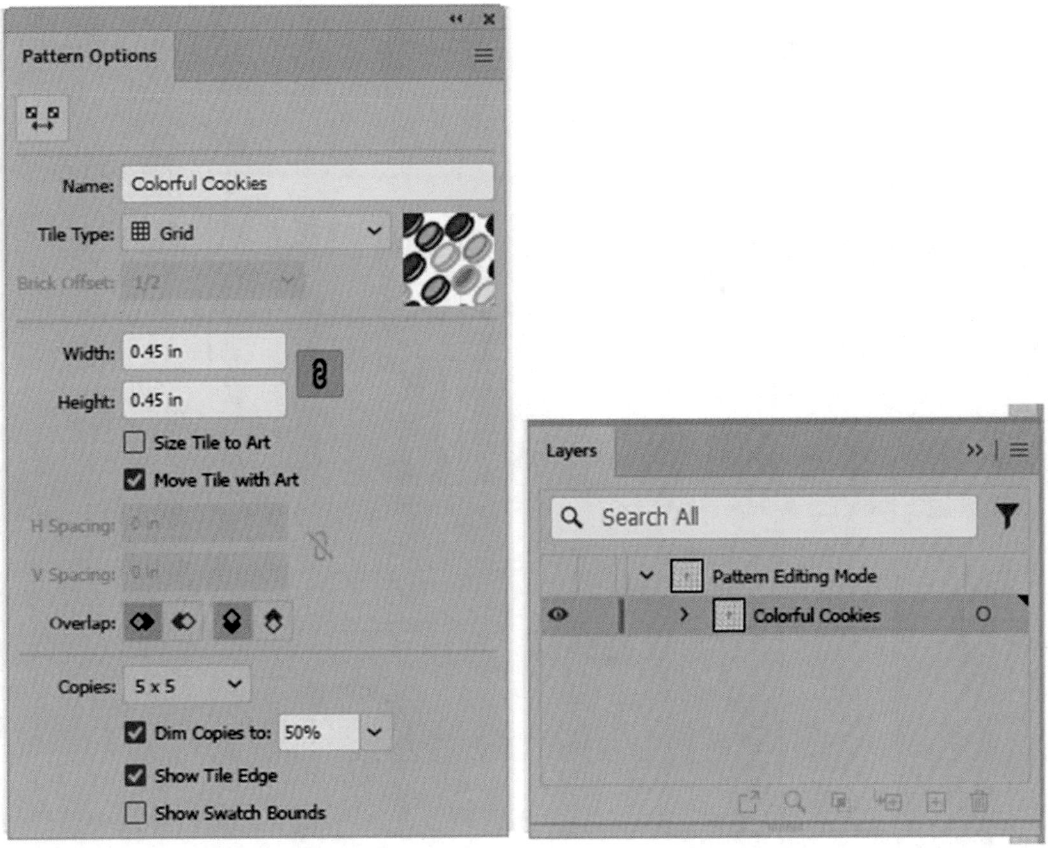

Figure 2-41. *Final settings in Pattern Options panel and how the mode appears in the Layers panel*

Save your work by clicking the Done button to exit pattern editing mode; the button is near the arrow in the upper left corner below the rulers. Refer to Figure 2-42.

Figure 2-42. *Click Done to save your changes and exit the pattern editing mode*

You can also use the arrow if you need to exit a pattern without saving changes or click the cancel button. The Save a Copy button will allow you to save a copy of an updated pattern to the Swatches panel as a separate item.

You can then use the Group Selection tool and click twice on the legend rectangle to apply that pattern to the bars or wedges that you want to using the Swatches panel. Refer to Figure 2-43.

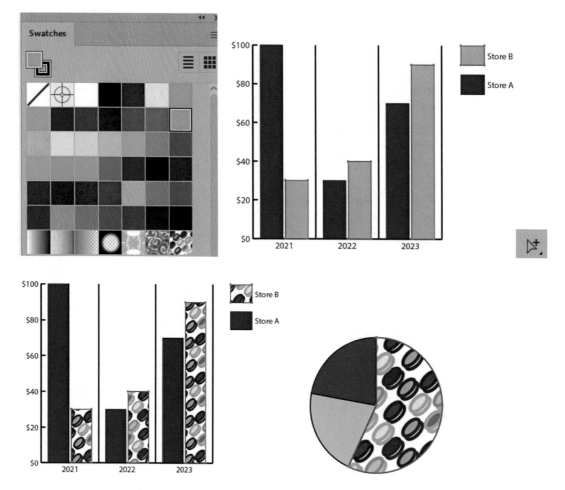

Figure 2-43. *Use the Group Selection tool to select the rectangle in the legend and columns, and use the Swatches panel to add the swatch to columns or part of a pie graph*

If you find that the pattern is still too large, you can always go back into your pattern and scale a copy of it. However, another way to correct this is, while the pattern is selected in the column graph (with legend) or on the pie chart, choose Object ➤ Transform ➤ Scale.

In this case in the dialog box, you only want to transform the pattern, so select Uniform. Change the setting to about 50%, and in the options, only check Transform Patterns, click the Preview, on and off check that it is scaling, and click OK to commit and exit the dialog box. Refer to Figure 2-44.

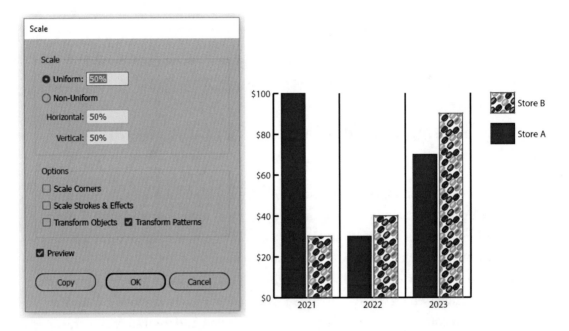

Figure 2-44. *Use the Scale dialog box when you need to scale a selected pattern in a graph*

Now only the pattern in the graph and legend is reduced. Make sure to use patterns sparingly as it can be difficult to focus on the graph if there are too many competing patterns. Refer to the file Graphs4_final.ai for reference.

More details on the Pattern Options panel can be found on this page:

`https://helpx.adobe.com/illustrator/using/create-edit-patterns.html`

While not being used in this book specifically, make sure on your own to check out Illustrator's new feature Text to Vector Graphic (Beta) powered by Adobe Firefly. You can access this panel either from the Window menu or directly from the Properties panel. When you don't require it, you can just collapse the toggle in the Properties panel which you will see in the upper area. This feature is very similar to Generative Recolor mentioned in Volume 1 in the sense that you can use text prompts, but this time they can be used to generate a subject, scene, icon, or even a pattern from a selected rectangular path rather than build the item yourself from scratch. In the case of patterns, they can be reedited using the Pattern Options panel as you just reviewed.

Our focus in this section was to explore drawing your own patterns using your own artistic abilities, but you can learn more about this panel from the following links as well as its current user guidelines due to the fact it is currently in beta:

https://helpx.adobe.com/illustrator/using/text-to-vector-graphic.html
www.adobe.com/legal/licenses-terms/adobe-gen-ai-user-guidelines.html

Altering Graphs with Symbols and Designs to Column and Marker

Rather than have an overall pattern, graphs can have illustrations added to columns and markers. A graph design is often a simple drawing or logo or even a symbol used to represent the values on a graph. It can also be a complex object that contains a pattern and a guide object, which will allow you to scale the design.

Before you create a design, Adobe recommends that you practice with one of their preset graph designs which you can acquire from the Symbols panel. Later, from that symbol or design you create, you will create a graph design and then store it in the Graph Design dialog box.

Note that the following section does not give instructions on how to add a graphic to a pie graph. To add a design, refer to the earlier section on patterns. Refer to Figure 2-43.

How to Add a Graph Design to a Column

The following steps will work for column, bar, stacked column, and stacked bar graphs.

To begin, if you need to acquire a graph column design, you can do so via Window ➤ Symbol Libraries ➤ and choose a symbol from one of the Library panels to add to your Symbols panel and then drag it out of the Symbols panel and then use the Break Link to Symbol icon. Do that now for practice. Refer to Figure 2-45.

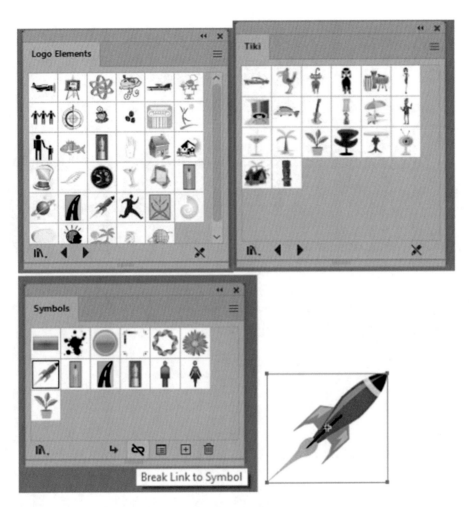

Figure 2-45. *Use a long-shaped symbol from one of the Symbol libraries, add it to your Symbols panel and then break the link to the Symbol and make your own modifications such as the Rocket Symbol*

Some Libraries may have better symbols than others for your graph needs, but for practice, locate some symbols that look like this, and Break Link to Symbols panel to each one first. Refer to Figure 2-46.

Figure 2-46. *Symbols or your own artwork are good items to practice with for column designs*

After you break the object, make sure that, with the Selection tool, you marquee drag around the shape and Object ➤ Group. Refer to Figure 2-47.

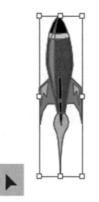

Figure 2-47. *Group your design with the Selection tool*

Refer to file Graph5.ai if you need to follow along a reference as you practice in your own blank file (File ➤ New).

Advanced Note: You may have an (.ai) document that you may want to acquire custom symbols from. Via your Symbols panel, choose the option of Other Library and locate that file on your computer. If you open it, it will contain the symbols in its panel that you can access, and click to add to your current Symbols panel. Refer to Figure 2-48.

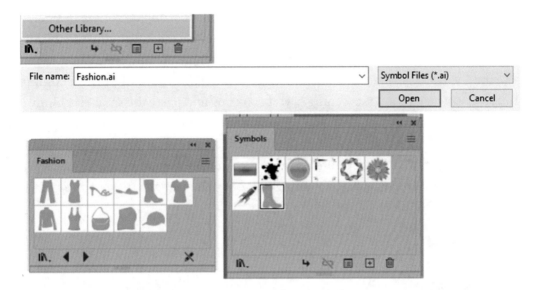

Figure 2-48. *Use the Symbols panel to locate a file that contains custom Symbols*

How to Create a Graph Design

If you want to create your own column design, do so using your various vector shapes and the Pen tool and group the shapes together. For this example, we will just use the rocket, or another broken object, from the Symbols panel. Refer to Figure 2-49.

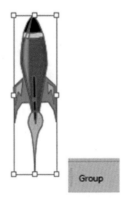

Figure 2-49. *The former Rocket Symbol was rotated, so it is no longer at an angle and has been grouped*

Then you'll create a transparent rectangle as the backmost object. For the design, this will be the boundary of the graph design. To get the design the way you exactly want for all your columns in the column or bar graph you plan to use, it may take a bit of practice until you are satisfied with the result as some designs may not work for columns.

To get an exact size for your rectangle, you can copy and paste the smallest column in your graph to guide you as to how wide your graphic should be. Use your Group Selection tool to select a column and Edit ➤ Copy and then Edit ➤ Paste. And then with the Selection tool, move it somewhere on the artboard next to your rocket. To place your rocket on top, use Object ➤ Arrange ➤ Bring to Front and place the rocket on top of the bar. Refer to Figure 2-50.

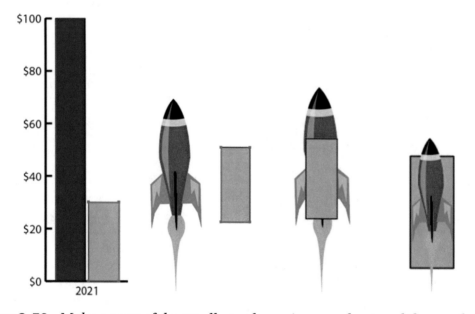

Figure 2-50. *Make a copy of the smallest column in your chart and then scale the rocket to the same size the column and place the column behind the rocket*

You do not need to scale the height of the rectangle to match the height of your graphic.

Alternatively, you can fill or leave the rectangle with a solid color, in this case, set the Stroke and Fill to None so that it is invisible. Check in your Layers panel if the Group rocket design is above the rectangular path. Refer to Figure 2-51.

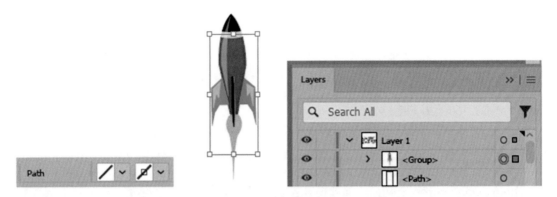

Figure 2-51. *Set the copied column path to no fill or stroke using the Control panel and use the Layers panel to confirm it is behind the rocket*

If it is not, you can alternatively, as you saw in Volume 1 Chapter 8, use your Layers panel square that indicates the selected art to move one sublayer above another.

Use the Selection tool marquee and select the entire design and then Choose Object ➤ Group. Now the design is one unit. Refer to Figure 2-52.

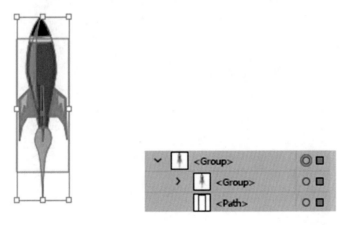

Figure 2-52. *Group the Rocket pattern with the invisible rectangle*

Select with the Selection tool the group.

Now choose Object ➤ Graph ➤ Design.

In the Graph Design dialog box, click the New Design button. Refer to Figure 2-53.

Figure 2-53. *Graph Design dialog box*

You can then see a preview of the selected design. In some situations, only the portion of the design that is first inside the backmost rectangle may appear visible, but the whole design appears when used in the graph. Refer to Figure 2-54.

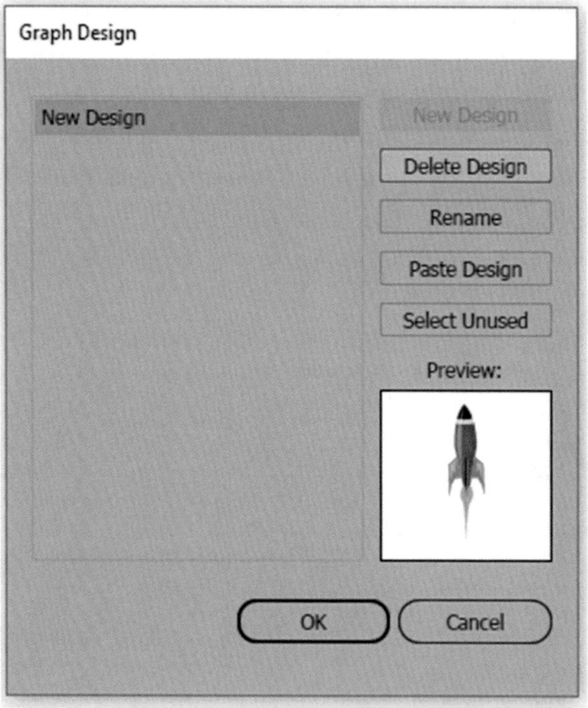

Figure 2-54. *Graph Design dialog box for New Design Preview*

Click Rename to rename the design. And Click OK. Refer to Figure 2-55.

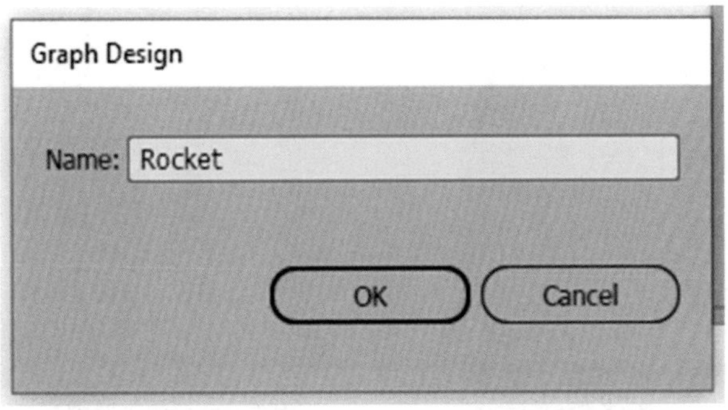

Figure 2-55. *Graph Design dialog box, rename the New Design*

From this dialog box, you can also Delete Design, Paste Design, and Select all Unused designs.

Click OK to exit the Graph Design dialog box. Proceed to the next section, apply a column design to a graph, or continue reading for additional options in graph design.

Sliding Column Graph Design

A sliding column design can also be created in a similar fashion. Refer to the earlier steps, and as before, behind a graphic, you need to create a rectangle boundary of the same column width behind your artwork. Make a copy (Alt/Option+Drag) of your artwork if you want to keep the original.

Now use the Line Segment or Pen tool and create a horizontal line to define where you will stretch or compress the design. Refer to Figure 2-56.

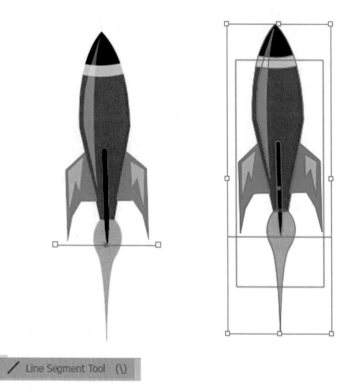

Figure 2-56. *Creating a New Design for a sliding column graph adding a line segment which will be a guide*

Use the Selection tool to marquee select all parts of the design (rectangle, art, and horizontal line).

Use Object ➤ Group and the design is now one unit.

Use the Direct Selection tool or Group Selection tool to select the horizontal line only and nothing else. Choose View ➤ Guides ➤ Make Guides. Refer to Figure 2-57.

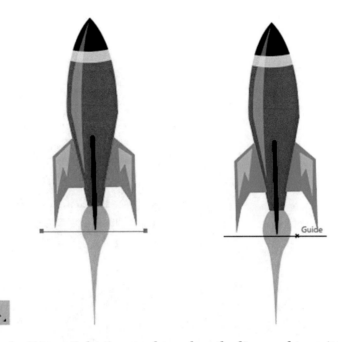

Figure 2-57. *Use the Direct Selection tool to select the line and turn it into a guide*

Then choose View ➤ Guides ➤ Unlock Guides from the menu to remove the Lock setting so that all guides are unlocked. If they are already unlocked, then you do not need to do this step. You will know because the menu will read View ➤ Guides ➤ Lock Guides.

You can see that it is a guide when you hover over it with your smart guide setting on.

To test, use the Selection tool to move the grouped design around to make sure that the guide moves with the design. The whole design should be currently selected.

Like you did earlier, choose Object ➤ Graph ➤ Design.

Click New Design to see the preview. Refer to Figure 2-58.

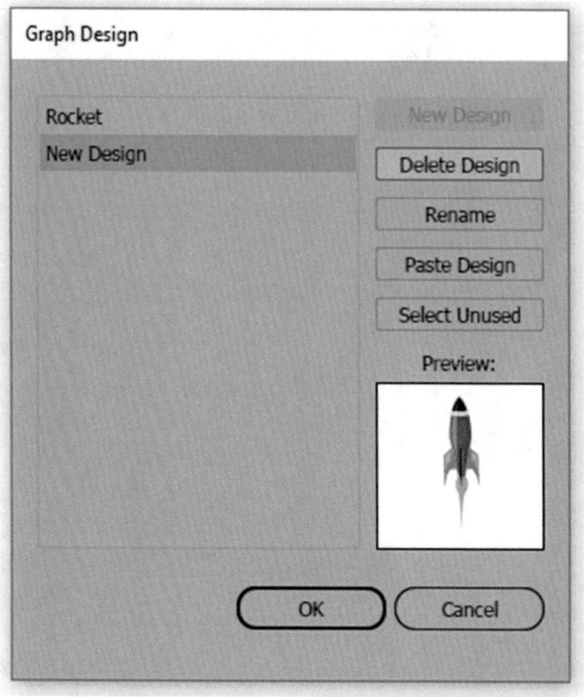

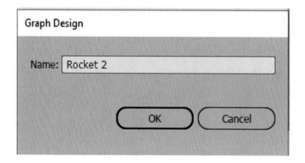

Figure 2-58. *Add the New Design to the Graph Design dialog box*

Then click Rename to name the design. And click OK and then click OK to exit the Graphic Design dialog box. Refer to Figure 2-59.

Figure 2-59. *Rename the New Design*

Apply a Column Design to a Graph

After you have created the design for the column, use the Group Selection tool to select the legend rectangle in the graph, and click again to select the columns or bars you want to fill with the design. Refer to Figure 2-60.

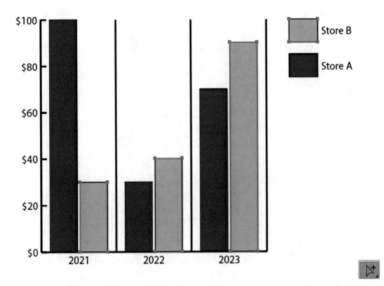

Figure 2-60. *Use the Group Selection tool to select the rectangle in the legend and the columns that you want to alter*

This area is probably the most complicated part of modifying your graph.

Go to Object ➤ Graph ➤ Column.

From the Graph Column dialog box, choose the column design that you created. The default is none. In this example, try Rocket or Rocket 2, which you created with the guide. Refer to Figure 2-61.

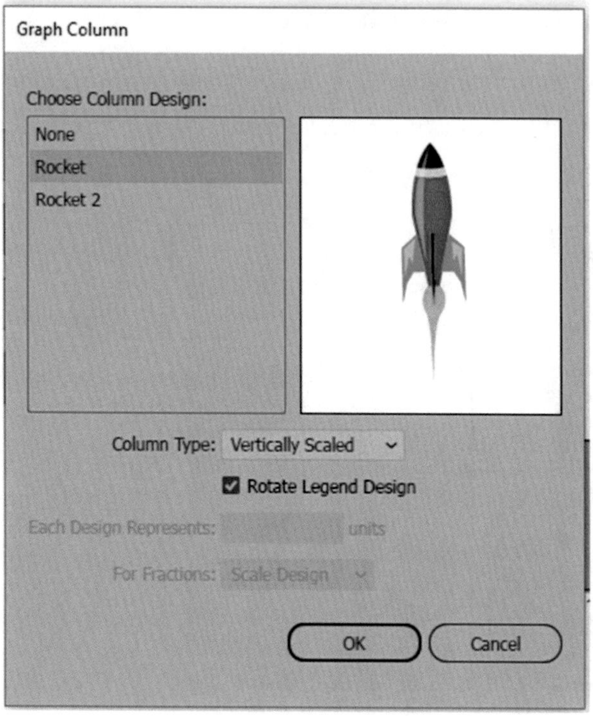

Figure 2-61. *Column Graph dialog box with artwork selected and a chosen column type*

Once you have selected a new column design, you can then set the following options in the Graph Column dialog. Depending on the column type chosen, some will work better with one design than another. You will only be able to view these settings after you click OK, as there is no preview.

- Vertically Scaled Design: It is stretched or compressed vertically, but the width does not change. Notice that because I built some of my rockets above and below my column height, that part of the design extends below the Category Axis. This may be something you do not want. Refer to Figure 2-62.

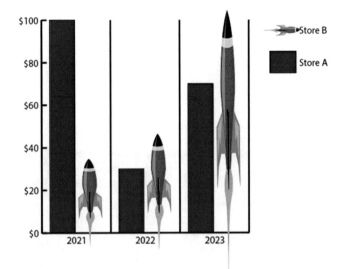

Figure 2-62. *An example of a vertically scaled rocket*

You may want to scale another version inside of the column so that this extension does not happen. Outside the dialog box, you can Object ➤ Ungroup and modify artwork. Object ➤ Group it again with the invisible column. Select with the Selection tool. You can then go back and add a Rocket 3 to the Graph Design dialog box and preview to see what that looks like. Click OK and exit. Refer to Figure 2-63.

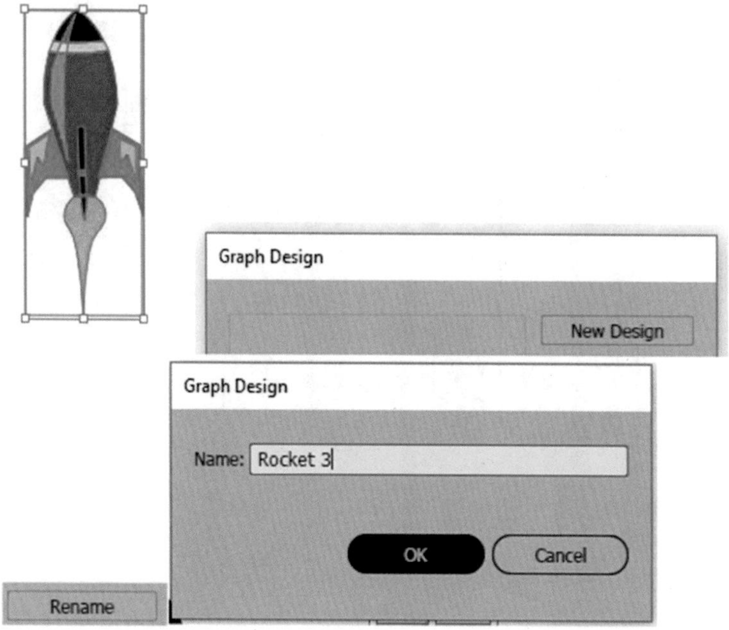

Figure 2-63. *If you want the graph to be more accurate, then make sure to scale a new copy of your rocket so that it matches the smallest column height as well and then create a New Design and rename it*

Now you will want to update the graph column again.

Now you use the Group Selection tool, at this point, to select the older rocket in the legend and columns you will need to click a few more times to ensure that you select both the legend and your columns before you enter Object ➤ Graph ➤ Column to try other options. Select Rocket 3 and Click OK to see how it changed on the graph. Refer to Figure 2-64.

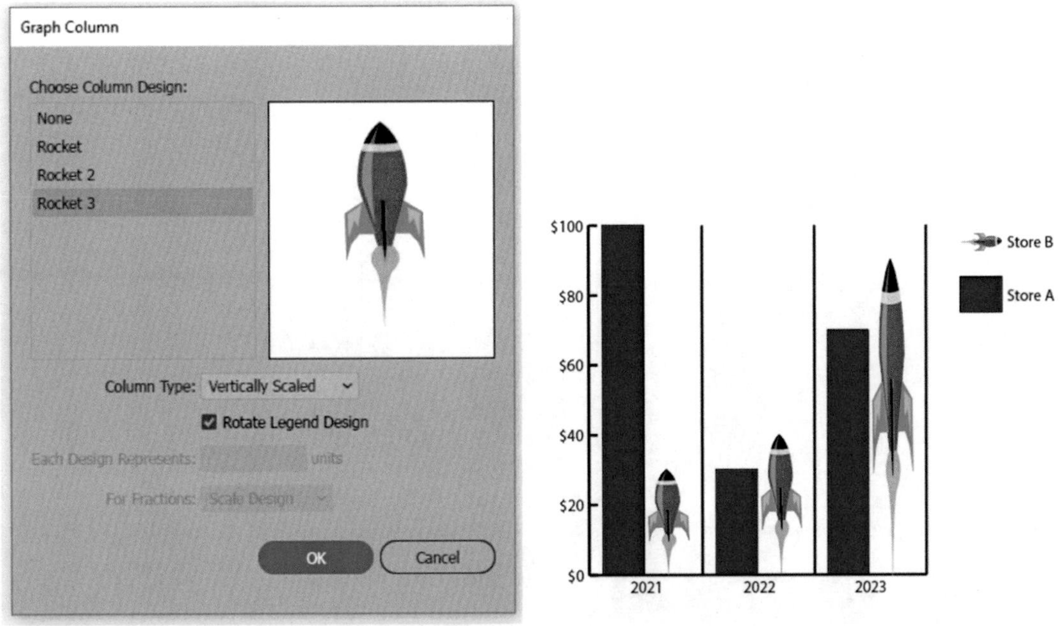

Figure 2-64. *Make sure to select the whole rocket in the legend and the related columns so that you can make your update in the Graph Column dialog box*

- Uniformly Scaled Design: Scaled vertically and horizontally. The horizontal spacing of the design is not adjusted for different widths. We can see that if other column/bar types are incorporated, there is some overlap, so this kind of design would likely be best for a single column design rather than a cluster. Refer to Figure 2-65.

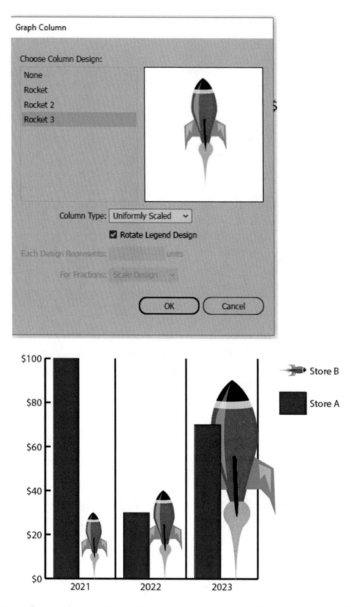

Figure 2-65. *Use the Column Graph dialog box to uniformly scale the rocket on the graph*

- Repeating Design: Stacks the designs to fill the columns. You are able to specify the value that each design represents in units and if you want to chop or scale the design to represent fractions. Refer to Figure 2-66.

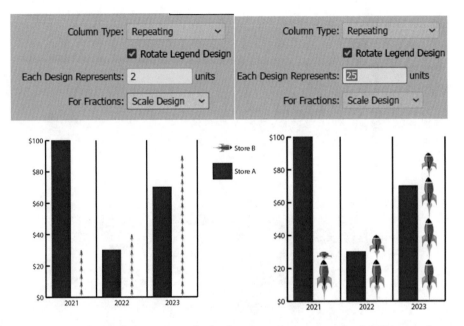

Figure 2-66. *Use the Column Graph dialog box to repeat the rocket on the graph for fractions scaled*

As with the all the other column types so far, you can also Rotate Legend Design. Unchecking this would cause the rocket to be straight up as it is on the column. Refer to Figure 2-67.

Figure 2-67. *For the graph legend design, you can rotate it*

Each design represents number units, so you need to enter a value in the text box. For Fractions (Chop Design and Scale Design) will now be available. Chop Design cuts off a fraction of the top design as required, and scale design scales to the last top design to fit in the column. Refer to Figures 2-66 and 2-68.

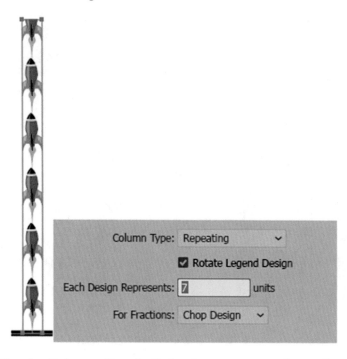

Figure 2-68. *Use the Column Graph dialog box to repeat the rocket on the graph for fractions Chop Design*

- Sliding Design: Similar to the vertically scaled design, except that you can specify where in the design you want to stretch or compress using the guide line. Some areas can remain proportionate. While the vertical scale, as we saw earlier, would scale the whole design. I will use Rocket 2 to test this. Refer to Figures 2-69 and 2-70.

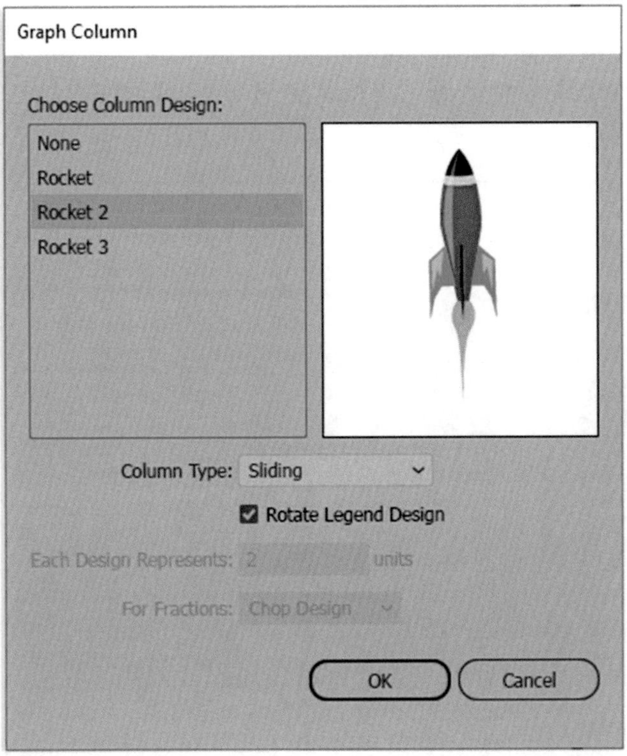

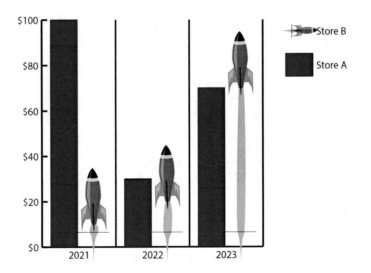

Figure 2-69. *Use the Column Graph tool to set a sliding design with your rocket with a guide line*

Figure 2-70. *A rocket with a sliding guide will stretch at a set point*

Note   In this example, the guide line was left visible so that you can see where the stretch occurred. However, like all guides, it will not print when you print directly from Illustrator.

Once you select the design and column type you want to use, then Click OK to exit.

You can also create a fourth rocket, outside of the dialog box if you do not want the stretch to extend below the Category Axis line. Refer to Figure 2-71.

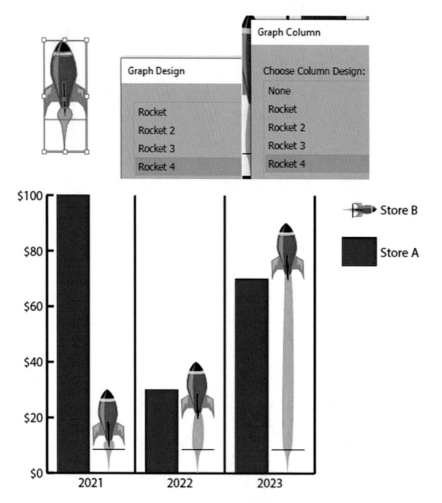

Figure 2-71. *Adjust the rocket and its guide to match the height of the column, create a new graph design, renamed design, and then apply it to the updated column graph using the Graph Column dialog box*

Tip When editing a grouped design on the artboard rather than ungrouping your whole design from the column and guide, you can use the Group Selection tool to select the parts of the rocket only. Then switch to the Selection tool. Use View ➤ Outline so that you can accurately scale just the rocket inside of the column. Then choose View ➤ Preview Click off the artwork to deselect and then select the whole design with your Selection tool before returning to Object ➤ Graph ➤ Design and creating your new design. Refer to Figure 2-72.

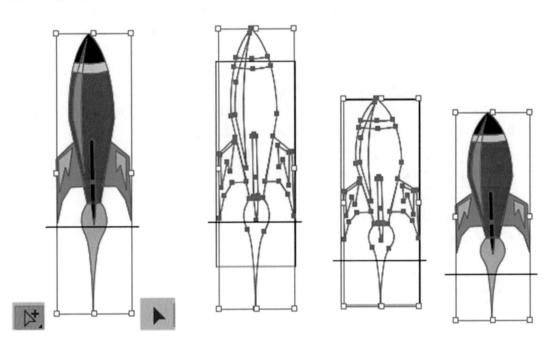

Figure 2-72. *Adjust your artwork while in a grouped state using Outline mode*

Totals Can Be Added to a Column Design

After your column design has been created, select the Type tool. Position the pointer at the location where you want the value to appear in or near the rectangle guide. Type can be placed, in, above, below, left, or right of the design. Refer to Figure 2-73.

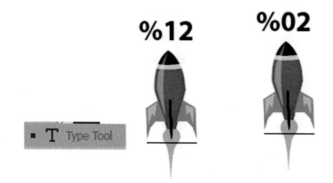
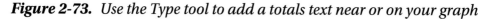

Figure 2-73. *Use the Type tool to add a totals text near or on your graph*

Click and type a percent sign (%) followed by two digits from 0 to 9, for example, %12. This is a code, in that the first digit determines how many places appear before your decimal point, for example, if the total is 134, a digit of 3 will display 134. However, if you entered 0 for the first digit, the program adds the number of places required for the digit.

The second digit determines up to how many places appear after the decimal point. Zeros are added as necessary, and values will round up or down as required, similar to how you see them in the Graph Data window. These numbers can be varied depending on how many digits are required.

Use your Control panel or Character and Paragraph panels to adjust the Attributes for the text, as required. Refer to Figure 2-74.

Figure 2-74. *Highlight the text and make adjustments*

Use Text Align Right when you want to align decimal points. You may need to use your Selection tool to move the text over to center it over your design. Refer to Figure 2-74.

Now use the Selection tool to marquee the design within the rectangle (which was already grouped with a guide line), and now the type is selected.

Object ➤ Group the New Design so it is one unit.

Choose Object ➤ Graph ➤ Design.

In the dialog box, click New Design to see the preview. Refer to Figure 2-75.

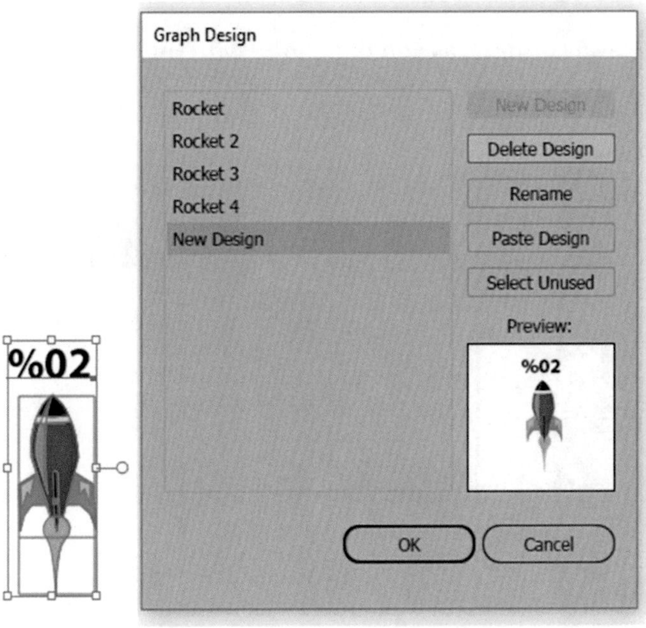

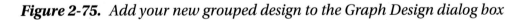

Figure 2-75. *Add your new grouped design to the Graph Design dialog box*

Click Rename then give the design a new name. Click OK and OK again to exit the dialog box.

Refer to Figure 2-76.

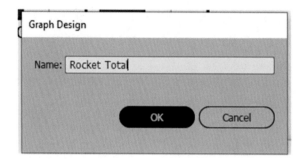

Figure 2-76. *Rename your New Design*

Select the legend and columns as you did before with the Group Selection tool. Refer to Figure 2-77.

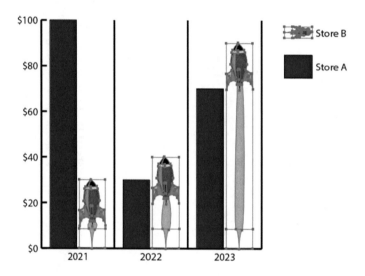

Figure 2-77. *Select your legend and columns to update your graph design*

Then apply your new graph design as you did in earlier examples to the Object ➤ Graph ➤ Column dialog box, and this number will update if you change it using your Graph Data window and clicking the check icon to confirm. Refer to Figure 2-78.

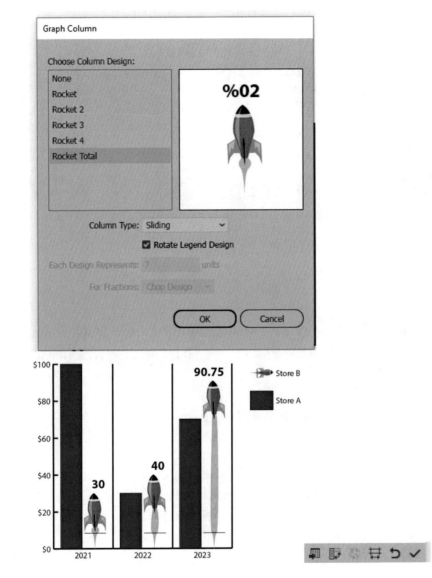

Figure 2-78. *Update your graph design in the Column Graph dialog box to display the latest data totals when you update the data*

Note   If you try to delete a design from the Graph Design dialog box that is already in use, you will receive the following warning. Refer to Figure 2-79.

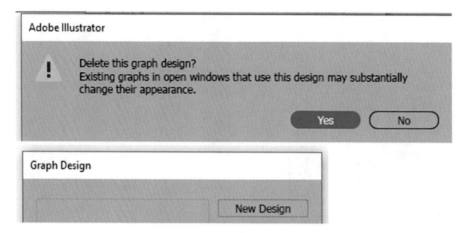

Figure 2-79. *Warning message if you try to delete designs that are already in use by a graph*

Note   Click No and then switch the graph design, first in the Graph Column dialog box, before returning to the Graph Design dialog box, and now click Delete Design.

How to Create and Add a Graph Marker

These steps work for line and scatter graphs.

As you created column graph art, you can also create a marker design. In this example, I have already colored the point markers and lines using the Group Selection tool, similar to how I colored the column graph using the Control panel. However, you will need to select the line in the legend separately if you want to color the lines on the graph. Refer to Figure 2-80.

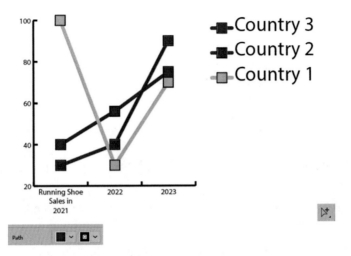

Figure 2-80. *Color markers and lines on a graph using the Group Selection tool and the Control panel*

To change the marker, you need to select one with the Direct Selection tool from a line graph and then choose Edit ➤ Copy. Then choose Edit ➤ Paste, and with the Selection tool, move it on the artboard to where you are going to create your design. Refer to Figure 2-81.

Figure 2-81. *Make a copy of your marker from the graph to edit*

Like the column, this will become the backmost object in the design and will be the size of your new marker. You can leave it solid with a stroke or if you want or make it invisible with no fill or stroke.

Above it, add some marker artwork; it can be the same size as the marker or slightly larger. Refer to Figure 2-82.

Figure 2-82. *Add some artwork to your marker and group it*

Make sure to Select the Art and the marker with the Selection tool and Object
➤ Group.

Then as you did earlier, choose Object ➤ Graph ➤ Design and click the New
Design button.

Click the Rename button to rename the design, and click OK and then OK to exit the
Graph Design dialog box. Refer to Figure 2-83.

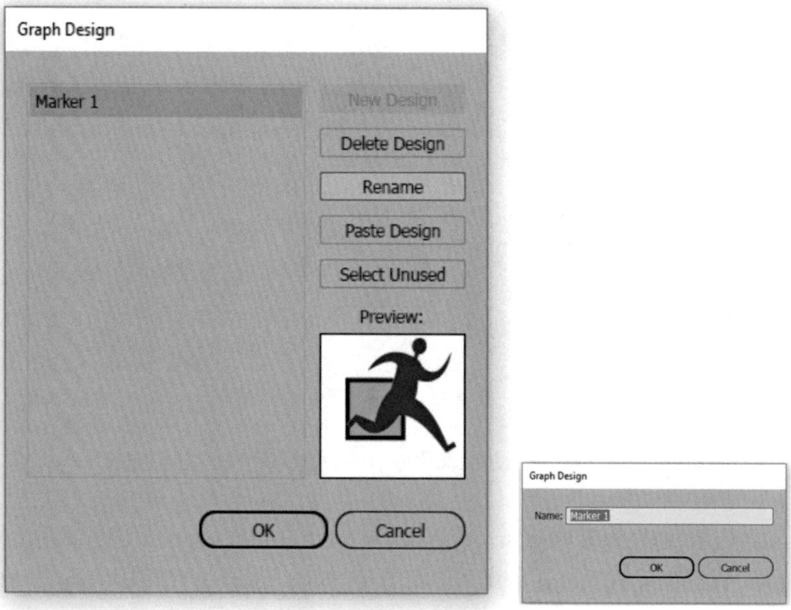

Figure 2-83. *Add the marker to your Graph Design dialog box, and you can
rename the marker*

Now you can apply it to a line or scatter graph.

After you create the design, use the Group Selection tool to select the rectangular
legends and square marker in the graph that you want to replace the design with, but do
not select any of the lines. Here I have selected the orange markers. Refer to Figure 2-84.

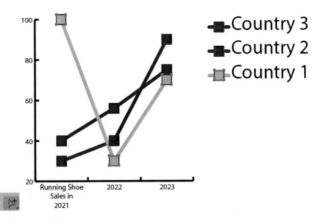

Figure 2-84. *Use the Group Selection tool to select the square marker on the legend and graph*

Choose Object ➤ Graph ➤ Marker to select the name of the Marker Design from the list, none is the default. Choose, in this case, Marker 1, look at the Preview, and click OK; the design will be scaled so that the backmost rectangle in the design is the same size as the default square marker on the line or scatter graph. Refer to Figure 2-85.

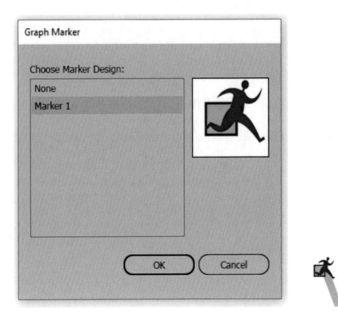

Figure 2-85. *Choose the marker from the Graph Marker dialog box*

Keep this in mind when you design a marker: If you want a larger marker, then make sure that the design fits within the marker. Likewise, you could also cover your markers with your own artwork later, but it would not actually be part of the graph.

Refer to the following files graph_design5.ai and graph_design6.ai to review this artwork and graphs. Refer to Figure 2-86.

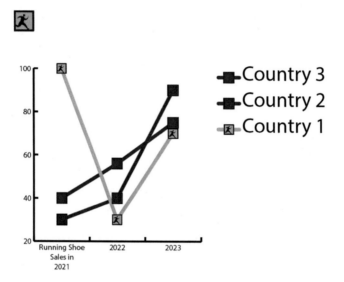

Figure 2-86. *Try adding another marker that has the icon fit within it*

Recycle/Extract a Graph Design

In some situations, you may have received a graph with a design applied but do not have the original artwork. Most times it would be best to keep a backup or save the artwork as a symbol, which you can break the link to after you drag it onto the artboard again. Refer to Figure 2-87.

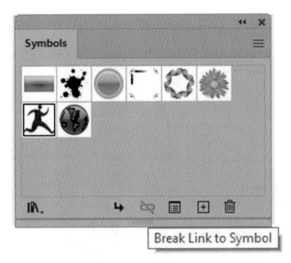

Figure 2-87. *Store markers you create on the Artboard or Symbols panel to drag onto the artboard to edit when your break the link to the Symbol*

Original artwork, as you discovered when you practice the earlier steps, can always be added again to the Graph Design dialog box with a new name, and the old design deleted.

However, when you must create a new design or edit the original design and the artwork is not on the artboard, you can extract it from the Graph Design dialog box.

Make sure that nothing is selected on your artboard while using your Selection tool or Choose from the main menu Select ➤ Deselect.

Go to Object ➤ Graph ➤ Design, and from the dialog box, select the design that you want to paste onto your artboard and click the Paste Design button. Refer to Figure 2-88.

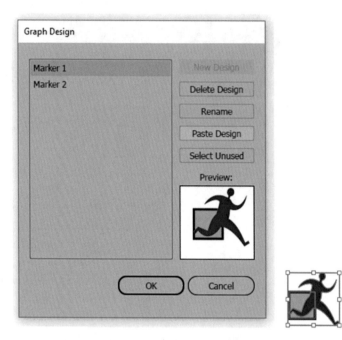

Figure 2-88. *Retrieve a marker or design from the Graph Design dialog box with Paste Design and OK to exit, and the art is on the artboard*

Click OK to exit, and that design is now on your artboard. You can now edit it and then add it back later using the earlier mentioned steps in the Object ➤ Graph ➤ Design dialog box and then later to your Graph Column or Graph Marker dialog boxes.

Make sure that you File ➤ Save any of your work at this point.

Note that we will look at more design enhancements in Chapters 5 and 6 for 3D. Refer to file graph7.ai for reference.

For more details on this topic, you can visit the following page:

`https://helpx.adobe.com/illustrator/using/graphs.html`

Summary

In this chapter, we looked at how to alter symbols and designs to suit your needs for your graph. We also looked at working with type, colors, and patterns on your graph.

In the next chapter, you will be using the Image Trace panel to extract designs from a line drawing or copied graph/chart that came from another application.

Altering Graphics Using the Image Trace Panel and Project Ideas

This chapter looks at how to edit graphs that are copied from another Microsoft application and pasted into Illustrator. We will also look at using the Image Trace panel to create unique graphic creations. As we progress through the chapter, we will look few graph projects and consider some ideas.

Note This chapter does contain projects that can be found in the Volume 2 Chapter 3 folder. Some of the text on Image Trace in this chapter has been adapted and updated from my earlier books *Accurate Layer Selections Using Photoshop's Selection Tools* and *Perspective Warps and Distorts with Adobe Tools: Volume 2*.

Copy/Pasting Graphs from Other Microsoft Products

What about using Word, Excel, or PowerPoint to create my forms first?

In some situations, you may feel more comfortable creating your charts with the data in Microsoft Word, Excel, or PowerPoint. These programs have more chart options such as histogram and box and whisker, as well as a few 3D options. That's OK to do that if you need to create a chart quickly because the data and the chart are in the same location and easy to update. Refer to Figure 3-1.

© Jennifer Harder 2024
J. Harder, *Creating Infographics with Adobe Illustrator: Volume 2*,
https://doi.org/10.1007/979-8-8688-0041-2_3

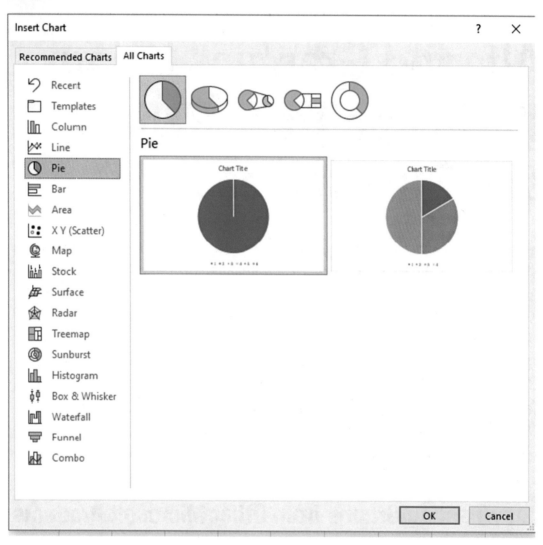

Figure 3-1. *Use Excel to create different chart designs not available in Illustrator*

While I will not go into any depth on how to do that because the focus of this book is Illustrator, you can find notes on how to do that here in Excel:

```
https://support.microsoft.com/en-us/office/create-a-chart-from-start-to-
finish-0baf399e-dd61-4e18-8a73-b3fd5d5680c2
```

However, keep in mind that if you use MS Word to create a chart, when you copy and paste that graph/chart into Illustrator, only a grouped, low, blurry resolution image will be available, and you will not be able to do any final editing in Illustrator. You can use the Image Trace panel to make parts of the image into a vector drawing or draw over it with your shape tools, but this will not turn it back into a graph. We will look at Image Trace panel in a moment.

However, if you copy Ctrl/CMD+C the graph out of Excel (refer to file Chart1.xlsx if you need an example) or PowerPoint, the graph/chart will be pasted Ctrl/CMD+V into Illustrator as a grouped vector for scaling and high-resolution work. Here you can select each of the wedges. Refer to Figure 3-2.

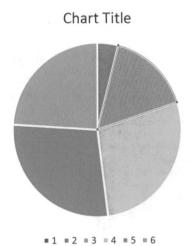

Figure 3-2. *Some parts of an Excel chart like paths and text are still editable after they are copied to Illustrator but not the data*

With certain 2D graphic charts, you will be able to edit the surrounding default text and some of the graphics. Choose Object ➤ Ungroup to do this and then use your Selection tool to move paths or Type tool to edit text.

For 3D charts copied from Excel, because the resolution is higher, you may have more success with Image Trace on the 3D shapes should you want to recreate them for other projects. We will look at how to do that in the next section of this chapter.

Regardless of how you create your chart/graph, each method works well whether you start your work in Illustrator or Excel. But ultimately it all depends on how you want to store the data and then how you will manipulate it afterward in regard to colors or 3D. Remember, color and effect manipulation should always be the last steps for charts, and we will look at that in more detail in Chapters 4, 5, and 6.

How to Edit Graphics That Are Copied Directly from Microsoft Excel

Lastly, I will just demonstrate quickly how you can use the Image Trace panel and some of its new and improved features to trace your graph or some simple line art when you need to make it into a vector shape for your graph or graphic art.

In this first example, I will show how this can be done with a chart/graph that was copied and then pasted into Illustrator from Microsoft Excel.

Use my file Chart2.xlsx. In this case I selected the Chart Edit ➤ Copy from Excel and Edit ➤ Paste it into Illustrator. From Excel to copy you can use (Home >Copy) or (Ctrl/CMD+C). It is in the file graph_trace_start.ai. Unlike a 2D graph mentioned earlier, this other 3D graph is not selectable and requires that I use the Image Trace settings, either from the Control panel or from the Image Trace panel itself. I will now show you how to make it into a vector image. Refer to Figure 3-3.

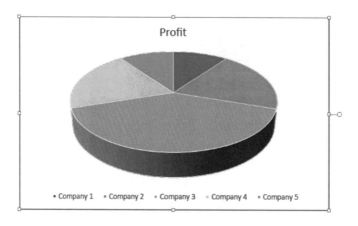

Figure 3-3. Copy a complex chart from Excel to Illustrator, and it is just a grouped image

Once the image is pasted onto the Illustrator artboard, it is a grouped object. In this case we only want the embedded image. Images in Illustrator can be linked or embed. When directly copied, it is embedded. Later, you can refer to the Window ➤ Links Panel to confirm this. Refer to Figure 3-4.

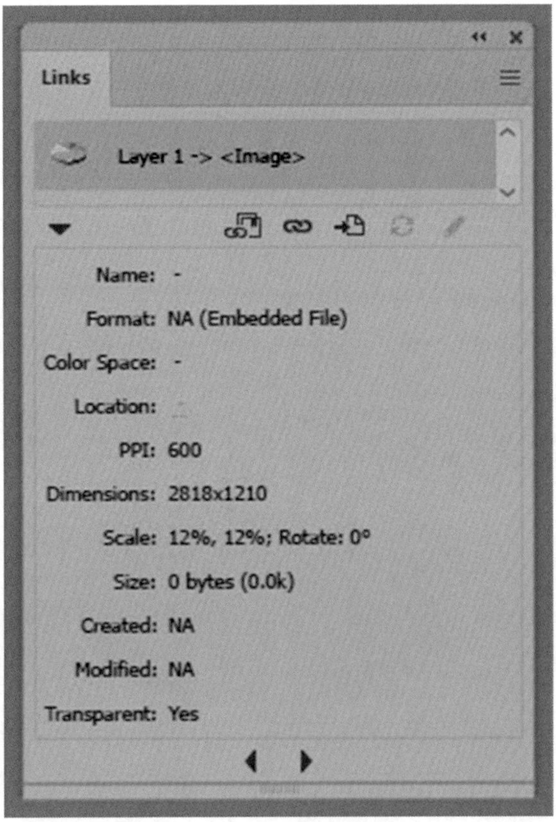

Figure 3-4. *Links panel indicates that the image is an embedded file*

To access just the image while selected, choose Object ➤ Ungroup and then select the clip group pie chart. Move it out of the box, and notice the text is still editable and not a graph or outlines, which is good to know. Refer to Figure 3-5.

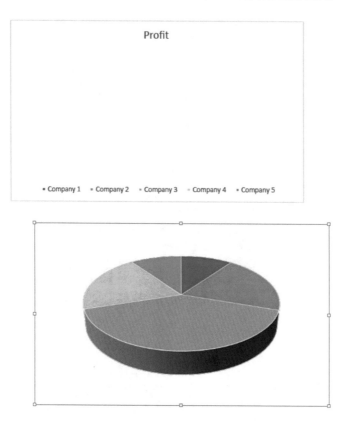

Figure 3-5. *Ungroup the image clipping mask from the text*

For the clip group, choose Object ➤ Clipping Mask ➤ Release. Select the image layer with the Selection tool, move it out of the way, and then select the extra hidden path and Backspace/Delete the extra surrounding invisible path. Use View ➤ Outlines if you are having difficulty locating the invisible path. Refer to Figure 3-6.

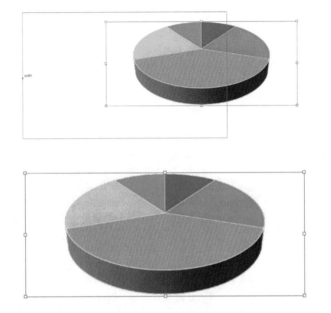

Figure 3-6. *Release the clipping mask to extract the image*

Now select the image again then from the Control panel, click the Image Trace button Arrow list and choose in the preset list the option of 16 colors. This will start the Image Trace. Depending on the Illustrator version you are using, instead of seeing the text in the drop-down, it may appear as thumbnail preview graphics instead, if you do not see these graphic previews. Refer to Figure 3-7 and use it as a visual; note that this area and its related Image Trace panel are often subject to change.

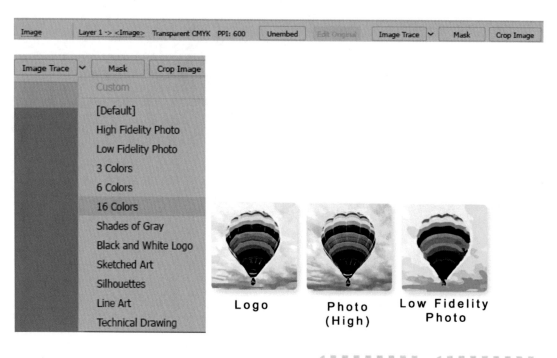

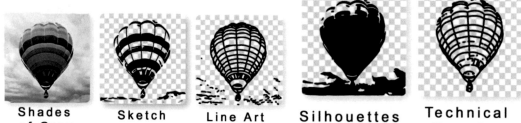

Figure 3-7. *Use the Control panel to do an Image Trace with either the old or new settings depending on your app version. Images are preview examples from Adobe of some settings*

Regardless of how your interface appears, next you may get a warning message that it may take time to trace if it is a high-resolution image. Do not, in this case, click cancel and use Object ➤ Rasterize. In this case, click OK and proceed with the trace. Refer to Figure 3-8.

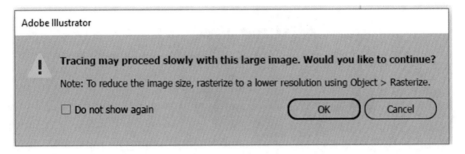

Figure 3-8. *Warning you may receive if the graph image is quite complicated and large*

It may take a moment, but you will know it is complete when you view the Control panel. Refer to Figure 3-9.

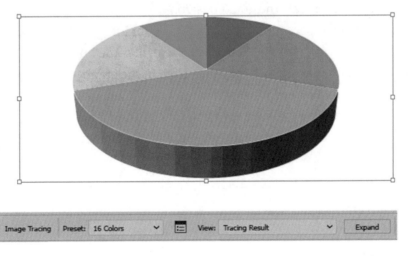

Figure 3-9. *Allow the graph a moment to trace based on the selected preset*

Colorwise, this is pretty close to the original, and to complete the process, click the Expand button in the Control panel. Refer to Figure 3-10.

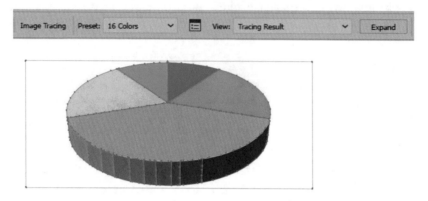

Figure 3-10. *Click Expand in the Control panel to complete the tracing*

This is a fast way to recreate a vector chart from Excel for artwork purposes, but keep in mind that it is no longer a graph and cannot be altered in Illustrator with the Graph Data window. Nevertheless, this is much faster than tracing by hand using the Pen tool, and now you can edit and scale the graph design.

There are many other uses for Image Trace and your infographic projects. For example, in situations where you need to trace a scan of some line art or a logo, where you do not have the original artwork available. Here in the graph_trace_start.ai, you can see how this is useful for line art drawing such as a map that is placed using File ➤ Place as a Linked file (see file globe_background.tif). In the same way, as with the Excel chart, you will see how easy it is to trace a high-resolution (300ppi) map. Refer to Figure 3-11.

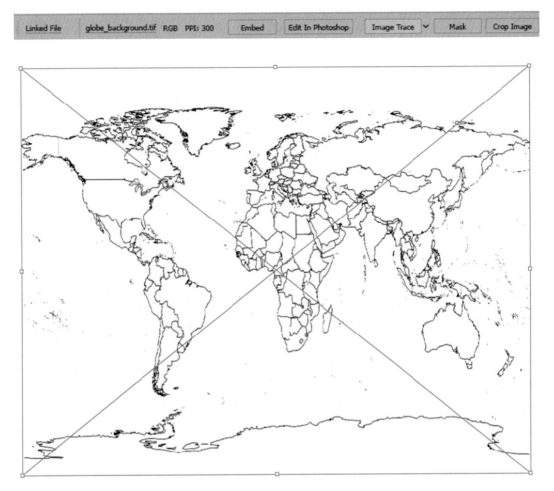

Figure 3-11. *Use Image Trace on high-resolution line drawings when you want to trace them quickly*

When the image is selected with the Selection tool, just click Image Trace with the default setting; in this case, you do not need to select any option from the preset list and click OK to the warning you saw earlier with the chart. The map is traced, then click the Expand button to complete the trace as a grouped image. Refer to Figure 3-12.

Figure 3-12. *Once the trace is complete, click the Expand button*

Choose Object ➤ Ungroup, and you can now, with the Selection tool, select parts of the map that you need for your art as well as Backspace/Delete other parts not required. Refer to Figure 3-13.

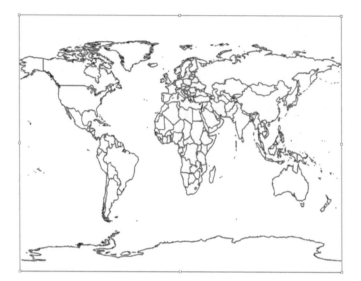

Figure 3-13. *Use elements for the vector line drawing for your project*

Note   While Image Trace is fast, it is not always perfect. As well, the higher the resolution file, the more accurate the trace will be. However, when you want more accurate settings, you must refer to your Image Trace panel. I will not go into any major detail on this topic, just explain some key settings that have been recently updated or may be available for your current interface depending on the version you are viewing. As mentioned, this panel is subject to change. More information can be found on the following page:

`https://helpx.adobe.com/illustrator/using/image-trace.html`

Refer to my file graph_trace_final.ai to see the final traced results of the pie chart and map.

Image Trace Panel Settings

Here is an overview of some of the settings for the Window ➤ Image Trace panel. As mentioned, the basic settings are found in the Control panel when an image is selected. Refer back to Figure 3-12. In regard to Presets, I will explain what they mean next.

Note that your interface may resemble the original interface on the left or the newer one on the right, depending on your current version. Recently Adobe has reverted back to the older interface on the left. Both for the most part have very similar settings. Adobe is often updating and improving this panel, so it is subject to change. Refer to Figure 3-14.

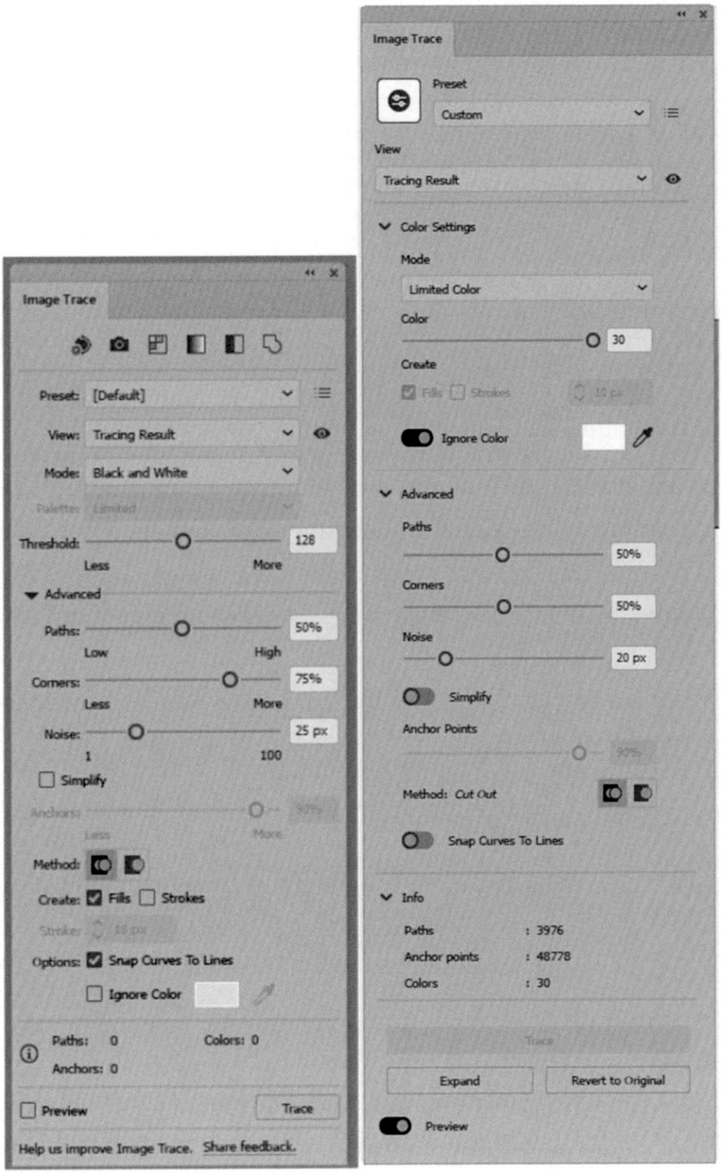

Figure 3-14. *Depending on your version of Illustrator, the Image Trace Panel may look slightly different*

Presets: Rather than extra presets running across the top of the panel or just a textual list in the panel on the right, you will notice that the Presets are now simplified into thumbnail previews. You will see such options as Auto Detect (Sketch, Logo, Line Art, Photo, Low Fidelity Photo, 3 Colors, 6 Colors, 16 Colors, Shades of Gray, Silhouettes, Technical Drawing) as seen earlier in Figure 3-7. You can refer to the thumbnail images earlier if you need to compare them. Note that the older Black and White Logo is similar to Sketch (refer to Figure 3-14 for your comparison). Other equivalent preset conversions are

- Auto-Color uses Logo

- High Color uses Photo

- Low Color uses Low Fidelity Photo

- Grayscale uses Shades of Gray

- Black and White uses Sketched Art

- Outline uses Line Art

As you select each one, as the image is in auto Image Trace mode, it will update the image, and the settings in the panel will change as well. Later if you alter any of the panel settings, a Preset of Custom will appear. Likewise, you can use the panel to set your settings ahead of time, while just the image is selected before you click the Trace button in the panel, but then preview results will update.

Beside the Preset is a Menu icon that will allow you to Save as New Preset, Delete, or Rename a preset. Refer to Figure 3-15.

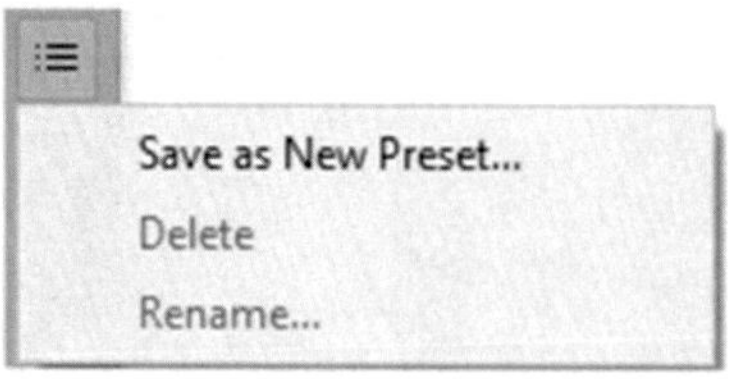

Figure 3-15. *Use the Preset menu to save a new preset*

View: This menu will allow you several viewing options: Tracing Result, Tracing result with outlines, Outlines, Outlines with source image, and source image. You can preview these options while the image is in Image Trace mode. However, they do not actually affect the final trace. Use the eye icon when you want to turn the viewing on or off and revert back to the original preview or source image. This example is based on the preset of 16 colors in the center of the pie chart. By default, leave on Tracing result as you work in the panel. Refer to Figure 3-16.

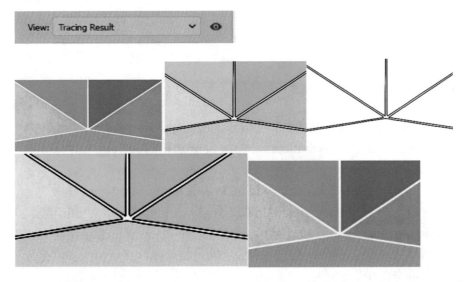

Figure 3-16. *View Tracing results settings when using the Image Trace panel: Tracing Result, Tracing result with outlines, Outlines, Outlines with source image, and source image*

Color Settings

In the version on the right, Mode and Palette and its related settings have been moved under the Color settings area. The drop-down lists of Mode and Palette have been amalgamated into one called Mode. Refer to Figure 3-14.

Mode/Palette consists of the following options:

Limited Color: Using your color slider, you can limit the number of colors in the design, for example, between 2 and 30 colors. This is useful when you want a specific amount and not the default presets of 3, 6, and 16. Refer to Figure 3-17.

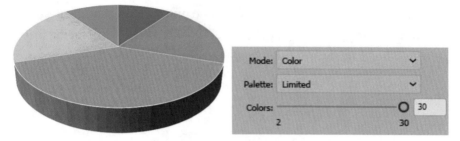

Figure 3-17. *Mode Color settings result for Limited Color*

- Full Tone Color: Allows for the full range of colors up to 100 colors. This is good for areas that contain gradients. However, you can set the colors to more or less with the slider. More colors will make more paths, while less colors will make less paths, but the image may appear more posterized. In Grayscale and Black and White, this slider setting may be referred to as a Grays or Threshold. Use this setting if you no longer can find the Automatic Palette setting. Refer to Figure 3-18.

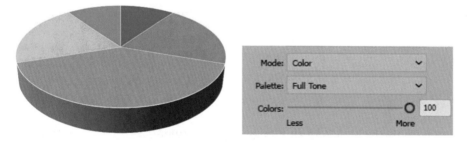

Figure 3-18. *Mode Color settings result for Full Tone Color*

- Grayscale: You can set the level of grays to less or more using the grays slider. This will generate a grayscale tracing result (0–100). By default, it is set to 50. Refer to Figure 3-19.

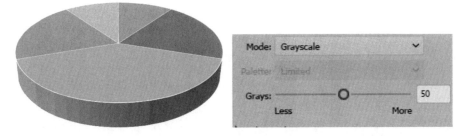

Figure 3-19. *Mode Color settings result for Grayscale*

- Black and White: Use the Threshold slider to generate a black and white tracing result (1–255). The default is 128, and those original colors that fall below a threshold setting will disappear and be white, a higher threshold setting, and then become black. Refer to Figure 3-20.

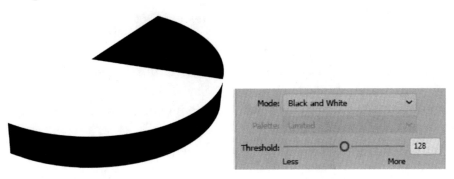

Figure 3-20. *Mode Color settings result for Black and White*

- Document Library: Uses an existing color group for the tracing palette, originally from the Swatches panel. Note that you can add to the Swatches panel color groups from other Swatch Libraries (Window ➤ Swatch Libraries) or your Creative Cloud Libraries panel, which may contain color themes. These were created using Adobe Color in Volume 1 and stored in your Libraries panel. When you add these new color groups or themes to the Swatches panel, they will be available to your Image Trace panel as well. Refer to the link provided earlier for more information on this topic if you are not able to find the available color groups. Refer to Figure 3-21.

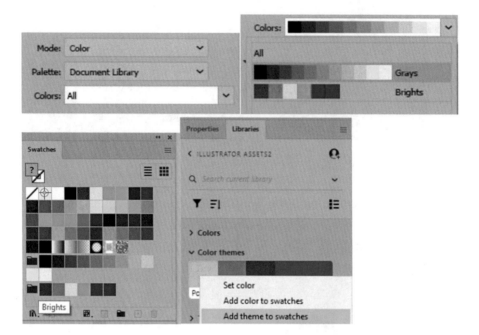

Figure 3-21. *Document color groups that are available from the Swatches panel or can be imported to the Swatches panel from the Libraries panel*

Alternatively use your Color Guide panel, as mentioned in Volume 1, to edit color after the images is traced.

Depending on the Mode settings chosen, the following will be available:

- Color/Grays/Threshold Slider: Which we just reviewed.

- Create: Fill or Create: Stroke check boxes with the Stroke Weight Point settings (moved from the Advanced area in example on the right Figure 3-14): By default, the Fills is checked, but you can also add a strokes as well to your trace and add a pixel setting to that for the stroke weight. The stroke and its weight option are only available when the color mode is set to black and white. Refer to Figure 3-22.

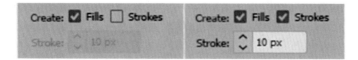

Figure 3-22. *Image Trace panel creates fills and strokes with a stroke weight*

- Ignore Color Settings (moved from the Advanced area in example on
  the right in Figure 3-14): Ignore if color is set to the setting of white
  so that it is not part of the trace, but it can be turned on or off using
  the check box/toggle button if you want white to be included, and
  you can also set a new color using the eye dropper to select a color
  from the source image. You cannot use this eye dropper setting in
  Grayscale or if the method is set to Overlapping, then ignore color is
  not available to any Mode. Refer to Figure 3-23.

Figure 3-23. *Ignore a color as part of the trace in the Image Trace panel*

Advanced Settings

Use the sliders to set the following:

- Paths: Path Fitting – a higher value means a tighter fit to the original
  pixel shape. A lower value is a looser fit to the original. The range is
  1%–100%. Refer to Figure 3-24.

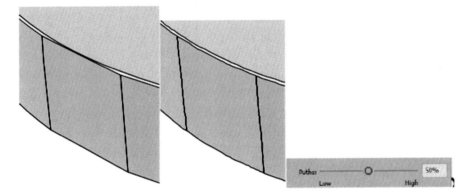

Figure 3-24. *Adjust the Paths slider in the Image Trace panel*

- Corners: Corner emphasis – higher values mean more corners, while lower values mean less corners. The range is 0%–100%. Refer to Figure 3-25.

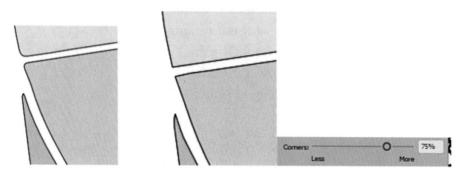

Figure 3-25. *Adjust the Corners slider in the Image Trace panel*

- Noise: Reduces noise by ignoring areas of specified pixel size. Higher values mean less noise. The range is 1–100px. When working with high-resolution images, Adobe recommends moving the slider to higher values such as 20–50. However, when working with low-resolution images, set it lower from 1 to 10. Changes in Noise, when using the slider, are often more apparent when starting with a detailed photograph or artwork rather than a lower-resolution image of a logo or chart with limited colors. Refer to Figure 3-26.

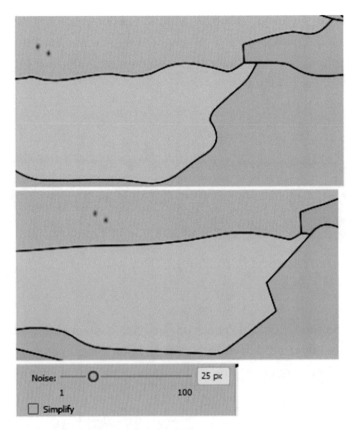

Figure 3-26. *Adjust the Noise slider in the Image Trace panel; changes are more visible on a detailed image*

- Use the check box or toggle for simplified anchor points to access the slider for anchor points. This will allow you to simplify the paths you output, and the image is not as accurate. The range is 0%–100%, and the default is 90%. This option does not work with the method of overlapping. Refer to Figure 3-27.

Figure 3-27. *Simplify the paths in the Image Trace panel*

- Method: Has two toggle settings – abutting and overlapping. Abutting creates cut out paths; the edge of one path is the same as its neighbor. Overlapping creates stacked paths; each path will slightly overlap its neighbor. Refer to Figure 3-28.

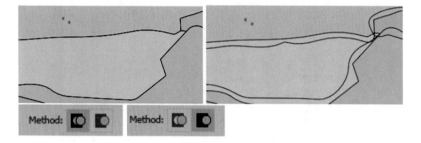

Figure 3-28. *Choose a method in the Image Trace panel of abutting or overlapping*

- Snap Curves to Lines: This check box/toggle, when enabled, will replace slightly curved lines with straight lines. If the lines are very near 0 or 90 degrees, they will snap to a straight line. Refer to Figure 3-29.

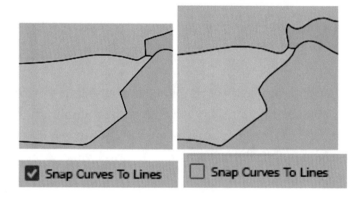

Figure 3-29. *Snap the Curves to Lines using the Image Trace panel*

Info Settings (Tracing Result Information)

The info area informs you of how many paths, anchor points, and colors your trace contains. As you make adjustments elsewhere in the panel, this area will update. Refer to Figure 3-30.

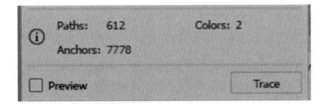

Figure 3-30. *Image Trace panel Info area for Preview check box and Trace button*

Click the Trace button when you want to begin tracing selected images to bring them into Image Tracing mode. Refer to Figure 3-30.

Click the Expand button when you want to complete your tracing settings and apply them. If you cannot see this button in your Image Trace panel, then use the button in the Control panel, Properties panel (under Quick Actions), or Object ➤ Image Trace ➤ Expand.

Click the Revert to Original button if you want to cancel out of Image Trace mode and just return to the original pixel image. If you cannot see this button in your panel, then go to Object ➤ Image Trace ➤ Release.

Use your Preview check box/toggle when you need to compare the before and after of your settings, before clicking the Expand button. Refer to Figure 3-30.

This concludes the topic on graphs and charts for now. Make sure to File ➤ Save your work, and you can close the current files you have open.

Project Idea: Creating a Graph and Chart Based on Research/Data You Have Collected

Now that you have seen what a graph can do in the last three chapters, take a moment to research your own topic and compile some data. Make sure to enter the data into your Excel worksheet as described earlier. Then take a moment to start creating one of the charts mentioned in this chapter that fits with your data and modify it to suit your needs.

Here is an example of a graph that I am starting that will be used in Chapter 6; it will be on the topic of coffee. You will notice that I have colorized each of the bars for different countries to make them appear separate. Or I could color the bars in coffee-related colors or even add a coffee-themed pattern swatches. Refer to my file graph_ideas.ai. Refer to Figure 3-31.

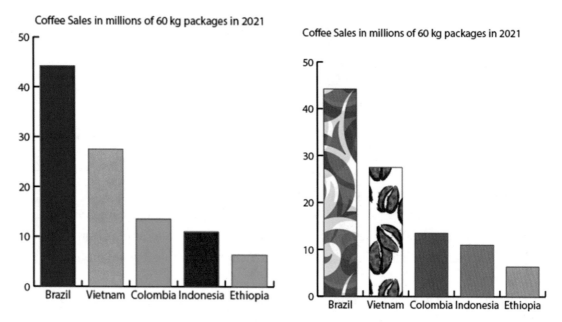

Figure 3-31. *Adjusting colors and swatches on a graph to fit a theme*

Going a step farther, you could add a column design, as in this case, coffee bags, or if about beverages, you could try to add coffee cups or try another beverage. Refer to Figure 3-32.

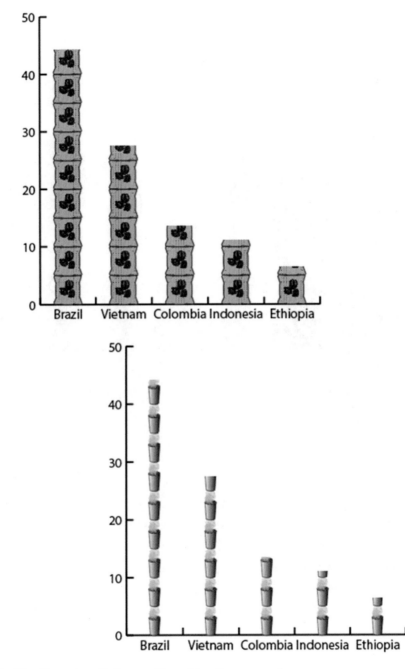

Figure 3-32. *Creating Column Graphics for a graph*

In this case I am keeping it pretty simple, as I plan to make it appear more 3D later on and will leave it at the solid color bars for now.

Here are a few other ideas: medical bottles or smokestacks in regard to fossil fuel or nuclear, which also could be adapted to a column graph that acts as my guide. I could then place paths or symbols over the top of the graph after I entered my final data to give a more custom and creative look. Refer to Figure 3-33.

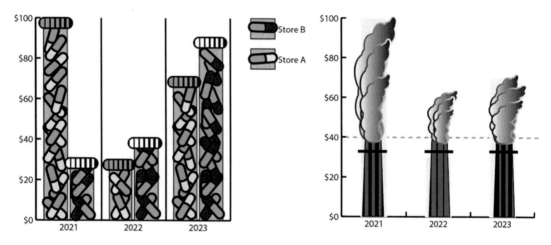

Figure 3-33. *Overlay your own designs over an existing graph*

Summary

In this chapter, we reviewed the following topics copying and pasting a graph from another application and using Image Trace to extract designs from a graph and a line drawing. Later you also looked at some additional creative graphing ideas.

In the next chapter, we will be enhancing our 2D drawings with effects that include giving the graph a more 3D appearance.

CHAPTER 4

Illustrator's 2D Effects for Creating Infographics

In this chapter, we will focus on applying a 2D look to your infographics.

The graphs are not just limited to the effects found in their options in the Graph Type dialog box, you can apply 2D and 3D effects to them as well, some of which are better than others, depending upon the effect settings chosen.

While in this chapter, we will look at a few 2D effects found in the Effects menu, later in Chapters 5 and 6, the main focus will be on using the 3D and Material Effects panel with its newly updated settings. Later, in Chapter 6, we will look briefly at one other advanced toolset we can use to add perspective and create a final project. For now, let's review some of the main 2D effects that could be used with infographics, logos, and just type. Practice in a File ➤ New document that you created if you want to follow along.

Note   This chapter does contain projects that can be found in the Volume 2 Chapter 4 folder. Some of the text in this chapter on 2D effects has been adapted and updated from my earlier book, *Perspective Warps and Distorts with Adobe Tools: Volume 2*, in regard to infographics and logos.

Effects (FX) List Overview

The Effects menu was mentioned briefly in Volume 1. It can be used to add various filters and styles to a shape or path, which can later be edited using the Appearance panel, then saved as a Graphic Style, and later applied to other paths or shapes. In this book, we will not focus on all the effects. However, I will just point out a few common stylize effects that you may want to use for your basic infographics, which are not overly distracting

© Jennifer Harder 2024
J. Harder, *Creating Infographics with Adobe Illustrator: Volume 2,*
https://doi.org/10.1007/979-8-8688-0041-2_4

or affect readability if used correctly. Some of these you will be familiar with if you have used Photoshop, but in this case, they are in a different location. You cannot access them from the Layers panel and must be applied to a selected path or grouped object, using the Effect menu or Appearance panel instead. Refer to Figure 4-1.

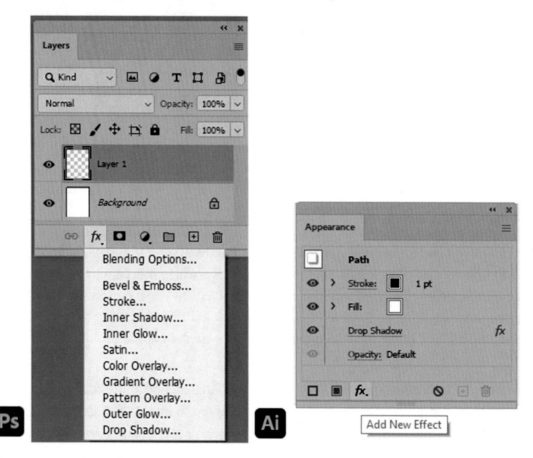

Figure 4-1. Photoshop Layers panel accessing layer styles. In Illustrator, similar styles are applied in the Appearance panel to a path

Applying 2D Effects

There are many 2D effects to choose from the Effects list, which you can explore on your own for warping and styling. They are divided into two kinds: Illustrator Effects and Photoshop Effects. Photoshop Effects are very similar to Photoshop Filters in that they can change the color of a vector path or image. Illustrator Effects affect the vector and often warp the shape when the effect is applied, but several of them are more like Photoshop Layer styles instead. Here are four that we will focus on in the menu Effect ➤ (Illustrator Effects) Stylize ➤:

- Drop Shadow

- Feather

- Inner Glow (Inner Shadow)

- Outer Glow

- Refer to Figure 4-2.

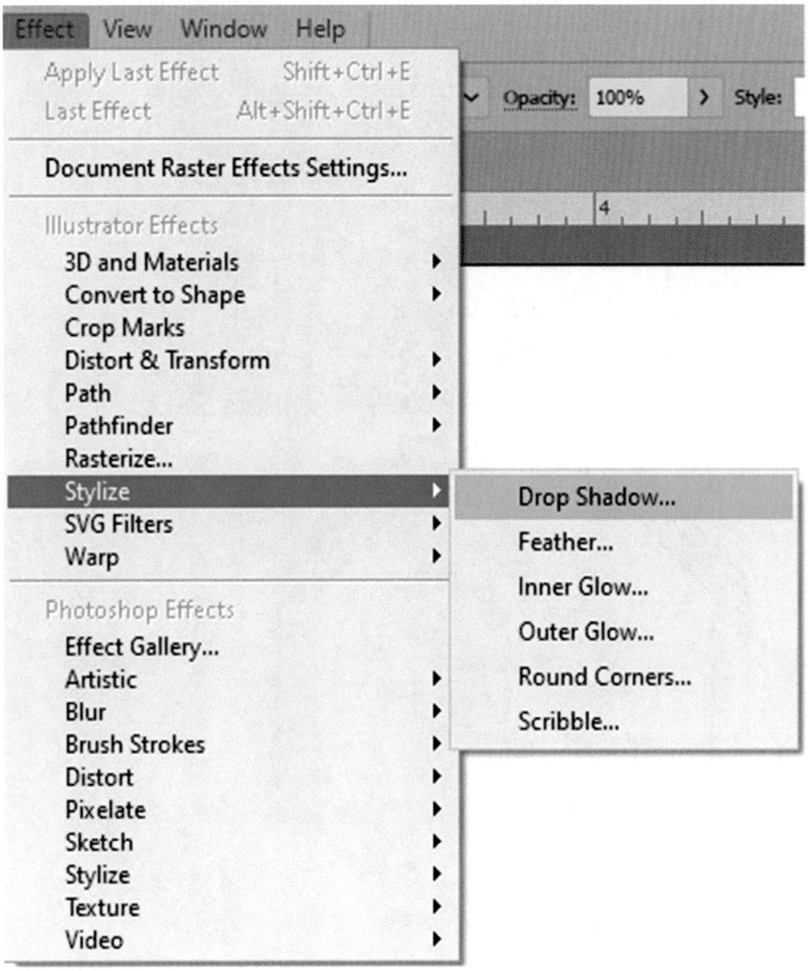

Figure 4-2. *Use Illustrator's Effects menu to access various Stylize effects*

Try the following effects on a selected shape on the artboard for practice. You can create a new file for practice.

Drop Shadow

This effect that can be used to add a shadow behind a shape or path or grouped shape. Refer to Figure 4-3.

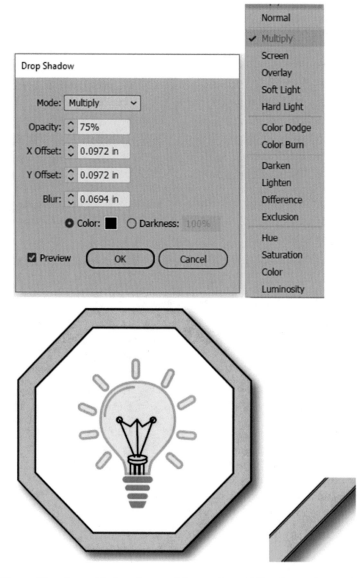

Figure 4-3. *Drop Shadow dialog box with various blend mode settings and drop shadow applied to a graphic*

It can have a Blending mode setting similar to the ones seen in the Transparency panel; by default for shadows, it is set to Multiply. You can also set the opacity (0%–100%), X and Y Offset of the Shadow, as well as you can set the Blur range so that the shadow appears fuzzy or out of focus. You can then set a color; by default, it is black K=100%, but you can use the color square to click on to set a new color using the Color Picker. Refer to Figure 4-3 and Figure 4-4.

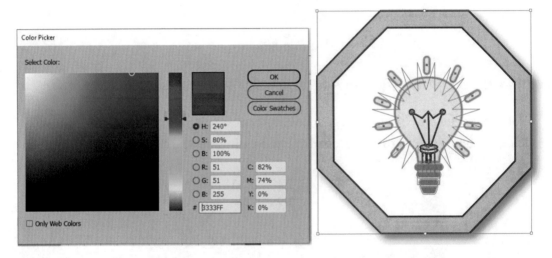

Figure 4-4. *Color Picker Dialog box and the color of the drop shadow changed on the edge of the grouped object*

Or you can set by darkness 0%–100% which appears like a fading of the original color in the current overlayed stroke and fill color. Darkness Numbers lower than 100% will have an alert message that warns how custom spot colors may be affected if they overprint. Refer to Figure 4-5.

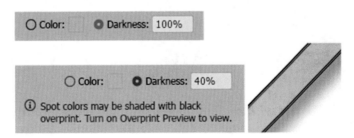

Figure 4-5. *Drop Shadow dialog box setting the drop shadow to darkness*

Enable your preview check box to see the effect of drop shadow, set your settings, and click OK to commit. Refer to Figure 4-3.

You can also use the effect on large text as well. It will often be more apparent in text with a different stroke color. Refer to Figure 4-6.

Figure 4-6. *A drop shadow is more apparent behind lighter text with a stroke*

Notice how the drop shadow appears when the text has a stroke but no fill. By reducing the blur, you can make some of the text outline appear. Refer to Figure 4-7.

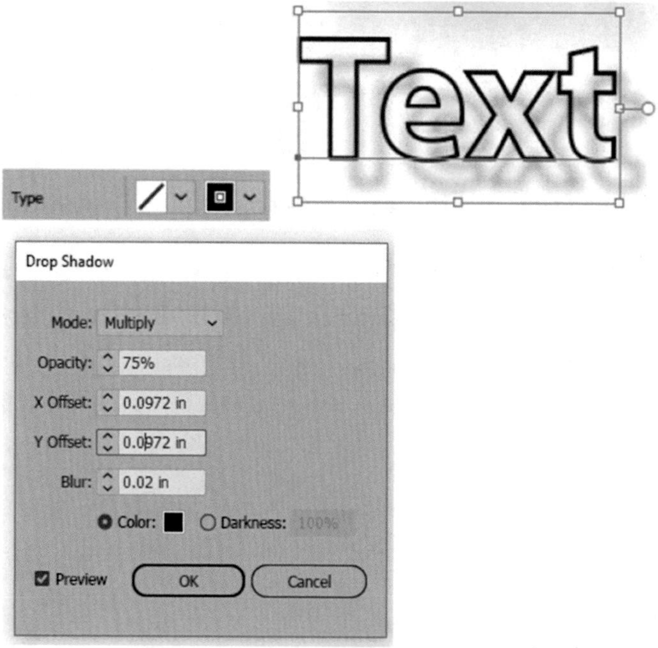

Figure 4-7. *Control panel with a fill of none and stroke outlined text with a drop shadow added using the dialog box*

These settings will now appear in the Appearance panel for that select shape (path), type, or group as they will for all of the following effects. Refer to Figure 4-8.

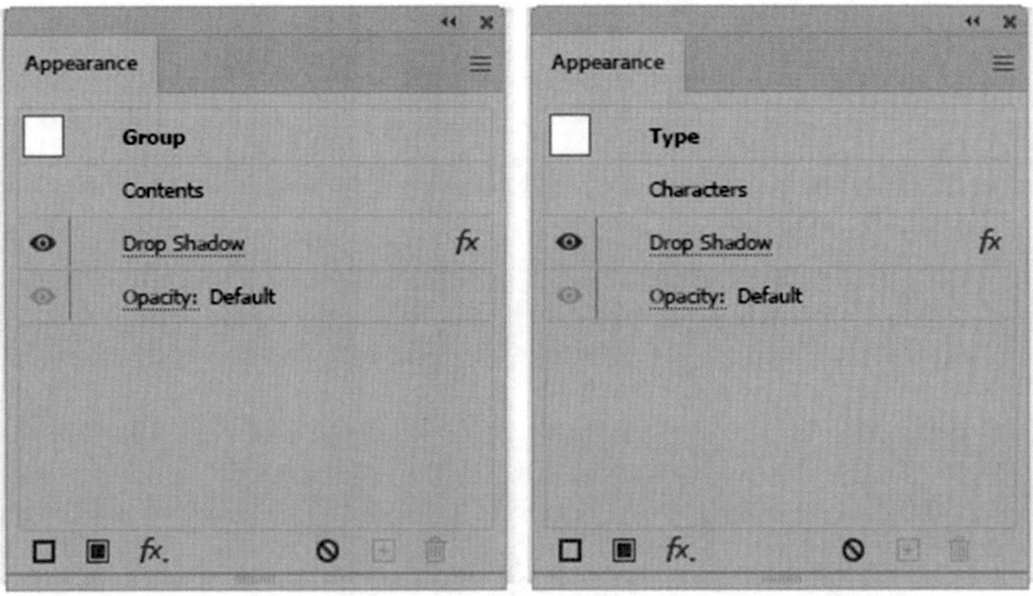

Figure 4-8. *Use the Appearance panel to set and edit a drop shadow for a grouped shape and type*

If at any point in time you need to go back and edit the Drop Shadow effect on the selected path, just click the word in the Appearance panel to access that dialog box, and you can adjust it.

However, if you choose drop shadow again from the Effect ➤ (Illustrator Effects) Stylize ➤ menu, you may get a warning message that the effect will be applied again, and this is a way to darken the shadow effect further, and a second drop shadow will be added to the Appearance panel. Refer to Figure 4-9.

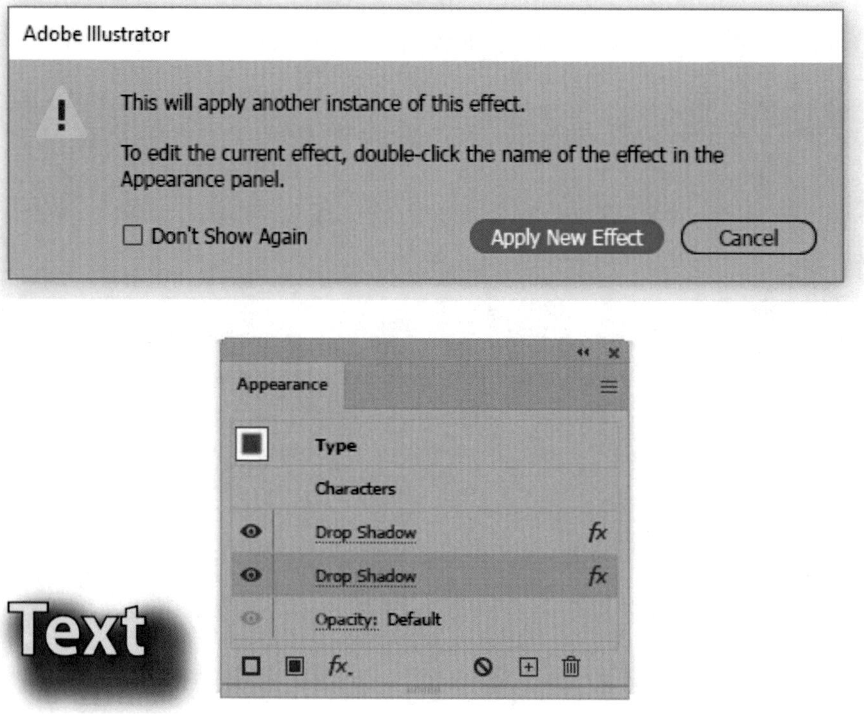

Figure 4-9. *Applying a second drop shadow using the Effect menu may result in this warning message and a darker drop shadow if the effect is applied*

As with any effect using the Appearance panel, you can select it and click the trash can icon (Delete Selected Item) to remove it from object or type.

Feather

Feather is a type of fading or blurring effect that can graduate the edges on a selected shape or path and make them appear fuzzy. The main setting is radius. After you set the radius, because there are no other text boxes to click into, toggle on and off the Preview checkbox so that you can see the changes you make. Click OK to confirm changes, and the effect is added to that selected path and the Appearance panel. Note that for text, the radius of feathering should be set quite low, or you may not be able to read the font, and the stroke can become lost. Refer to Figure 4-10.

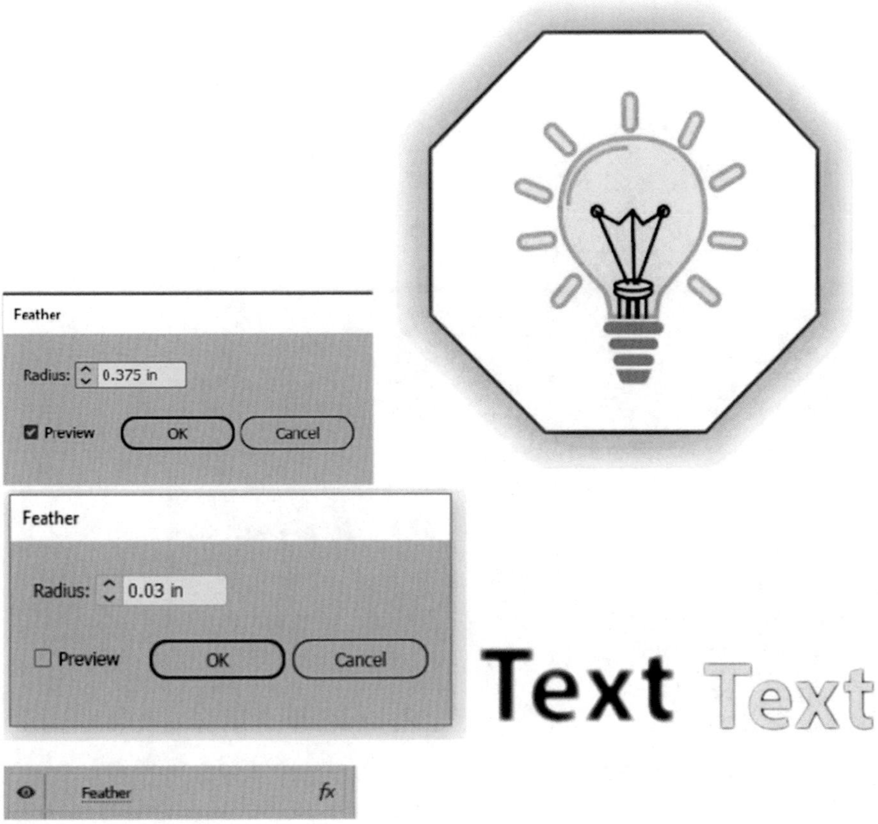

Figure 4-10. *Use the Feather dialog box to feather the edge of a grouped graphic or text, and the effect will appear in the Appearance panel*

Inner Glow (Inner Shadow)

Inner Glow allows you to add a glowing effect to your path, grouped shape, as well as text. The Blending mode in this case is set to Screen, but you can set it to any of the other modes found in the Transparency panel. You can then select a glowing color other than white, using the Color Picker, such as a yellow or other neon-looking color. You can set the Opacity (0%–100%), the Blur range, and whether the blur should come from the center or edge. Refer to Figure 4-11.

195

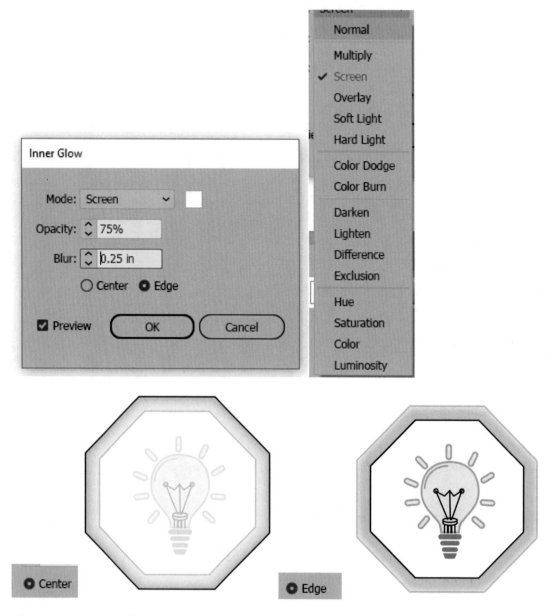

Figure 4-11. *Use the Inner Glow dialog box and its Blending modes to affect the glow on the center or edge of a graphic*

For Photoshop users, you will notice that in Illustrator there is no Inner Shadow effect available. However, you can use the Inner Glow dialog box to do this for you simply by changing the mode from Screen to Multiply and then color to black (K=100%) or a darker color using the swatch link to access the Color Picker and adjust your other settings as similar to the Drop Shadow effect. Refer to Figure 4-12.

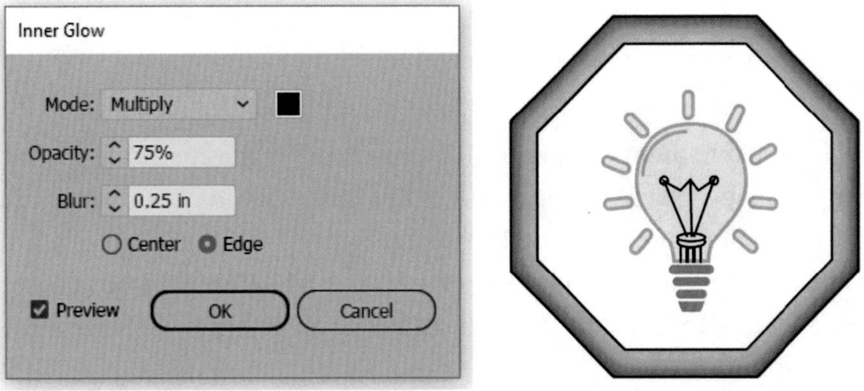

Figure 4-12. *Use the Inner Glow dialog box to create an inner shadow by resetting the blend mode and color*

This Inner Glow effect can be applied to text as well, but due to readability, keep the blur at a low setting, and using a color other than white, such as yellow, may make the glow stand out better. Refer to Figure 4-13.

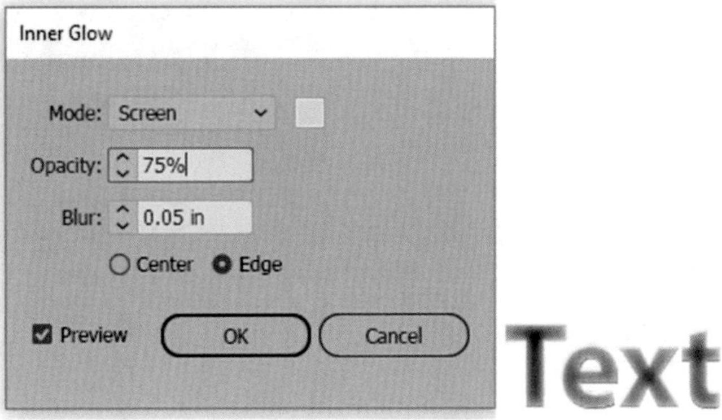

Figure 4-13. *Use the Inner Glow dialog box to affect type*

Use the Preview checkbox to preview your work and then click OK to commit, and the effect is added to that selected path and the Appearance panel. Refer to Figure 4-14.

Figure 4-14. *Inner Glow settings will appear in the Appearance panel*

Outer Glow

Outer Glow is similar to Inner Glow and allows you to add a glow to the outside of the path or grouped shape. The Blending mode, in this case, is set to Screen, but you can set it to any of the other modes found in the Transparency panel. You can then select a glowing color other than white using the Color Picker such as a yellow or other neon-looking color. You can set the Opacity (0%–100%) and the Blur range. Refer to Figure 4-15.

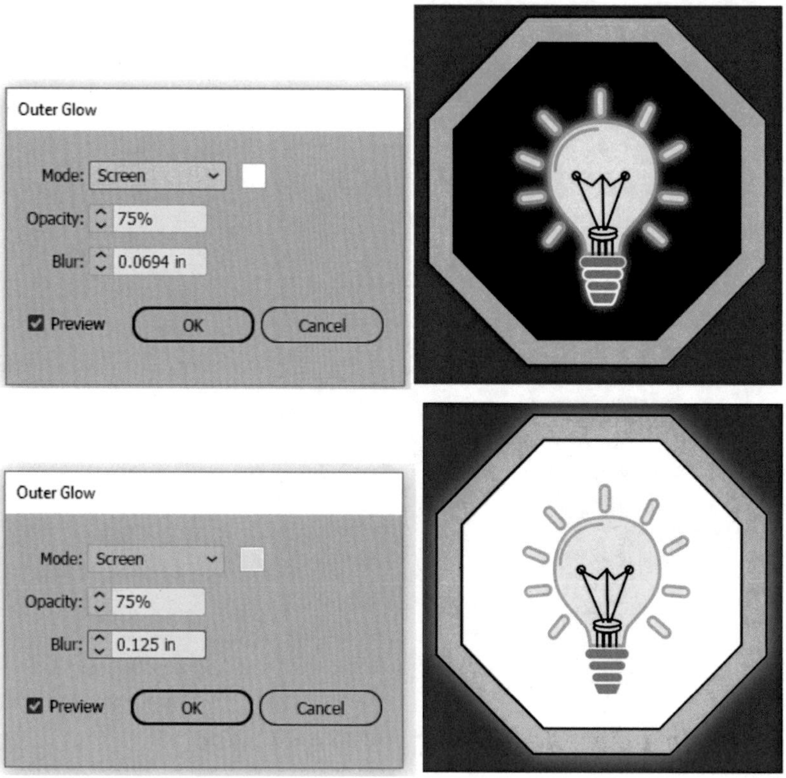

Figure 4-15. *Use the Outer Glow dialog box to affect a grouped light bulb or the entire graphic edge if it is grouped as one unit*

Note When you want to have the selected area of your design appear with just the outer glow, make sure to Object ➤ Ungroup your grouped shape. Then select with your Selection tool only the parts of the shape you want to apply the outer glow to and Object ➤ Group them again. Then apply to the object Effect ➤ Stylize ➤ Outer Glow again. Refer to Figure 4-15.

Use the Preview checkbox to preview your work and then click OK to commit, and the effect is added to that path in the Appearance panel. Refer to Figure 4-15 and Figure 4-16.

Figure 4-16. *The Outer Glow effect appears in the Appearance panel*

Outer glow can be applied to text as well, but again, adjust your blur settings as required, and it often looks best with brighter fill colors. Refer to Figure 4-17.

Figure 4-17. *Outer Glow applied to text*

Tip For a more controlled Outer Glow effect, try using the Drop Shadow effect set to a more neon color with a Mode of Screen. Refer back to Figure 4-3.

Using the Appearance panel, you can add and arrange multiple effects in the order that you want.

Also, if you are familiar with Photoshop Layer effects in Illustrator, try using your Appearance panel to recreate similar Photoshop effects (*fx*) such as Color Overlay, Gradient Overlay, and Pattern Overlay by overlaying various, solid, gradient, or pattern swatches found in the Swatches panel to recreate those effects. Multiple Strokes can be added as well using the Appearance panel. Refer to Figure 4-18.

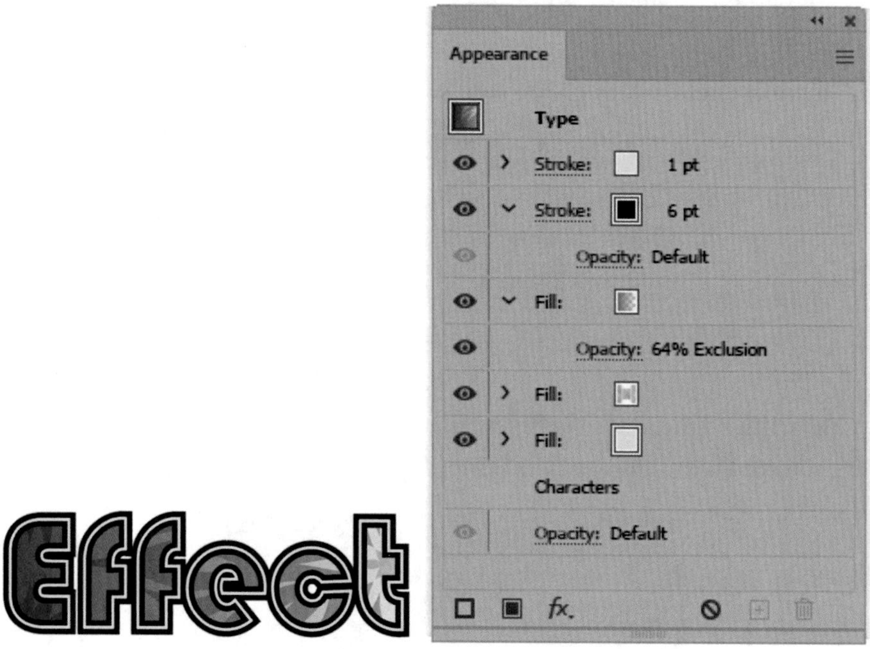

Figure 4-18. *Use Illustrator's Appearance panel to recreate some of the effects you may have created in Photoshop*

Remember, if you have applied multiple effects that you like to shape or path while the shape or group is selected, make sure that your Graphic Styles panel is visible, and click the New Graphic Style button to add it to the panel. Refer to Figure 4-19.

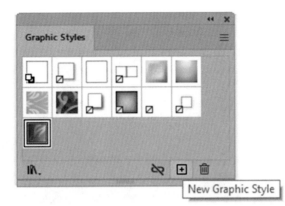

Figure 4-19. *Make sure to store your created effects found in the Appearance panel in the Graphic Styles panel afterward*

You can then select other paths and apply these Graphic styles to them.

On your own, take time to explore some of the other Illustrator effects and adjust them in the Appearance panel. You can refer to my file 2D_effects.ai for reference to the images I created. For Photoshop examples refer to the file photoshop_layer_styles.psd. Make sure to File ➤ Save any of your work so far.

Summary

In this chapter, we reviewed the 2D effects of Drop Shadow, Feather, Inner Glow, and Outer Glow and how to add them to your graphics. You saw how you could recreate some of the Photoshop Layer effects using the Appearance panel and then store them as Graphic Styles for later use.

In the next chapter, you will look at the 3D and Materials panel and learn how to add those related effects to paths and later a graph to appear more 3D-like.

CHAPTER 5

Illustrator's 2D and 3D Effects for Creating Infographics

In this chapter, we will look at how to apply 3D effects to your infographics.

The graph tools are not just limited to the effects found in their options in the Graph Type dialog box, you can apply 3D effects to them as well, some of which are better than others depending upon the effect settings chosen.

The main focus of this chapter will be on using the 3D and Material Effects panel with its newly updated settings. These effects can also be referenced from the Effect menu as well. Later in Chapter 6, we will look briefly at one other advanced toolset we can use to add perspective and create a final project.

Note This chapter does contain projects that can be found in the Volume 2 Chapter 5 Folder. Some of the text in this chapter on 3D Shapes has been adapted and updated from my earlier book, Perspective Warps and Distorts with Adobe Tools Volume 2, in regards to graphics and some new settings will be discussed in this chapter as well.

© Jennifer Harder 2024
J. Harder, *Creating Infographics with Adobe Illustrator: Volume 2*,
https://doi.org/10.1007/979-8-8688-0041-2_5

Working with the Effects of 3D and Materials Panel

As you saw in Chapter 4, the Effect menu has many options. However, you can also add 3D effects to the Graphic Styles panel as well. In this case, the focus will be on the newer 3D effects and not 3D (Classic) which I will just mention briefly. Refer to Figure 5-1.

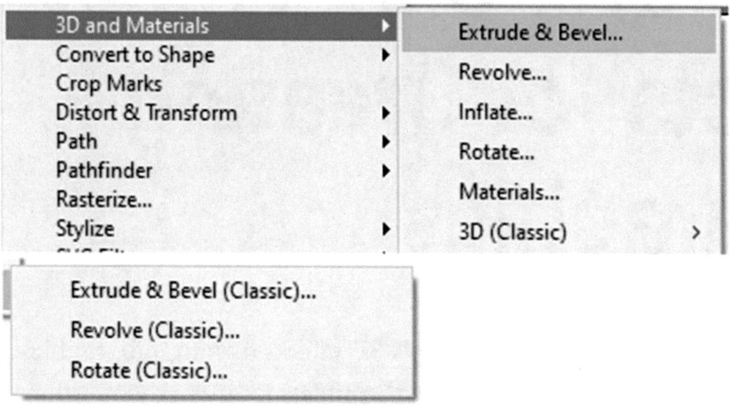

Figure 5-1. *Effects menu 3D and Materials options*

What About 3D Classic?

In the past, before the new 3D and Materials panel and effects were added to Illustrator, originally, on Photoshop, there were basic 3D effects in the Effects menu. They are now set under the 3D (classic) submenu, and you can still use them with their related dialog boxes for your own projects. You can refer to this page for more details on how to use them:

https://helpx.adobe.com/illustrator/using/creating-3d-objects.html

Also, for those interested, my book, mentioned at the beginning of this chapter, has some examples and ideas for using those 3D (Classic) effects though that information is not required for this book.

However, our topic for this chapter and this book will focus on the newer 3D effects which, for the most part, I find easier to edit and use than the original classic. There is only one item that I wish they would add to the new settings, which I will mention later in this chapter, as the classic version uses the bevel settings slightly differently.

Effect ➤ 3D and Materials Panel

Now, we will look at some new features in the Effects menu that have been updated and improved for 3D in Illustrator and are a good alternative if you need to create 3D objects that you can copy as Smart Objects into Photoshop, which I will mention briefly at the end of the chapter. Refer to Figure 5-2.

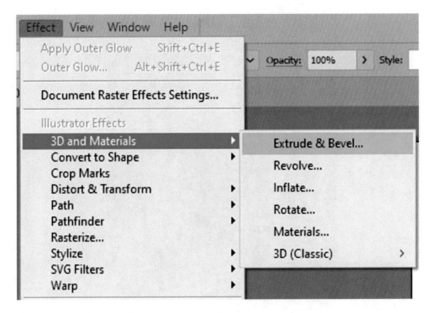

Figure 5-2. *Effect ➤ 3D and Materials panel*

The options include

- Extrude & Bevel

- Revolve

- Inflate

- Rotate

- Materials

All of this is combined and edited using the 3D and Materials panel which we will look at next. You can see those similar names when you look at the Object Tab. Refer to Figure 5-3.

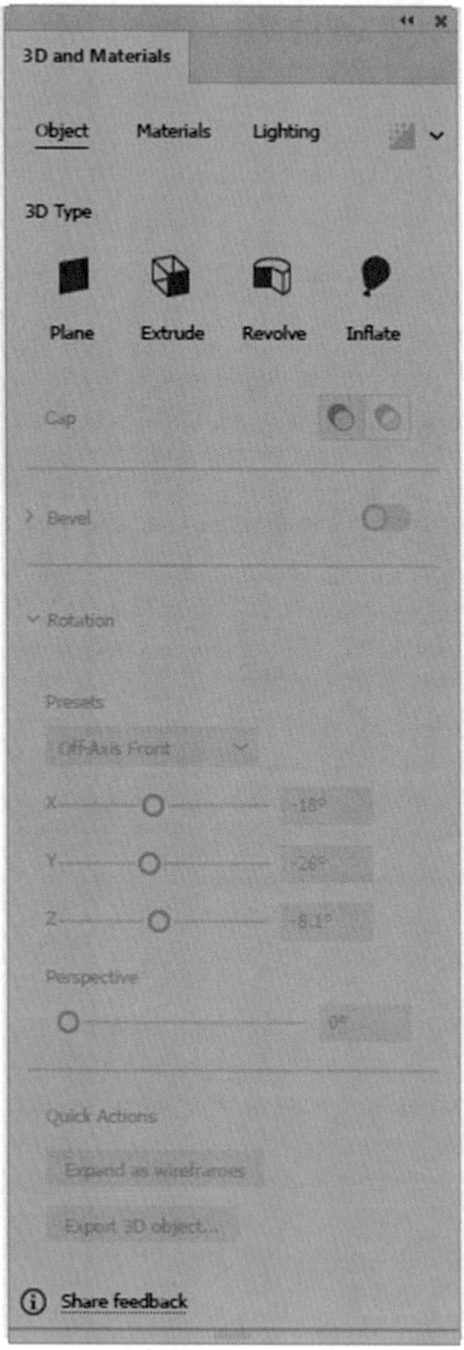

Figure 5-3. *3D and Materials panel*

Project: Coffee Cup Example

File ➤ Open 3D_effects.ai for reference and create your own graphics in a new file for practice. (File ➤ New).

In this example,

I will show you some same examples of a coffee cup and other objects that I recreated using the Window ➤ 3D and Materials panel. Refer to Figure 5-22.

Note   These 3D effects can only be applied as one instance to an object, however, you can use other non-3D effects in combination which will appear in the Appearance panel. Refer to Figure 5-4 for multiple 3D effect alert.

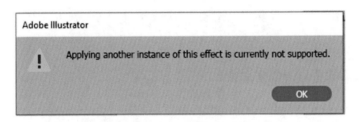

Figure 5-4. *Alert message for applying more than one 3D and Materials effect*

Rotate

In the first example, we can see that I used Effects ➤ 3D and Materials ➤ Rotate. You can apply this effect when you select your object with the Selection tool. Refer to Figure 5-5.

Figure 5-5. *Select the object with the Selection tool to apply the 3D effect of rotate*

3D and Materials Object Tab

In the 3D and Materials panel, this will come up as a 3D Type Plane or a Flattened object on a single plane, under the Object Tab. Refer to Figure 5-6.

Figure 5-6. *3D and Materials Panel Plane (Rotate) setting and preview*

Rather than using a cube, as you would in 3D Classic Rotate dialog box to do your rotating, you can now rotate, directly on the shape, or use the sliders under the rotation tab in the 3D and Materials panel. It has the same Preset for Rotation, based on direction axis and isometrics (Front, Back, Left, Right, Top, Bottom) and Off-Axis options. The X (horizontal), Y (vertical), and Z (circular) each with an axis range (-180,0,180°) sliders are clearly labeled, and you can change the Perspective (0–160°). Refer to Figure 5-7.

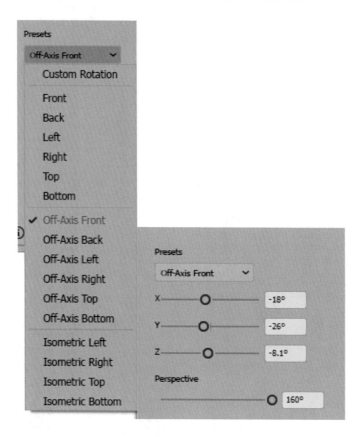

Figure 5-7. *3D and Materials Panel Plane (Rotate) setting Presets and preview*

In the current Preset of Off-Axis Front, to rotate on the shape itself, select and drag upward and downward on the horizontal line, if you want to rotate around X axis. Doing so will create a Custom Rotation Preset. Refer to Figure 5-8.

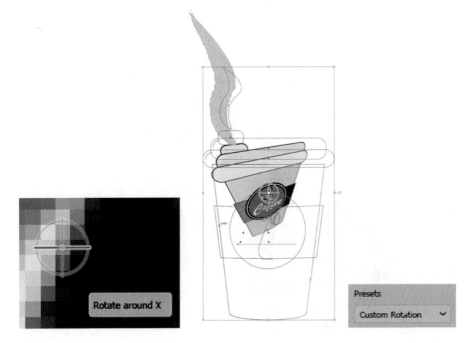

Figure 5-8. *3D and Materials Panel Plane (Rotate) setting and preview for Rotate around X*

Drag on the vertical line, left and right to rotate around the Y axis. Refer to Figure 5-9.

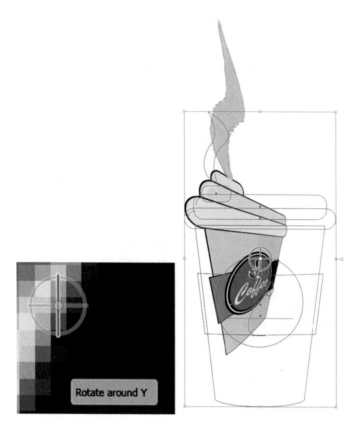

Figure 5-9. *3D and Materials Panel Plane (Rotate) setting and preview for Rotate around Y*

Drag on the circle and move in a clockwise or counterclockwise motion if you want to rotate around Z axis. Refer to Figure 5-10.

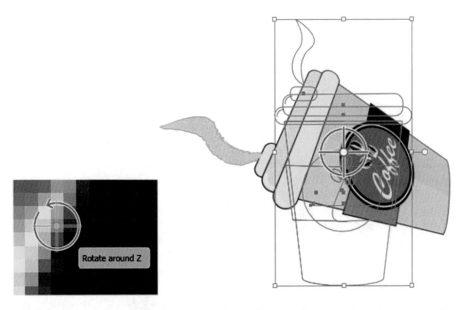

Figure 5-10. *3D and Materials Panel Plane (Rotate) setting and preview for Rotate around Z*

The dot in the center is Rotate Freeform. Drag on this dot in any direction to get a different random rotation. Refer to Figure 5-11.

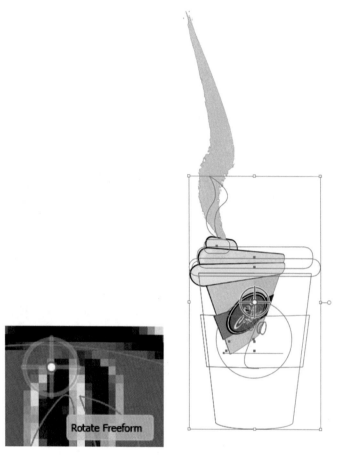

Figure 5-11. *3D and Materials Panel Plane (Rotate) setting and preview for Rotate Freeform*

Note   To undo any of the steps, you can choose Edit ➤ Undo or Ctrl/CMD+Z or use the History panel.

While in the Object Tab for Plane, you will notice that the cap and bevel options are not available. You do, however, have the option to "Expand as wireframes" in the Quick Actions area; this creates a type of grouped path outline of the object. Edit ➤ Undo that last step. I will mention it again later at the end of this section, as well as a new Quick Actions for Export 3D objects.

However, at any point in time, you could switch to another 3D Type, and these options would become active. We will look at that shortly; however, for now, remain on the 3D Type of Plane. Refer to Figure 5-12.

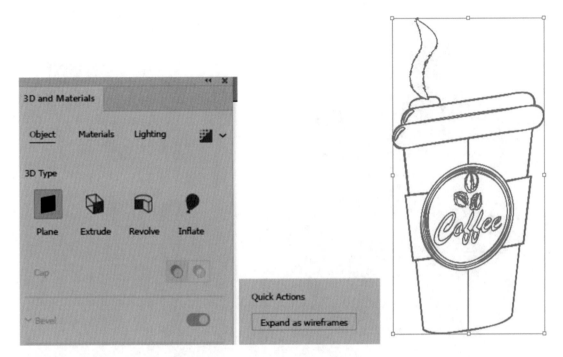

Figure 5-12. *3D and Materials Panel Plane (Rotate) setting Plane or set to another 3D Type or expand as a wireframe*

Besides setting the Object settings, you also have access to three other tabs: Materials, Lighting, and Render with Ray Tracing with Render settings.

Materials Tab

Materials Tab: this lets you set the Type of Materials that you can fill or cover the Object with. If, in the past. you used 3D features in Photoshop, this area will be familiar to you as many of the Materials will look similar. Note that in Photoshop, while 3D features are being phased out, you will still have access to the Materials panel and recently added Parametric Properties panel, which in previous versions was combined with the Materials panel, which is like using smart filters and Patterns in Layers. Refer to Figure 5-13.

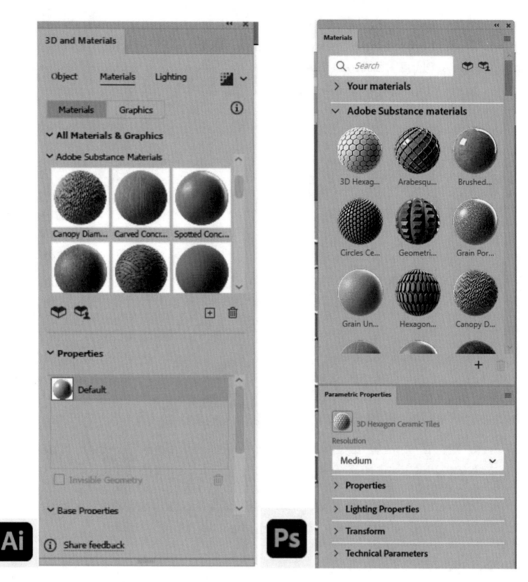

Figure 5-13. *3D and Materials Panel Plane (Rotate) Materials Tab, similar Materials can be found in the Photoshop Materials and Parametric Properties panels*

For details on that, you can refer to this page:`https://helpx.adobe.com/photoshop/using/substance-3d-materials-for-photoshop.html`

In Illustrator, under the Materials section, with the Materials Tab active, you can review all the Materials that are available. These include the Default Base Materials, which are like Plastic Shading. And if you scroll down a bit in the menu, you will see over 40 different Adobe Substance Materials. A Material is applied to the entire 3D surface. Refer to Figure 5-14.

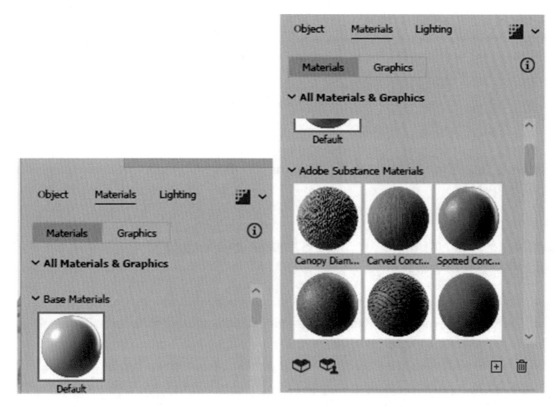

Figure 5-14. *3D and Materials Panel Plane (Rotate) Materials Tab*

Tip   If you need to expand this area to see more materials, then drag on lower edge of the panel to enlarge it. Refer to Figure 5-15.

Figure 5-15. *3D and Materials panel drag to lengthen the panel*

While looking at the Adobe Substance Materials, you can have the option to, from Adobe icons on the left side "Find more Materials on Substance 3D Assets" or "Find more Materials on Substance 3D Substance Community assets." You can also use the button options on the right to add your own Materials. These Materials come in the (.Sbsar) format if you have them downloaded on your computer. Refer to Figure 5-16.

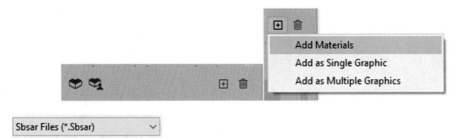

Figure 5-16. *3D and Materials Panel Plane (Rotate) Materials Tab Add Materials and file format*

Add Single and Multiple Graphics Symbols and Modify with Symbol Overlay

For adding Single or Multiple Graphics, you need to switch to the Materials Graphics tab. This is the same as using Map Art (Symbols), which is an option found with the 3D Classic options. Here all your Graphic Symbols are available to add to your art. This allows you to add a selected Object or Objects on your artboard as a Single Graphic to Symbols panel or Add as Multiple Graphics if more than one Graphic is selected. Refer to Figure 5-17.

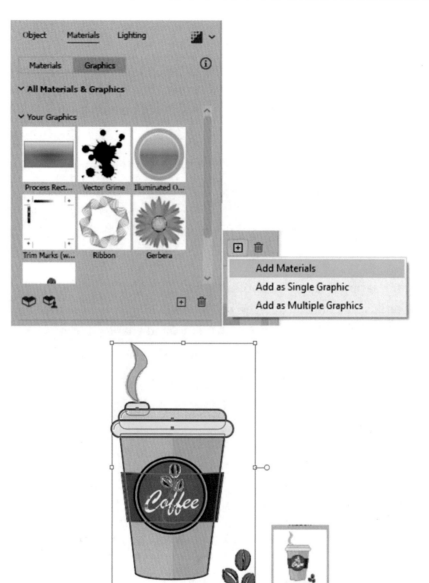

Figure 5-17. *3D and Materials Panel Plane (Rotate) Materials Tab, Adding Symbols Graphics and preview of Graphic on Object and add Single and Multiple Graphics to the panel and Symbols panel results*

You can also drag and drop selected items into this area in the panel, and they will be added to the Symbols panel at the same time.

You can click the Delete button if you want to remove a Graphic, and it will be removed from the Symbols panel as well. In this case, do not delete any graphics you did not create. Use Ctrl/CMD+Z right away if you deleted an item by mistake. Refer to Figure 5-18.

Figure 5-18. *3D and Materials Panel Plane (Rotate) Materials Tab Delete Graphic button*

You will look at how to apply symbols shortly.

In the Materials Tab, once you have a collection of Materials from the Substance Collection, you can select that Material in the panel and change it from the default to a different material. Some will appear more realistic than others depending on the shape you use. Refer to Figure 5-19.

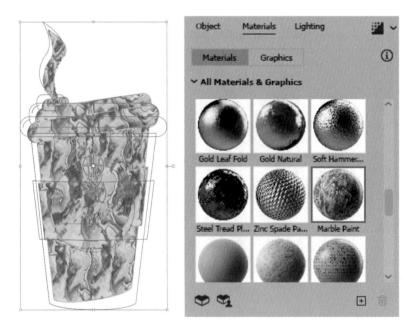

Figure 5-19. *3D and Materials Panel Plane (Rotate) Materials Tab with a Material selected*

Once a Material is selected, it will appear in the Panels Properties tab. Depending on the Substance Material that you choose, you will have different options known as Main Parameters and Additional Parameters below the Properties that you can further edit. These could include your resolution, repeat of pattern as well as paint colors, texture (roughness, pattern), warp, staining (density and color), position (offset x, offset y, and rotation), and additional technical parameters such as lighting effects that affect colors and ambient lighting intensity. These settings will vary from material to material. Refer to Figure 5-20.

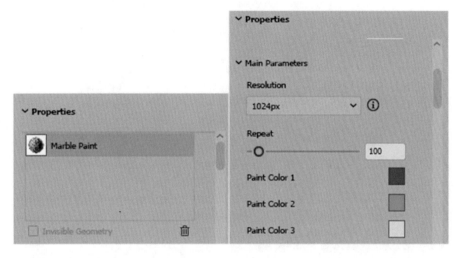

Figure 5-20. *3D and Materials Panel Plane (Rotate) Materials Tab with Material added to Properties panel and additional settings viewed in Main Parameters*

Some Main Parameters are complex, and other materials may only have a few options, so you need to spend time and look at each one after you select your Substance Material and experiment.

In this case, I just returned to my Base Default Property for now so that I could see my current design on my coffee cup. It has two Base Properties: Roughness (0–1) for texture and Metallic (0–1) to set a shinier appearance. Refer to Figure 5-21.

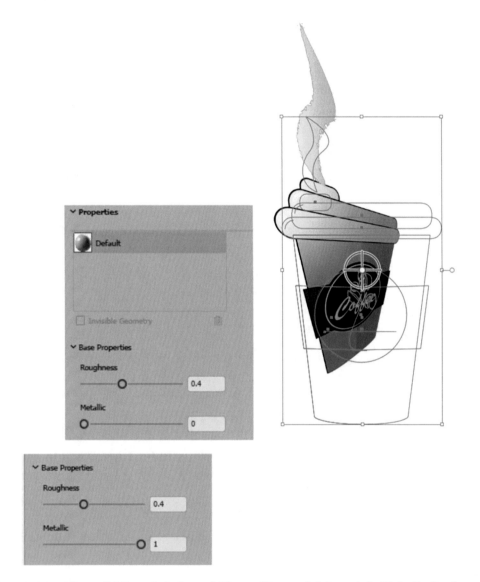

Figure 5-21. *3D and Materials Panel Plane (Rotate) Materials Tab, Default Material and Base Properties and preview of object with a higher metallic setting*

However, these properties are affected by a combination of perspective and lighting. We will look at lighting shortly.

Additionally, when you switch to the Graphics tab, you can click a symbol to add it to your Properties area and then further manage its Main Parameters. This includes setting Invisible Geometry and Scale and Rotation of the Symbol. You also have an additional option to replace a selected symbol when you click a new symbol's more options ellipse and click Replace to switch to the new symbol. Refer to Figure 5-22.

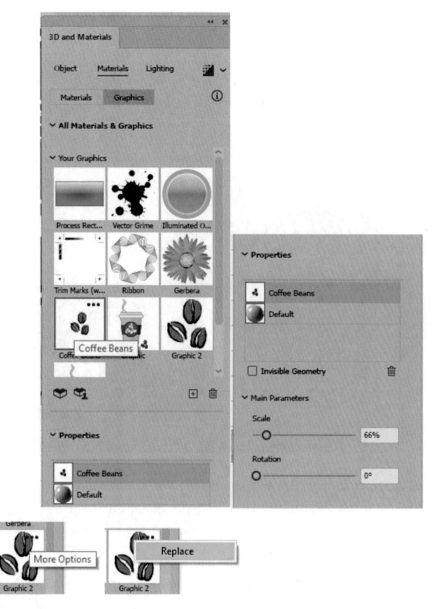

Figure 5-22. *3D and Materials Panel Plane (Rotate) Materials Tab, Graphic Properties and Main Parameters for selected Graphic*

You can move, scale, and rotate the graphic on the object. Also, you can later apply Multiple Graphics on top of a Material. They can be dragged above and below each other in the Properties area to reorder them. However, you cannot drag a symbol below a material. Refer to Figure 5-22 and Figure 5-23.

Figure 5-23. *Move, Scale rotated the selected Graphic on the Object*

We will look at the Properties area again when we look at the other 3D settings, but for now, you can select the graphic in the Properties panel and remove it, and the symbol is removed from the Object. Use Edit ➤ Undo to undo that last step. Refer to Figure 5-24.

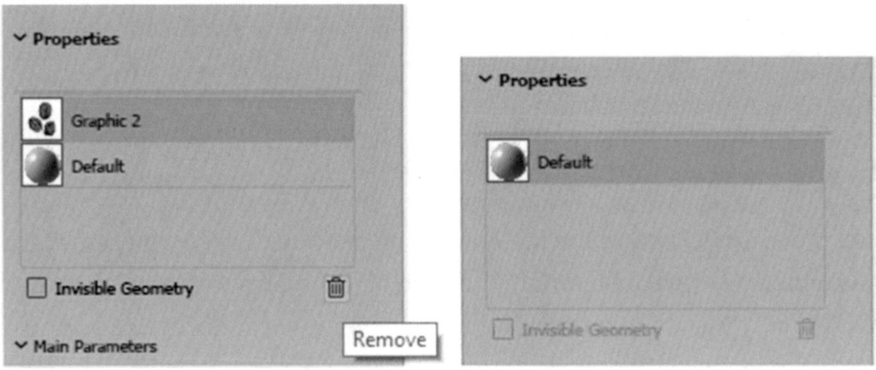

Figure 5-24. *Remove Graphic from Properties panel area*

Lighting Tab

The next tab is the Lightning; it has a few more options than what can be found in the Classic Rotate dialog box and also some recently updated features as well. Refer to Figure 5-25.

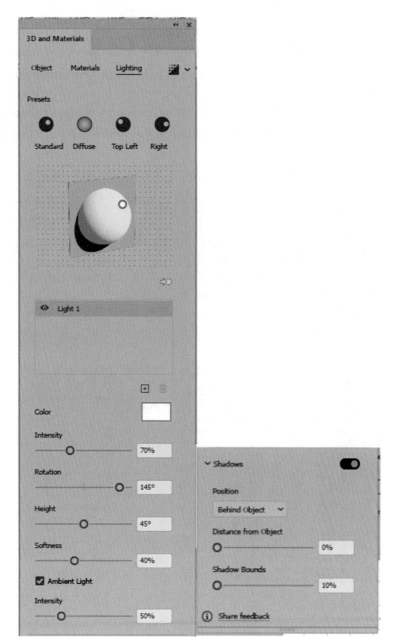

Figure 5-25. *3D and Materials Panel Plane (Rotate) Lighting Tab*

In this case you have some Lighting Presets: Standard, Diffuse, Top Left, and Right. Refer to Figure 5-26.

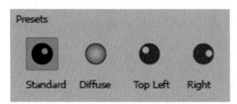

Figure 5-26. *3D and Materials Panel Plane (Rotate) Lighting Tab, Presets*

However, a new updated feature from the classic options has been added here that now allows you to add multiple lighting sources (dots) on the lighting widget. The default is one lighting source that you can drag around on the front of the lighting widget preview, and you can use the arrow toggle button below to send the selected lighting to the back of the object instead or return it to the front again. Refer to Figure 5-27.

Figure 5-27. *3D and Materials Panel Plane (Rotate) Lighting Tab, set more than one lighting source using the panels lighting widget and the result on the graphic*

You cannot move the selected light to the back of the object if it falls below the ground plane. This depends on the type of object rotation and shadow position that you will set later. Refer to Figure 5-28 and Figure 5-29.

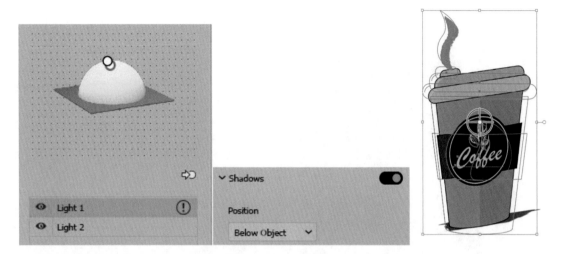

Figure 5-28. *3D and Materials Panel Plane (Rotate) Lighting Tab, lighting sources from Object and Shadows Position Below Object*

Figure 5-29. *3D and Materials Panel Plane (Rotate) Lighting Tab, one of the selected lighting sources set to the back of the graphic*

You can then set more than one light (up to 10) using the plus icon on the preview widget or delete lights using the trash can icon. There will always be at least one light. To see the multiple shadows, you may need to turn on the Ray Tracing render which we will look at later. Refer to Figure 5-30.

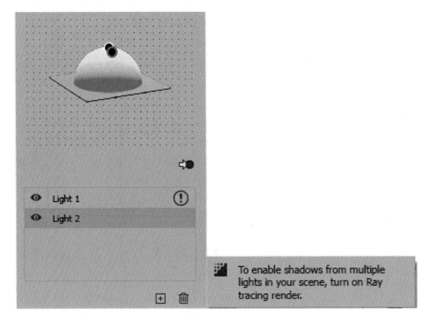

Figure 5-30. *3D and Materials Panel Plane (Rotate) Lighting Tab, informational note about how shadows are affected by settings*

For now, just work with one lighting source in front. Refer to Figure 5-31.

Figure 5-31. *3D and Materials Panel Plane (Rotate) Lighting Tab, lighting source adjusted on graphic*

Selecting a lighting Preset changes some of the settings in the lower sliders below the Lighting Color for each light source selected. A new color can be chosen with the Color Picker when you click the swatch. For example: C=36%, M=7%, Y=0%, K=0%. Refer to Figures 5-25 and 5-32.

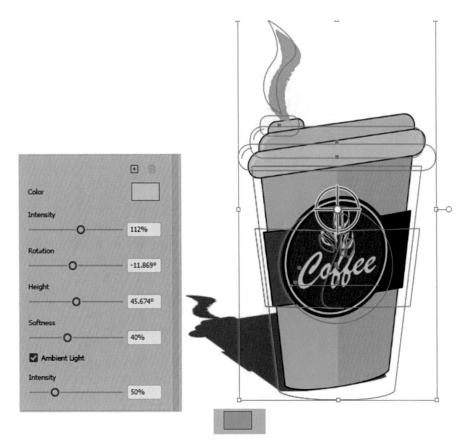

Figure 5-32. *3D and Materials Panel Plane (Rotate) Lighting Tab setting and set new color preset and view the result*

Other Lighting settings include

Intensity (0%–200%): Brightness of light.

Rotation (-180,0,180°): Rotates the focus of light around object.

Height (0°–90°): Brings or moves light closer or farther away from object. This can affect shadows.

Softness (0%–100%): Determines how the light spreads and creates a fuzzy effect that can override the diffuse preset. This is more apparent after the Object is rendered.

Ambient Light: Currently enabled and controls the global setting of the intensity of the ambient light (0%–200%). Refer to Figure 5-32.

Many of these settings are more apparent when a Shadow settings toggle is enabled for the Shadows. However, Lighting may need to be adjusted as well, as you can see when the shadow is set to a position of Behind Object. Refer to Figure 5-33.

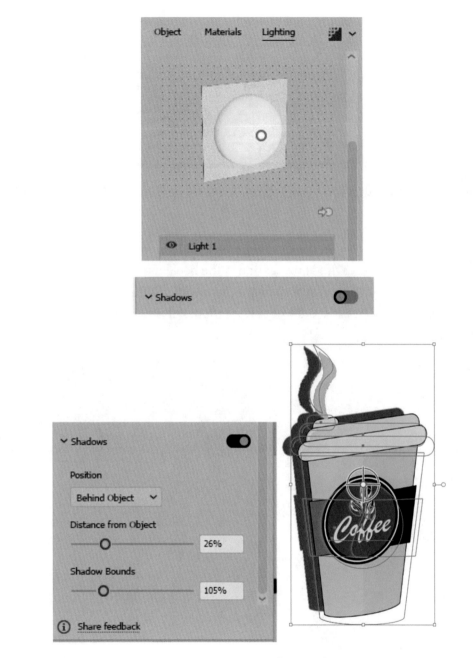

Figure 5-33. *3D and Materials Panel Plane (Rotate) Lighting Tab, Lighting Shadow settings*

This kind of shadow is a newer feature, and you do not have to use a separate Drop Shadow effect to create this shadow. Likewise, when you have multiple lighting sources, this will affect how the shadow is rendered.

Settings for the Shadows include Position where you choose a ground position of either Behind Object or Below Object. Refer to Figure 5-34.

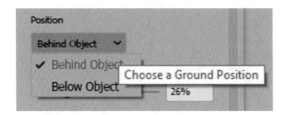

Figure 5-34. *3D and Materials Panel Plane (Rotate) Lighting Tab, Shadow set ground position*

Behind Object, while it can set the distance from Object and Shadow Bounds, you will not have access to setting with your lighting to the back of the object if it falls below the ground plane. Note that as you switch to another position or adjust light sources, the lighting widget may adjust to a different orientation. For now, stay with one lighting source. Refer to Figure 5-35.

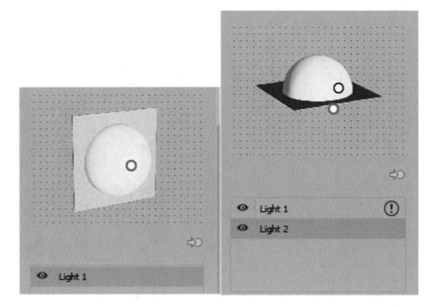

Figure 5-35. *3D and Materials Panel Plane (Rotate) Lighting Tab, plane of lighting widget adjusts based on ground position choice*

If you choose Below Object, you can move your selected light to the back of the object. You will have to adjust the distance of the shadow from Object (0%–100%) and the Shadow Bounds (10%–400%) so that the shadow does not appear chopped off, too far away, or compressed around the object. Refer to Figure 5-36.

Figure 5-36. *3D and Materials Panel Plane (Rotate) Lighting Tab, Shadow Options set distance from Object and Shadow Bounds*

In this case, I changed the rotation of the lighting to 22.758° as well so that the shadow position was below the object but behind the object as well. Note that the selected lighting source is in front of the object. Refer to Figure 5-37.

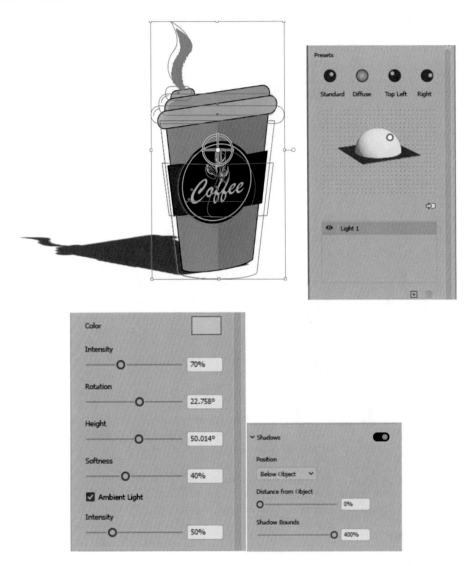

Figure 5-37. *3D and Materials Panel Plane (Rotate) Lighting Tab settings and preview*

The Render Tab

This area now allows for wireframe rendering with a wireframe mesh.

If you choose later, to render your Real-time Preview, you can use this tab to choose a Ray Tracing option. With Ray Tracing toggle active, you can set the Quality to Low, Medium, or High, and Raster settings. Raster pixelates the image.

Reduce Noise: Enabled to reduce the grainy appearance that may come from rendering.

Alternatively, with or without the Ray Tracing toggle active in Real-time Preview, you can Render as Vector the object and the map artwork which renders a resolution-independent appearance based on your document raster effects settings. Note that Render as Vector is not supported for Materials and Graphics with gradients or raster contents. Refer to Figure 5-38.

Figure 5-38. *3D and Materials Panel Plane (Rotate) Render Tab and effect on graphic*

The setting "Remember and apply to all" applies these Render settings to all existing and future 3D Material Effects.

If you want to render a graphic, then click the Render button or the square icon. It will take a few seconds to process depending on the quality setting that was used. It will then be a grouped object or path that has the setting applied; you can use Edit ➤ Undo if you need to undo that step and return to its original state before you choose to render.

In this case, we will disable the Wireframe and Ray Tracing options and remain in Real-time Preview for the rest of the chapter. Refer to Figure 5-39.

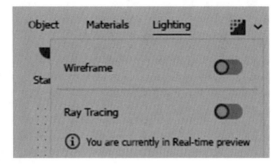

Figure 5-39. *3D and Materials Panel Plane (Rotate) Render Tab toggle off Wireframe and Ray Tracing*

Note   The effect will appear in the Appearance panel, and this effect, like the others, can be added to the Graphic Styles panel as well. Refer to Figure 5-40.

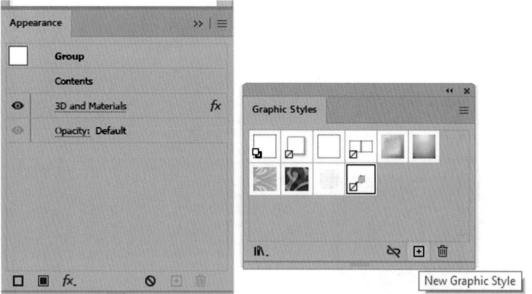

Figure 5-40. *Appearance panel with 3D and Materials effect. Effects added to New Graphic Style panel*

Materials

In the Effects panel for 3D and Materials, this setting, when chosen from the menu, will appear as a Plane Type in the 3D and Materials panel in the Object Tab with a default Rotation Preset of Front. Refer to Figure 5-41.

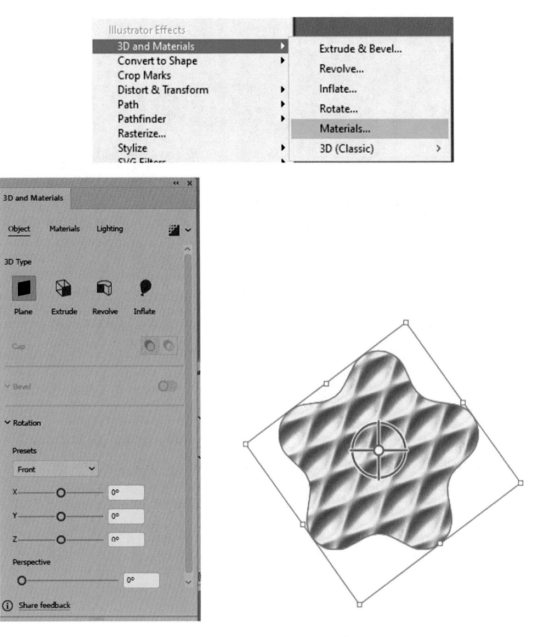

Figure 5-41. *3D and Materials Panel Plane (Material) Object found in the 3D and Materials menu*

However, you can then set the Rotation Presets for X, Y, Z axis and Perspective angle using the panel. As with the Rotation options, you can apply Materials and Graphics and Lighting and Shadow to alter the graphic as well as render. So otherwise, there are no real differences between this setting and Rotate for a Plane. Refer to Figure 5-41.

Revolve

Revolve has many of the same settings as the 3D Classic Effect Revolve, and much of what you have learned now about the Rotate Effect and the 3D and Materials panel so far can be applied to this effect as well. And you can refer back to that section if you need to review it. Refer to Figure 5-42.

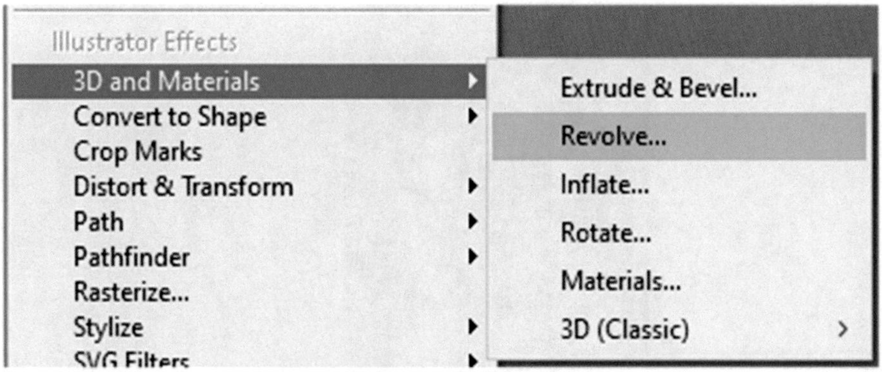

Figure 5-42. *Effect ➤ 3D and Materials ➤ Revolve*

In this case select an Open path with the Selection tool. Go to Effects ➤3D and Materials ➤ Revolve and look at the 3D and Materials panel. The path then sweeps or revolves around a point in a circular direction. Refer to Figure 5-43.

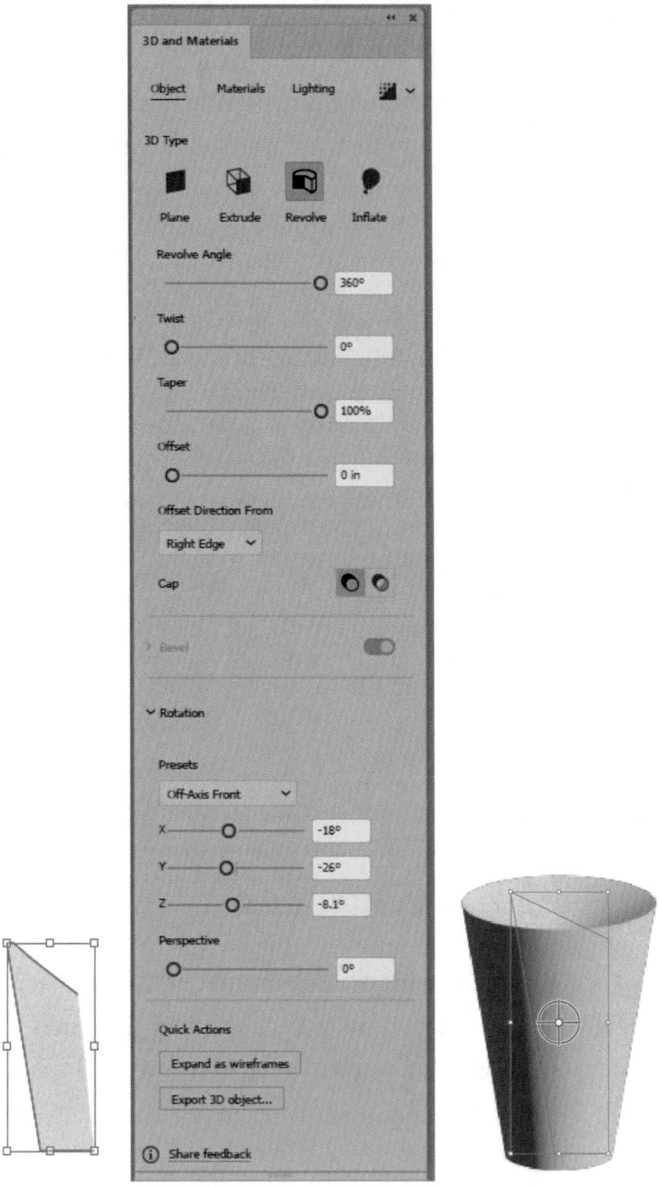

Figure 5-43. *Open path, 3D and Materials Panel Revolve Object Tab, and preview of revolve*

In the panel, you can see that many of the Panel Options are the same, so refer to the section "Rotate" for more details. I will just point out the main differences.

In the Object Tab, the 3D Type in the panel is now set to Revolve. Refer to Figure 5-44.

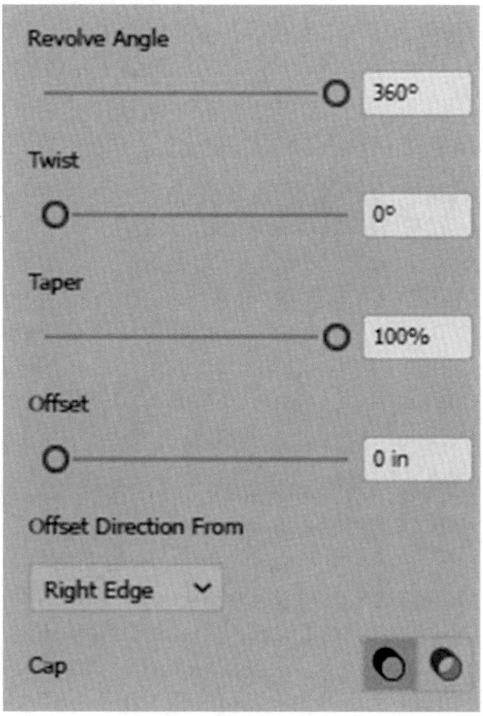

Figure 5-44. *3D and Materials Panel Revolve Object Tab and Revolve settings*

You now have access to the Revolve angle, which determines how much of a revolution occurs or if it is segmented and stops at a certain point. By default, it is set to 360° for a full rotation, but you can set it from 0° to 360°. Refer to Figure 5-45.

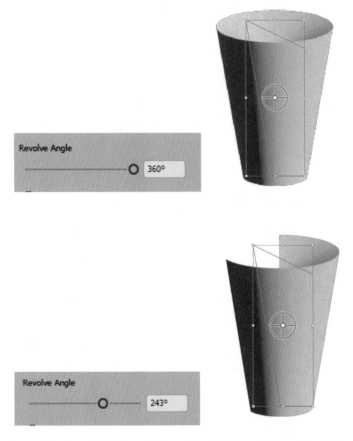

Figure 5-45. *3D and Materials Panel Revolve Object Tab with different Revolve angles*

Twist can be set from 0° to 360°. This can make a shape appear mangled and distorted. Leave at 0 degrees for now. Refer to Figure 5-46.

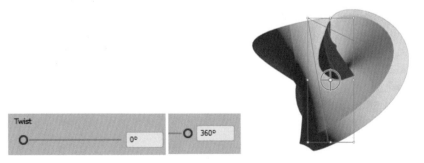

Figure 5-46. *3D and Materials Panel Revolve Object Tab with a different Twist angle*

Taper can be set from 1% to 100%. This too can affect the compression and distortion of the 3D effect. Leave at the default of 100% for an undistorted effect. Refer to Figure 5-47.

Figure 5-47. *3D and Materials Panel Revolve Object Tab with a different Taper angle*

Offset can spread out the revolve. This can make the cup appear more bowl-like. Refer to Figure 5-48.

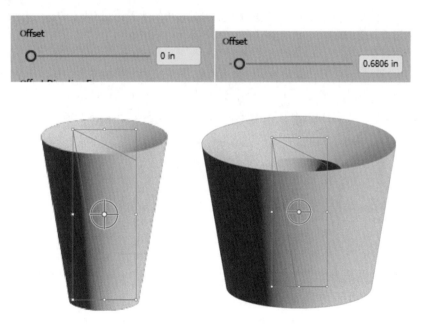

Figure 5-48. *3D and Materials Panel Revolve Object Tab with different Offset settings*

By default, the Offset is set to 0 inches, but you can move the slider to the right to increase the offset.

The Offset Direction can be set to either from Right Edge or Left Edge. I set it to Right Edge to create a cup rather than have it appear like a tent or a cone. For your own project, you will want to alter this depending on the shape you are trying to create. Refer to Figure 5-49.

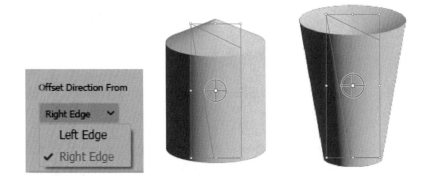

Figure 5-49. *3D and Materials Panel Revolve Object Tab with Offset Direction from settings of Left Edge and Right Edge and a preview*

Cap has two options: "Turn cap on for solid appearance" and "Turn cap off for hollow appearance." I leave the cap on by default; however, on some Objects, it may be more apparent when the cap off setting is chosen. Refer to Figure 5-50.

Figure 5-50. *3D and Materials Panel Revolve Object Tab with Cap setting on*

Note   For Revolve, Bevel is not an available option. We will be looking at that in the next section. Refer to Figure 5-51.

Figure 5-51. *3D and Materials Panel Revolve Object Tab with Bevel unavailable*

Rotation settings, as mentioned, are the same as for Rotate (Plain), and you can adjust your X, Y, and Z axis either from the panel or on the preview. You can also set your Perspective angle. Refer to Figure 5-52.

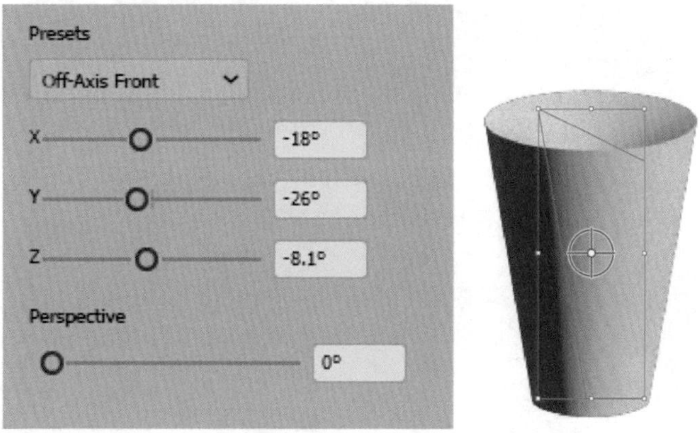

Figure 5-52. *3D and Materials Panel Revolve Object Tab with Preset settings for XYZ and Perspective and current setting for Object*

Materials Tab

In the Materials Tab, like Rotate, you have access to the Materials, Graphic Symbols, and Properties. Refer to Figure 5-53 and Figure 5-54.

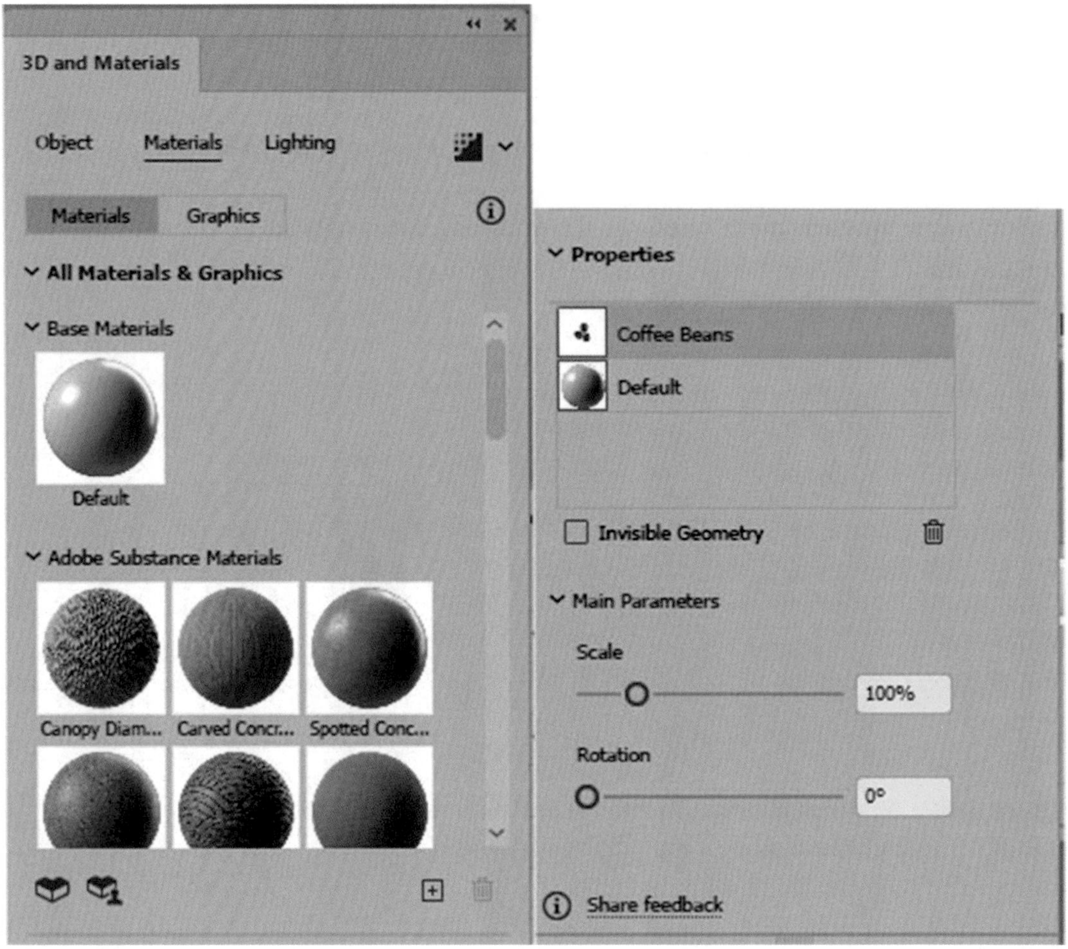

Figure 5-53. *3D and Materials Panel Revolve Materials Tab with Properties settings and a Graphic Symbol*

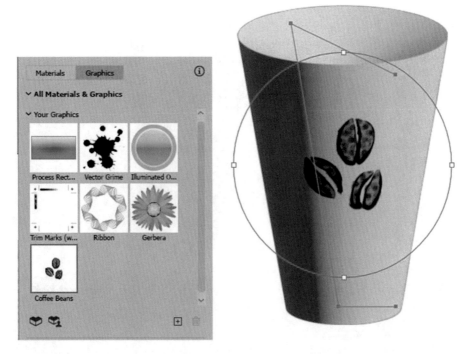

Figure 5-54. *3D and Materials Panel Revolve Materials Tab with Graphic Symbol options*

What I like about these new options for revolve, when working with Symbols, is that you can drag the symbol over one face and not have to worry if there are multiple faces to set the Graphic Symbol to; just drag the symbol to where you think it should be. Even if I add or remove stroke afterward, using my Control panel from the object, the symbol only flows over the material and the symbol is not lost or shifted. We will see an example of that later when we work on the Coffee Graph project in Chapter 6 with a complex 3D effect that requires multiple symbols. Refer to Figure 5-55.

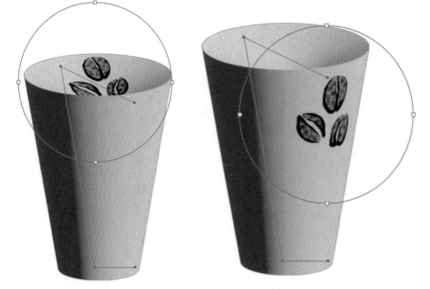

Figure 5-55. *3D and Materials Panel Revolve Materials Tab move graphic over cup*

Lighting Tab

In the Lighting area, as with Rotate (Plain), you can set the same settings. I like that with these new features, compared to classic, you can also set a shadow. Refer to Figure 5-56.

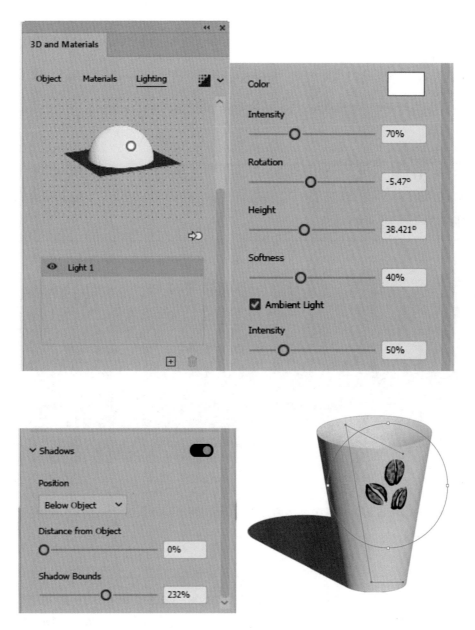

Figure 5-56. *3D and Materials Panel Revolve Lighting Tab with Shadow settings*

For details on Render setting, see the section "Rotate." Refer to Figure 5-57.

Figure 5-57. *3D and Materials Panel Revolve Render Tab*

Note   Like Rotate, this effect can be viewed and edited in the Appearance panel when selected and added to the Graphic Styles panel, which will also include the symbol. Refer to Figure 5-58.

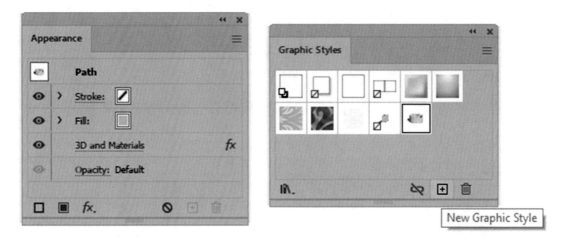

Figure 5-58. *Appearance panel with 3D effect that can be stored in Graphic Styles panel*

Note   An open shape can be revolved such as half circled to create spheres, half of a rectangle to create a cylinder, or half of a triangle to create a cone. Or you can use a combination of grouped open shapes to create a custom 3D revolve. Make sure that the Offset Direction is on the Right Edge. You can scale these shapes using the Selection tool. Refer to Figure 5-59.

Figure 5-59. *Simple shapes can be created from various open paths with a fill and no stroke*

Extrude & Bevel

Extrude & Bevel has many of the same settings as the 3D Classic Effect Extrude & Bevel, and much of what you have learned now about the Rotate Effect and the 3D and Materials panel so far can be applied to this effect as well. You can refer to those sections earlier in the chapter for more information. Refer to Figure 5-60.

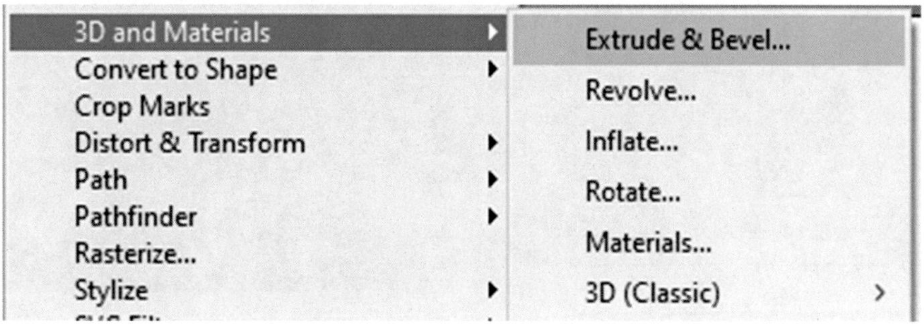

Figure 5-60. *Effect ➤ 3D and Materials ➤ Extrude & Bevel*

In this case, select a closed path with the Selection tool; it could be a shape or even some type. Go to Effects ➤ 3D and Materials ➤ Extrude & Bevel and look at the 3D and Materials panel. This extrudes the object or group objects to a certain depth. Refer to Figure 5-61.

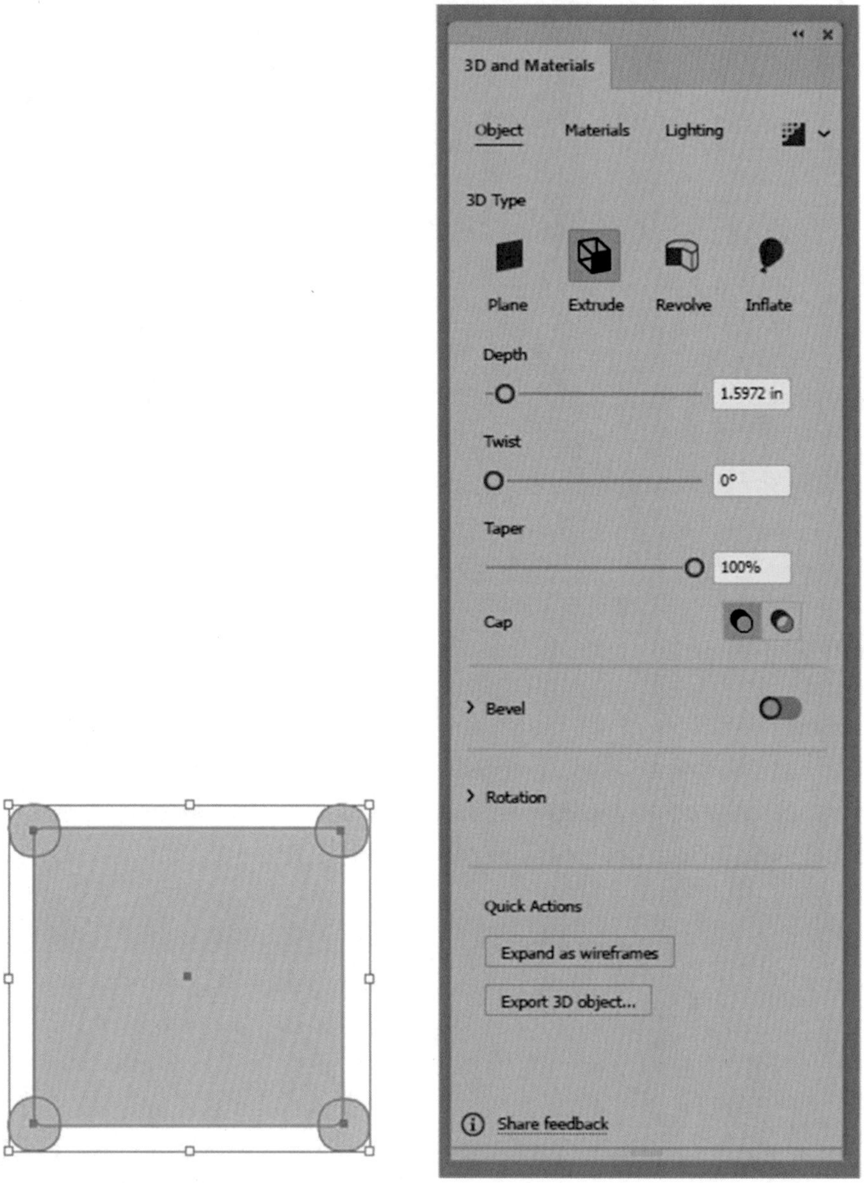

Figure 5-61. *Selected rectangle grouped shape with 3D and Materials Panel Extrude Object Tab*

In this case, the panel 3D Type will now be set to Extrude. You can set the depth of the extrusion. Refer to Figure 5-61, Figure 5-62 and Figure 5-63.

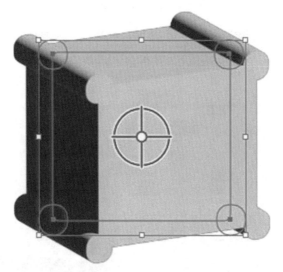

Figure 5-62. *Rectangle shape with extrusion applied*

As with the Revolve settings, you now have access to the Twist (0°–360°) and Taper (1%–100%) sliders. You can use these to distort the extrusion or give a more pointed shape, or give it a spin, or different perspective look. Adjust your rotation if you need to see this better. If you do not want to do this, then leave them in the default settings. Refer to Figure 5-63.

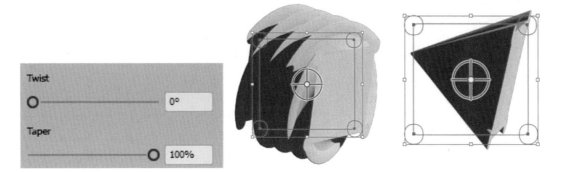

Figure 5-63. *Materials Panel Extrude Object Tab, rectangle shape with Twist of 360° and then a taper 1% applied*

Cap has two options: "Turn cap on for solid appearance" and "Turn cap off for hollow appearance." I leave the cap on by default; however, on some Objects, it may be more apparent when the cap off setting is chosen. Refer to Figure 5-64.

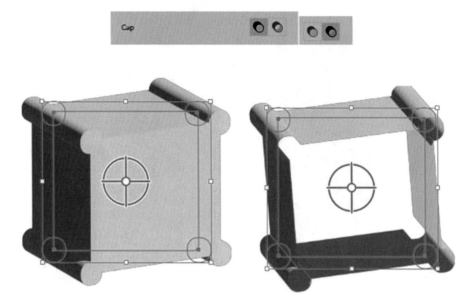

Figure 5-64. *3D and Materials Panel Extrude Object Tab with cap on and cap off*

The next section in the Object Tab in the panel is Bevel; enable the toggle to make bevel active. Refer to Figure 5-65.

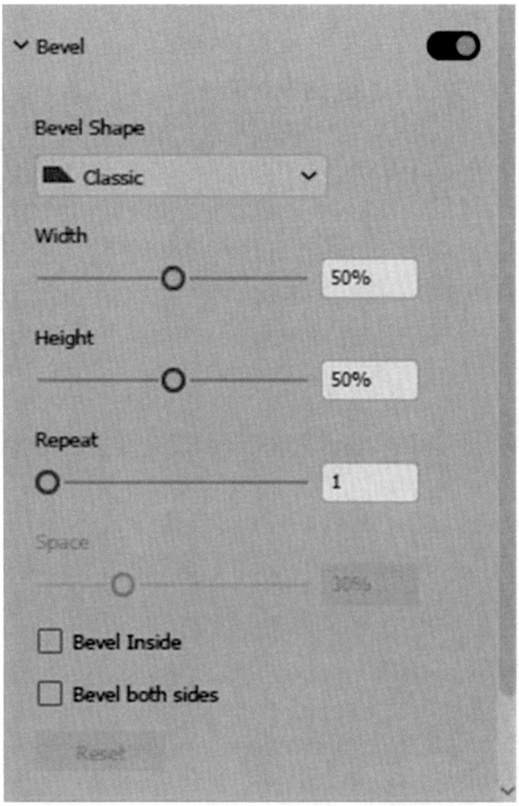

Figure 5-65. *3D and Materials Panel Extrude Object Tab with Bevel settings*

Bevel now has several updated options which affect the cap but not the extrusion depth as the Classic Extrude & Bevel Effect does. Currently, that setting is not available in this panel menu, but it would be a nice feature to have to give the body of the extrusion a more beveled effect. For now, first you can choose a bevel shape of seven options. I chose Classic from the list. This is often more apparent with graphics from the Materials Tab which are added as you did with the Revolve example. Refer to Figure 5-66.

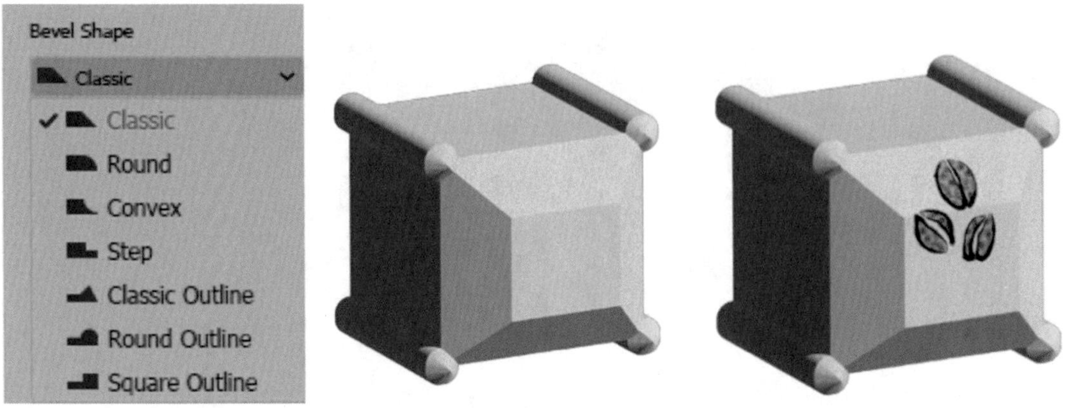

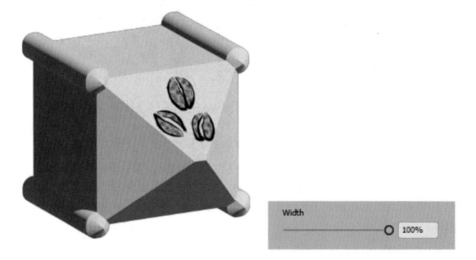

Figure 5-66. *3D and Materials Panel Extrude Object Tab with Bevel shape options*

An option is then applied along the Object's depth.

You can then make further adjustments to the bevel:

Width (0–100%): By default, it is 50%. Refer to Figure 5-67.

Figure 5-67. *3D and Materials Panel Extrude Object Tab with Bevel Width preview*

Height (0–100%): By default, it is set to 50%. Refer to Figure 5-68.

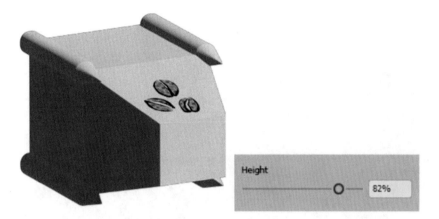

Figure 5-68. *3D and Materials Panel Extrude Object Tab with Bevel Height preview*

Repeat (1–10): Creates a type of stair step pattern. By default, it is set to 1. Refer to Figure 5-69.

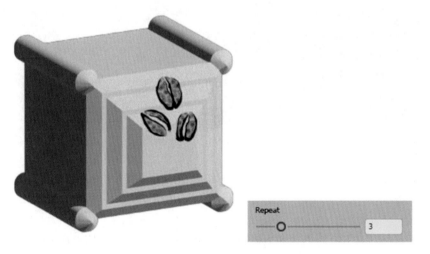

Figure 5-69. *3D and Materials Panel Extrude Object Tab with Bevel Repeat Preview*

Space (0%–100%): Is active when repeat is higher than 1. It sets the spacing of the repeat. By default, it is set to 30%, so make sure to set this before you set the repeat back to 1, or you might not see the bevel. Refer to Figure 5-70.

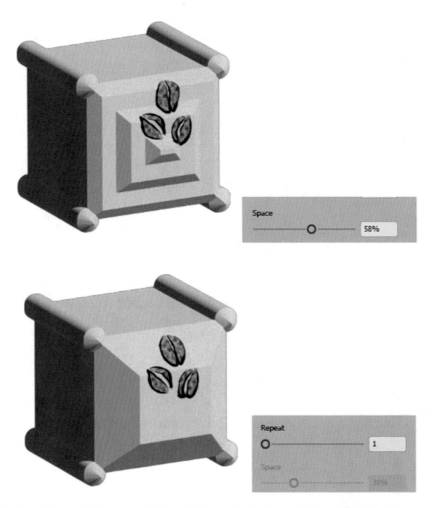

Figure 5-70. *3D and Materials Panel Extrude Object Tab with Bevel Space and Repeat options*

The next setting is Bevel Inside which makes the bevel go inward rather than outward on the end. Refer to Figure 5-71.

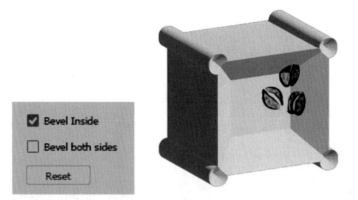

Figure 5-71. *3D and Materials Panel Extrude Object Tab with Bevel Inside option*

Next setting is Bevel both sides. It ensures that when you rotate the object, you can see the bevel on both sides, and this is good as one side might end up looking flat. Refer to Figure 5-72.

Figure 5-72. *3D and Materials Panel Extrude Object Tab with Bevel both sides options*

You can click the Reset button if you need to set the bevel setting back to the original state.

Another thing that I like about the improved bevel features was, in the past, I had difficulty creating pyramid shapes that are four or five sides with the classic setting. However, with the Improved settings, now I can choose whether to have one side beveled or not and adjust the depth and width, and this is much better. Refer to Figure 5-73.

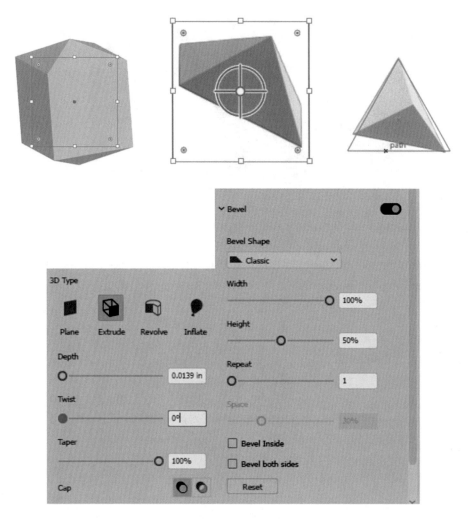

Figure 5-73. *3D and Materials Panel Extrude Object Tab with improved bevel options compared to Extrude and Bevel (Classic)*

As with Rotate, you can also set the Rotation setting presets for X, Y, and Z axis as well as the perspective which is by default 0°. Refer to Figure 5-74.

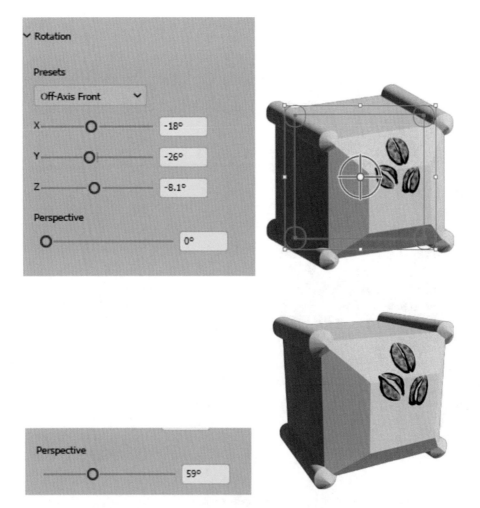

Figure 5-74. *3D and Materials Panel Extrude Object Tab Rotate and Preset options and Perspective settings*

Materials Tab

In the Materials Tab, like Rotate (Plane), you have access to the Materials, Graphic Symbols, and their Properties. You can refer to that section and the Revolve section as well for more details. I will point out that like Revolve, I like the fact that you do not have to hunt through faces to add symbols, as you do with Classic Extrude & Bevel. Just drag the symbol over the shape to the location you want it to be. Also, if you add or remove a stroke, you do not have to worry that the symbol will disappear or be covered as it rests on top of the material. Refer to Figure 5-75.

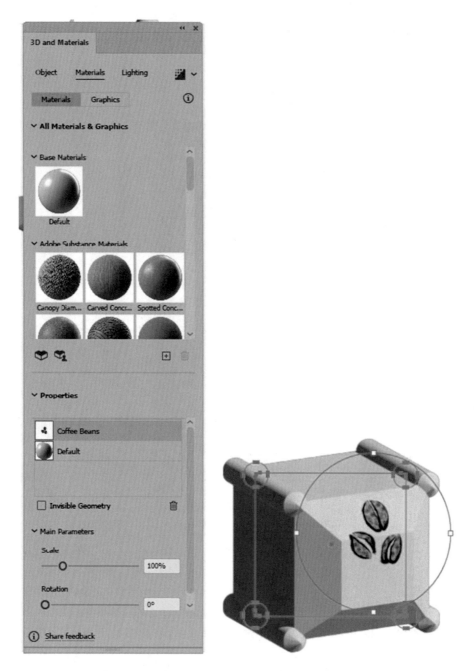

Figure 5-75. *3D and Materials Panel Extrude Materials Tab and Graphics on Object*

Lighting Tab

In the Lighting area, as with Rotate, you can set the same settings. I prefer these new features compared to classic as you can also set a shadow. Refer to Figure 5-76.

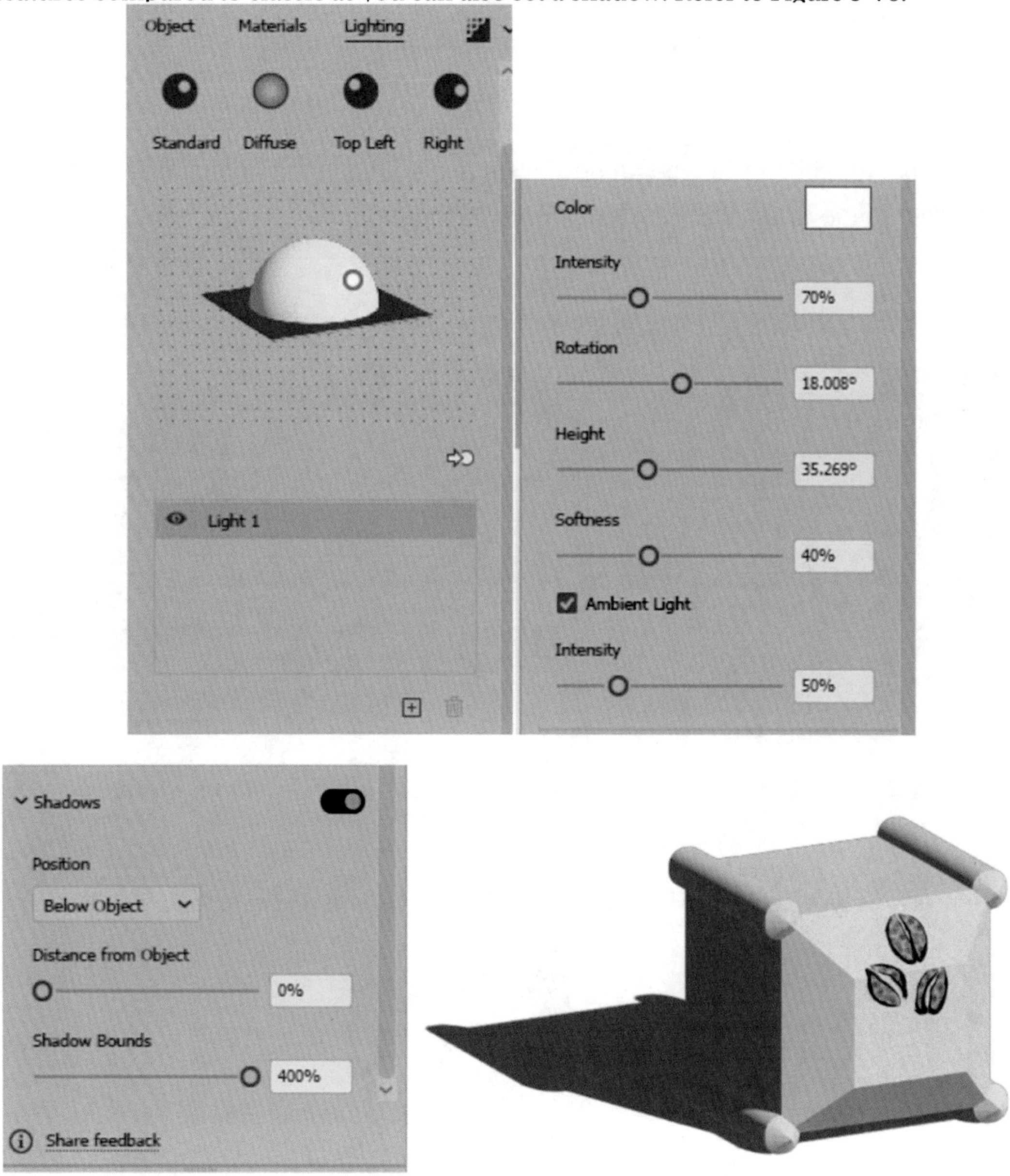

Figure 5-76. 3D and Materials Panel Extrude Lighting Tab with Shadow settings applied

For details on Render settings, see the section "Rotate." Refer to Figure 5-77.

Figure 5-77. *3D and Materials Panel for Extrude Render Tab*

Note   Like Rotate, this effect can be viewed and edited in the Appearance panel and added to the Graphic Styles panel. Refer to Figure 5-78.

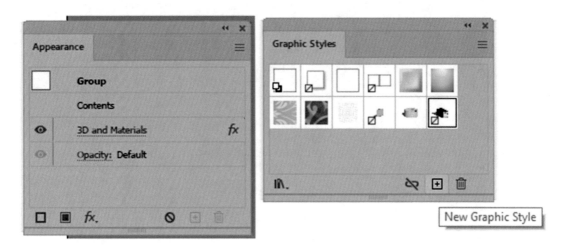

Figure 5-78. *3D effect applied in Appearance panel and added to Graphic Styles panel*

Here is how type appears when Extrude & Bevel is chosen. Refer to Figure 5-79.

Figure 5-79. *Text with 3D Extrude & Bevel effect*

We will look more at various shapes that can be extruded later in Chapter 6. But generally, shapes that you want to appear boxlike or add a tubular-like extension are best.

The gold bar, as we saw in Volume 1 in the mining poster, is a good example of an extrusion. It starts as a Trapezoid path which is extruded with a set depth and beveled slightly with a bevel on both sides. Adjusting the rotation angle also makes it appear more like a gold bar. Then, in the Materials section, use a material like Gold Natural. In this case, I left the image unrendered. Refer to Figure 5-80 and Figure 5-81.

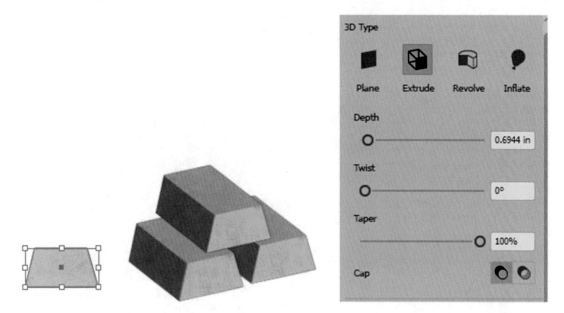

Figure 5-80. *3D and Materials panel with extruded gold bar shapes set to a new depth*

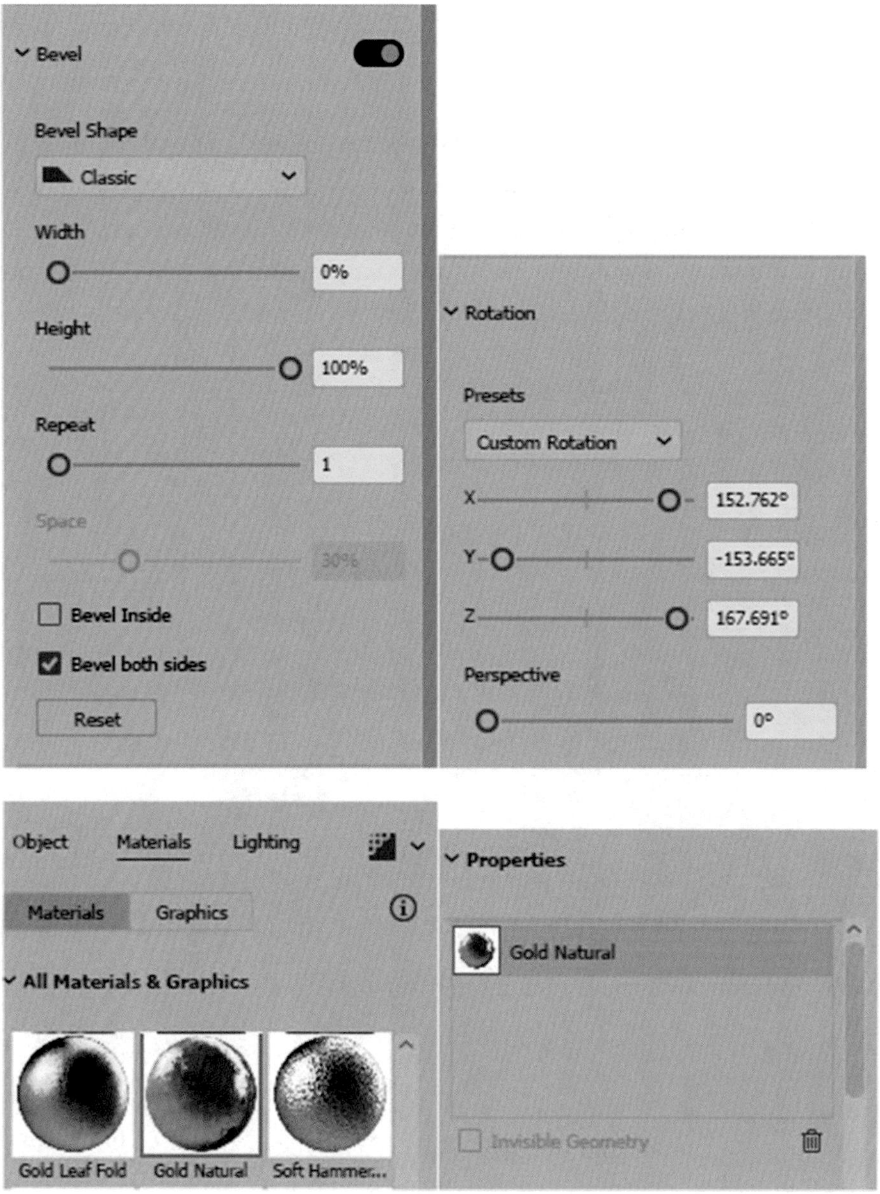

Figure 5-81. *3D and Materials panel use the Bevel, Rotation settings and the Materials Tab to add a new material to the surface of the object as seen in the Properties area*

Also, while there is a default light source, I did not add any Shadow settings, as Illustrator currently does not account for how shadows would fall over each other or how reflections would interact on separate object when placed on top of each other. Refer to Figure 5-80.

Inflate

Inflate is a newer option added to the 3D options, which is not found in the classic settings. However, it shares many of the new features of the Rotate Effect and the 3D and Materials panel, and those settings can be applied to this effect as well. You can refer to those sections for more information. Refer to Figure 5-82.

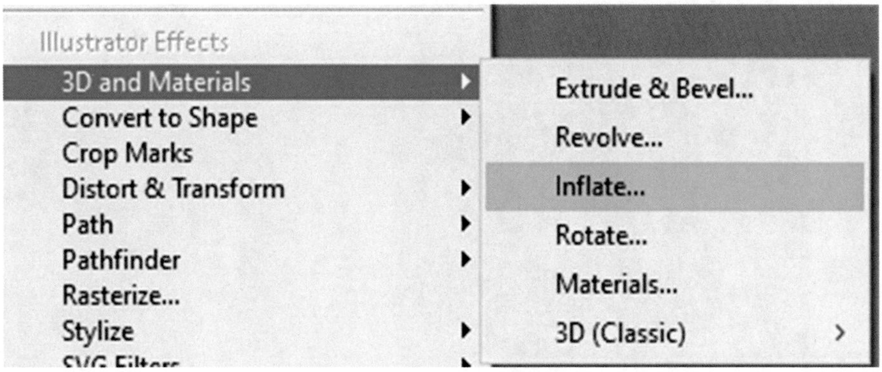

Figure 5-82. *Effect ➤ 3D and Materials ➤ Inflate*

In this case, select a closed path with the Selection tool; it could be a shape, a grouped object, or even some type. Go to Effects ➤3D and Materials ➤ Inflate and look at the 3D and Materials panel.

Much of what you have learned about the Rotate and Revolve Effects and the panel can be applied to this effect as well, so I will just point out the main differences. Refer to Figure 5-83.

Figure 5-83.   *Selected Object with Selection tool, 3D and Materials Panel Inflate Object Tab with Inflated 3D Object*

The 3D Type is now set to the Inflate setting, and the shape that is created is very much like a balloon. Refer to Figure 5-83.

In the Object Tab, you can set the Depth that will extrude the object, the Twist (0°–360°) for distortion, the Taper (1%–100%) for distortion, and Volume (0–100%) that will cause the object to expand more on the end. Currently, volume is set to the setting of 100%. This is more apparent if a graphic is added using the Materials Tab. Refer to Figure 5-84.

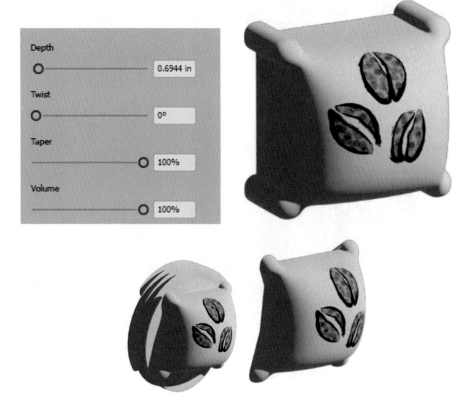

Figure 5-84. *3D and Materials Panel Inflate Object Tab with Object set to Depth and Volume settings*

Inflate Both Sides: When this check box is enabled, you can see that both sides are inflated when the object is rotated. Refer to Figure 5-85.

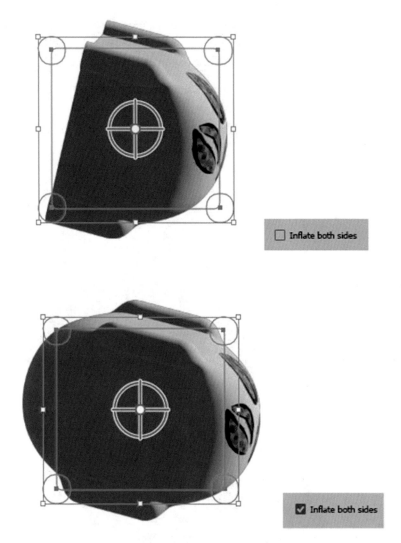

Figure 5-85. *3D and Materials Panel Inflate Object Tab with Object set to Inflate both sides disabled and enabled*

Cap has two options: "Turn cap on for solid appearance" and "Turn cap off for hollow appearance." I leave the cap on by default; however, on some Objects, it may be more apparent when the cap off setting is chosen. Refer to Figure 5-86.

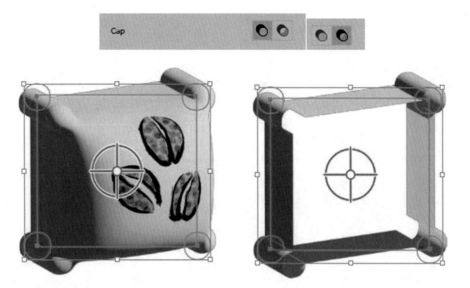

Figure 5-86. *3D and Materials Panel Inflate Object Tab with cap on and cap off preview*

Inflate has no Bevel options, but you can set the Rotation Presets for X, Y, and Z axis as well as Perspective, which is by default set to 0°. Refer to Figure 5-87.

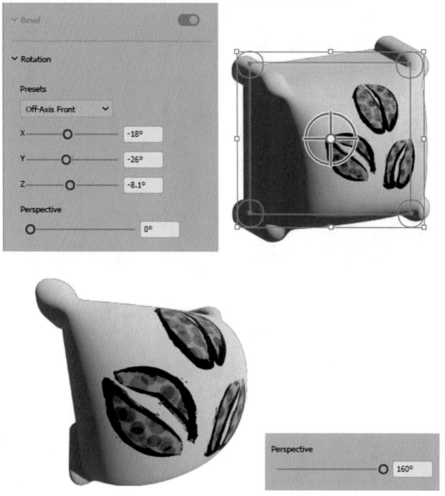

Figure 5-87. *3D and Materials Panel Inflate Object Tab with Rotation Presets and Perspective settings*

Note   Settings for the Materials, Lighting, and Render Tabs are the same, and you can refer to the Rotate, Revolve, and Extrude & Bevel selections to learn more about these tabs in the panel. Materials will allow you to overlay Symbols, and they will appear over the Material and not be hidden if you later add or remove a stroke from the object. With Inflate, you can also adjust the Shadows with your Lighting Tab. Refer to Figure 5-88.

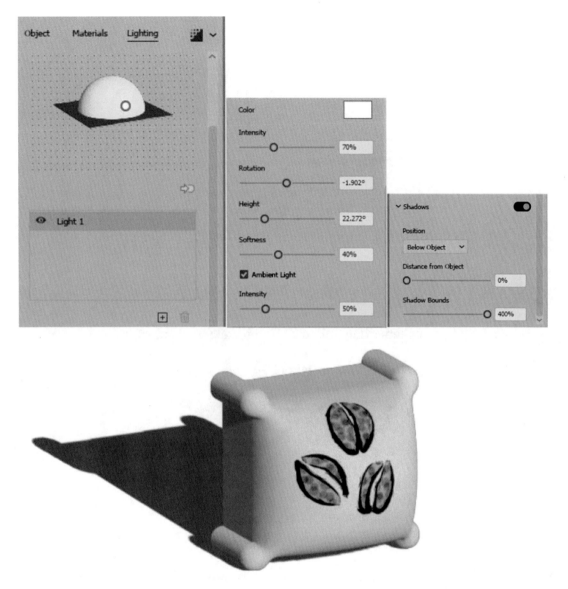

Figure 5-88. *3D and Materials Panel Inflate Tab settings for Lighting and adding shadow to object*

Like Rotate, this effect can be viewed and edited in the Appearance panel and added to the Graphic Styles panel. Refer to Figure 5-89.

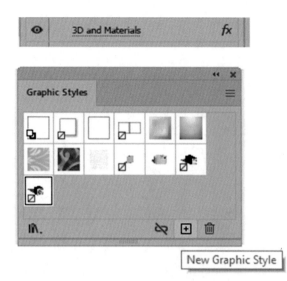

Figure 5-89. *Appearance panel with 3D Effect and added to Graphic Styles panel*

Here is how type appears when Inflate is chosen. Refer to Figure 5-90.

Figure 5-90. *Type with 3D Inflate effect applied*

Photoshop Tip for Infographic Use of 3D Files

You could then store these Objects as Symbols in Illustrator in the panel, or with an Object selected on the artboard with the Selection tool, you could Edit ➤ Copy the Object (Ctrl/CMD+C) and Edit ➤ Paste (Ctrl/CMD+V) into Photoshop as a Smart Object layer. Click OK and make sure to click the check to commit in the Photoshop Options panel. The smart object will appear on a new layer. See file 3D_Vector_Smart_Object. psd. Refer to Figure 5-91.

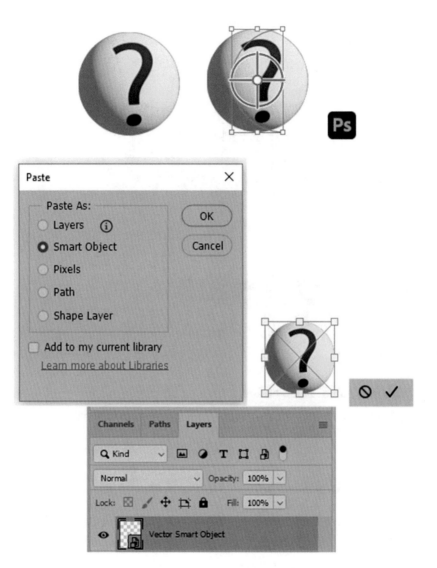

Figure 5-91. *Paste your Illustrator Graphics into Photoshop as Smart Object layers*

This is good if you need to scale your artwork or add other details using Photoshop. Use Layers menu or Layer ➤ Flatten image if at some point you need to render the entire graphic for printing if you notice any printing issues when you do a test print. I'll talk about this more about this in Chapter 6 and later in Volume 3 when I discuss using Adobe InDesign for layout.

In Illustrator, I found using a combination of two of the new 3D effects (revolve and inflate with a shadow) on separate, paths, allowed me to create a coffee cup with a plate, and you can see this example in my file coffee_cup_3D_effects.ai. Refer to Figure 5-92.

Figure 5-92. *Example of coffee cup with various 3D effects from the 3D and Materials panel applied*

To complete this design, I also added a circular ellipse with a gradient to cover the top of the cup and make it appear that there was liquid in the cup with no effects applied. Refer to Figure 5-92.

Using Quick Actions

Note in the Object Tab there is, like the Properties panel, a Quick Actions area that has two button settings, "Expand as wireframes" and "Export 3D object." Refer to Figure 5-93.

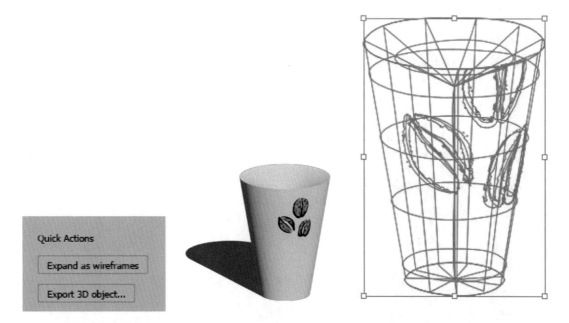

Figure 5-93. *Expand selected items as wireframes using the 3D and Materials panel's Quick Actions, resulting in grouped lines*

Expand as wireframes allows you to create a wireframe rendering of your 3D shape; it will no longer be a 3D effect, only a grouped object of lines.

Export 3D object will allow you to access the Asset Export panel, and we will look at that panel in more detail in Volume 3. 3D settings that you can export include Object (OBJ), Universal Scene Description (USDA and USDZ) the file extension (.usda) is ASCII encoded while the extension (.usdz) is a package or zip archive file and so do not end in the standard extension of (.usd), and GL Transmission Format (glTF). Various formats can be used with apps in the Adobe Substance Collection such as Substance 3D Stager which include (.usd) related files.

Note   These new 3D features, while they work best with solid color fills and strokes, can also use Pattern and Linear Gradient swatches to create material-like effects that bend over the object as you can see in these inflate examples. However, I would not recommend at this time using Radial Gradients in your designs as they can come out bitmapped. Grouped paths that already have an opacity applied to some paths may not translate the color exactly when transformed with the 3D effect, so it is generally best to stick to solid colors with 100% opacity. Also keep in mind that the more complex the pattern or group shape is, it will take longer to render. Refer to Figure 5-94.

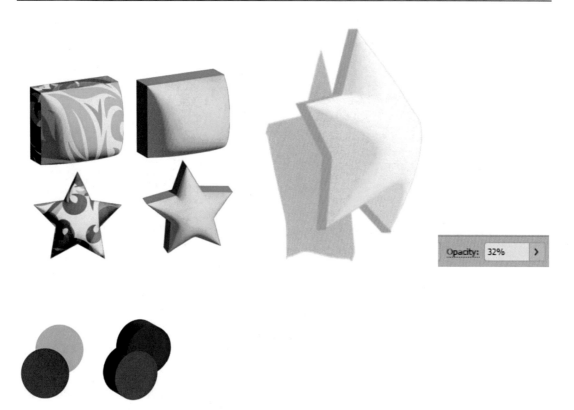

Figure 5-94. *The New and Improved 3D settings work better with Patterns and Linear Gradients on objects, and you can use Opacity from the Control panel as well; however, some opacities may not appear correctly if the 3D effect is added afterward*

Note   With 3D effects in Illustrator, when you adjust the opacity using the Control panel, it affects the object overall, and you will not see the back face. Refer to the file coffee_cup_3D_effects to see this example. Refer to Figure 5-94.

If you have not already done, so make sure that you File ➤ Save any of your work at this point.

For information on acquiring more Materials from the Substance Collection, you can visit

`https://helpx.adobe.com/illustrator/using/create-3d-graphics.`
`html?trackingid=YB1TGLWS&mv=in-product&mv2=ai`

For more information on the panel and its new improvements to revolve, shadow, and how to export 3D objects using the Asset Export Panel as OBJ, files here are some links:

`https://helpx.adobe.com/illustrator/using/create-3d-graphics.html`
`https://helpx.adobe.com/illustrator/using/whats-new/2022-3.html`
`https://helpx.adobe.com/illustrator/using/map-artwork.html`

Summary

In this chapter, we looked at the 3D and learned how to add that effect to paths and a graph to appear more 3D-like.

In the next chapter, you will create a 3D infographic project with a graph and then look briefly at the Perspective tools with their grid and how in combination with 3D items you could start to create an infographic landscape.

Creating 3D Infographic Projects and Perspective Basics

In this chapter, we will be creating an infographic project based on what you have learned in the past five chapters.

The graph tools are not just limited to the effects found in their options in the Graph Type dialog box, you can apply 3D effects to them as well. In this chapter, we will be using the 3D and Materials panel again to create our 3D graph. Then we will look at some additional 3D project ideas. Later, we will look briefly at one other advanced toolset we can use to add perspective and create a final project.

Note This chapter does contain projects that can be found in the Volume 2 Chapter 6 folder. Though not required for this chapter, you may also want to refer to the book *Perspective Warps and Distorts with Adobe Tools: Volume 2* after you have read this book as a topic of interest.

Project: Adding a 3D Effect with Symbol Overlay to Your Graph or 2D Item (Coffee Project)

Extrude and Bevel is the best 3D option to use with most column, bar, and pie graph charts as they are block or tube-like in design. Bar and column graphs are the easiest to adapt. Refer to file 3D_Coffee_Graph_Start.ai. You can File➤Save As a copy of this document if you want to follow along or refer to 3D_Coffee_Graph_Final if you just want to review the process.

© Jennifer Harder 2024
J. Harder, *Creating Infographics with Adobe Illustrator: Volume 2*,
https://doi.org/10.1007/979-8-8688-0041-2_6

Here is the example of the coffee project I began to adapt earlier. Refer to Figure 6-1.

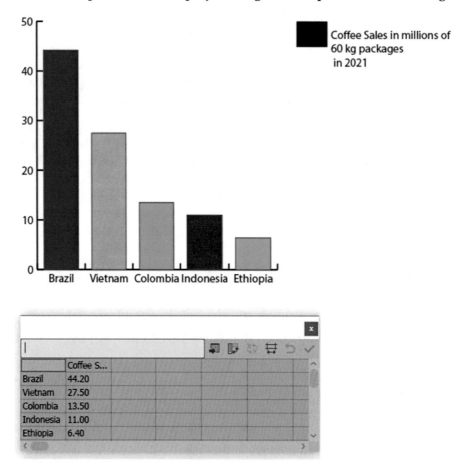

Figure 6-1. *Coffee column graph with data in the Graph Data window*

As you work with the 3D and Materials panel, you will discover that text and some colors and parts of the graph will work better with extrusion than others, and these are things to consider as you build your graph in regard to readability. Just doing a default Extrude from the current graph is not going to get you the results you want. That is why it is important to complete your data entry before you do the next steps and always save a backup copy of the original graph. Refer to Figure 6-2.

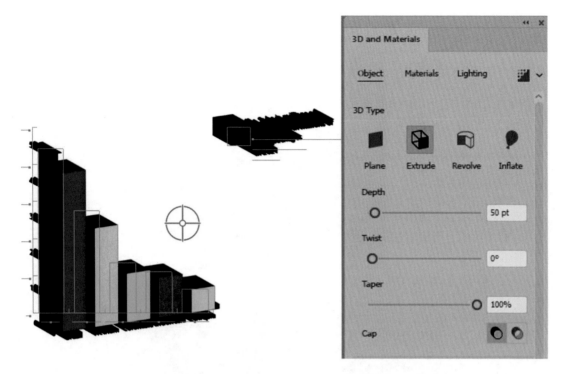

Figure 6-2. *Applying a 3D extrusion directly to a graph using the 3D and Materials panel is not a good idea*

Take a moment to go back to your original graph and remove the parts of the data that you do not want to have as part of the extrusion. In this case, we will not be needing the legend as we can always type that out to suit our needs later with the Type tool.

Also consider removing the text labels under each column category. Again, we can use the Type tool; these can still have a 3D effect, but the current extrusion is too much. The type can still have a 3D effect as you will see later.

You should reduce your graph copy with its data down to do something like this. In Illustrator for 3D effects, simple is best. Refer to Figure 6-3.

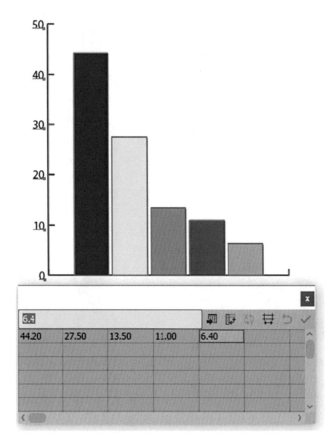

Figure 6-3. *The altered graph and Graph Data window as you prepare to make a 3D graph*

Once you have entered and saved your data, close the Graph Data window. Only your graph should be selected. You may also want to enlarge your graph at this point as well. At this point, I made a copy about 215% larger using Object➤Transform➤ Scale. The size change is optional, and each project will be different, but often a larger graph is easier to adjust in 3D. I used the scale option of Uniform and kept scale corners and scale strokes and effects unchecked. Refer to Figure 6-4.

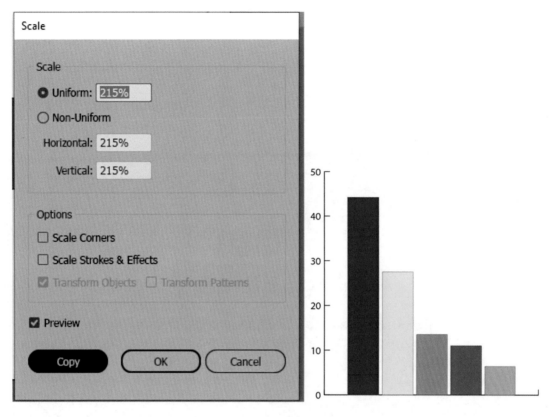

Figure 6-4. *Scale dialog box, making a copy of the graph larger so that you can make a better 3D extrusion*

Now take a moment to colorize parts of your graph columns as well as other parts of the graph so that they will later stand out as part of the extrusion. This step is tricky as you do not always know what colors will show up best. In my case, I used my Direct Selection tool to select the columns, and you will notice that I made the stroke color for them the same color as the fill as I did not want black to be part of the extrusion. Refer to Figure 6-5.

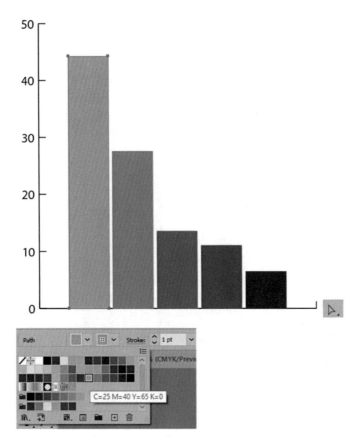

Figure 6-5. *Adjusting the colors of the column using the Direct Selection tool and the Control panel*

The following colors for the five bars that were used for stroke and fill are at 1pt:

- C=25 M=40 Y=65 K=0

- C=30 M=50 Y=75 K=10

- C=35 M=60 Y=80 K=25

- C=40 M=65 Y=90 K=35

- C=40 M=70 Y=100 K=50

Next, I then selected each of the value numbers and colored them in CMYK yellow fill. At the moment this will not turn up well, but once the extrusion is applied, it will look OK as there will be a partial shadow due to lighting effects. Refer to Figure 6-6.

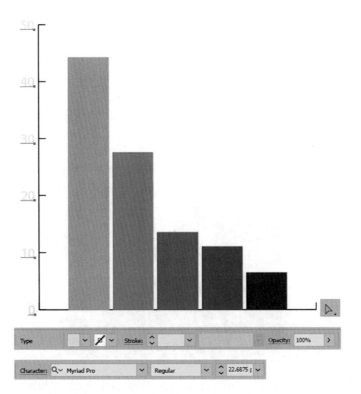

Figure 6-6. *Adjust the color of the value access number using the Direct Selection tool and the Control panel*

Then, with the Direct Selection tool, select only the horizontal line that goes below the columns and then the vertical value column (not the tick marks) and color them both orange (C=0 M=80 Y=95 K=0) stroke and increase the weight to 2pt as you want this to stand out during the extrusion. I left the tick marks at a weight of 1pt and black. Refer to Figure 6-7.

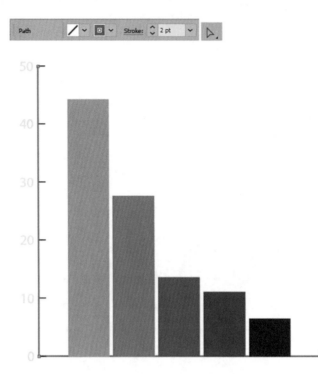

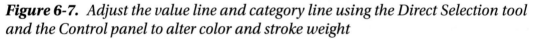

Figure 6-7. *Adjust the value line and category line using the Direct Selection tool and the Control panel to alter color and stroke weight*

Now you will be ready to create the 3D extrusion. Select the graphic with your Selection tool.

Using the 3D and Materials panel, use the 3D Type of Extrude, and for the moment, leave on the default settings to view your 3D graph. Refer to Figure 6-8.

Figure 6-8. *3D and Materials panel used to extrude the graph*

To make the graph appear more boxlike, adjust the depth slider from 50pt (0.6944 inches) to about 72pt (1 inch). Otherwise, in the Object Tab, I left the other settings at the default, including the rotation as I found this preset of Off-Axis Front the best layout so that I could see all the columns in the graph (X:-18°, Y:-26°, Z:-8.1°, Perspective: 0°). This graph also does not need any bevel, so I left that toggle inactive. Refer to Figure 6-8 and Figure 6-9.

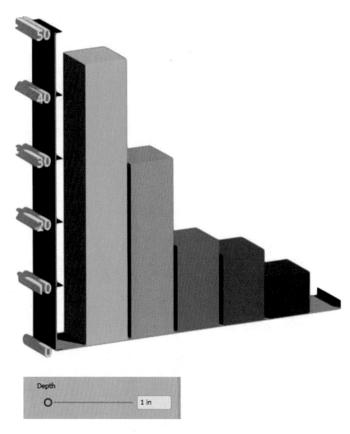

Figure 6-9. *3D and Materials panel is used to set the depth of the graph to make the columns more boxlike*

Next, before we add the materials, just check the Lighting tab. We will just leave it at the default settings with the Shadow setting turned off so that distracting shadows do not appear near the graph. Color: White, Intensity: 70%, Rotation: 145°, Height: 45°, Softness: 40%, Check Ambient Light and its Intensity: 50%. Refer to Figure 6-10.

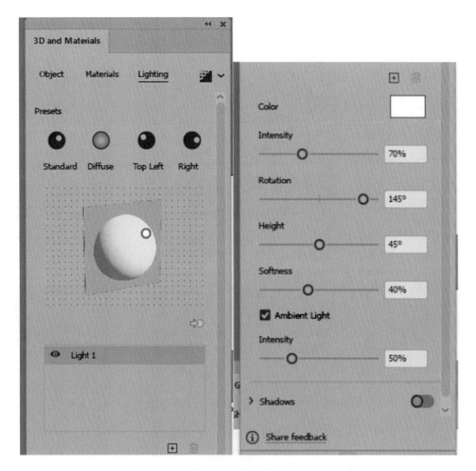

Figure 6-10. *3D and Materials panel review the Lighting tab and its default settings*

Make sure to File➤Save your work at this point.

Now you will want to add some Materials or Graph symbols to cover the columns and make them appear more boxlike, or that they contain coffee.

As I design it, I will show you how this appears on one column and then how it will appear on the other four. Remember, the graph is all one unit, so you will need to drag multiple symbols around so that they overlay and fit correctly, so this part of the project takes time to set up. The front is what is important, so we do not need to consider the back unless part of the design is visible. Go to the Materials Tab now and select the Graphics button. Refer to Figure 6-11.

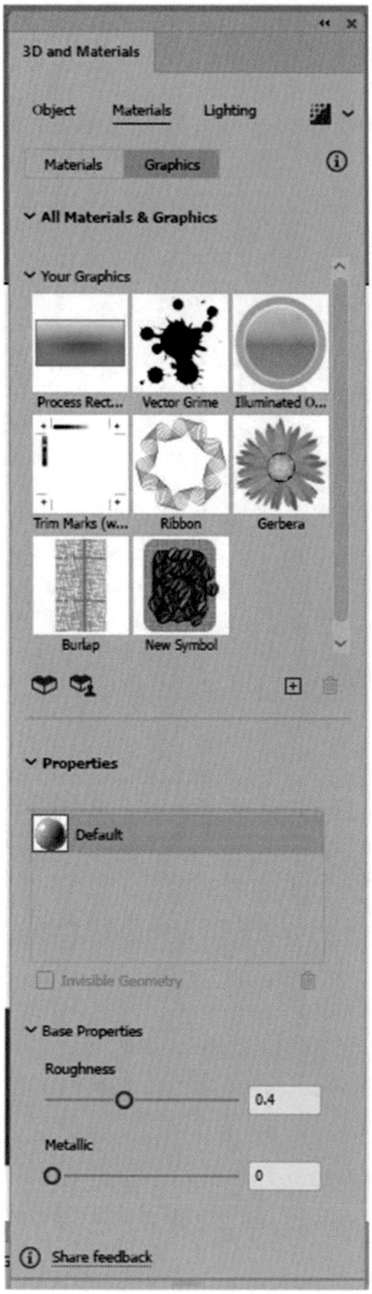

Figure 6-11. *3D and Materials panel review the Materials Tab and Graphics settings*

You will notice here and in the Symbols panel that I created two New Symbols, one for the top of my boxes and the other for the sides. After creating them on my artboard, they were selected and added to the Symbols panel when I clicked the new symbol icon [+] in the panel. The Burlap makes the boxes appear more textured, while the new symbol is some coffee beans that appear to be spilling out of the top of the bag. Refer to Volume 1 Chapter 8 if you need to review working with Symbols. Refer to Figure 6-12.

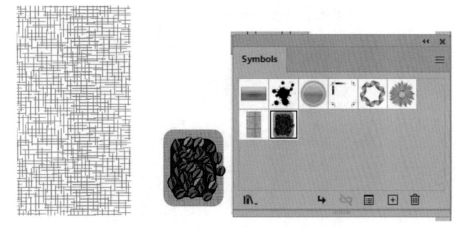

Figure 6-12. *Various symbols have been added to the Symbols panel that can be overlayed on a 3D graph*

Note   The Burlap is also saved as a pattern in the Swatches panel because it is part of the symbol. Refer to Figure 6-13.

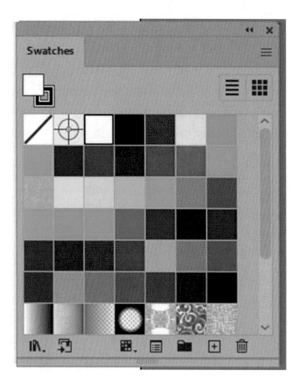

Figure 6-13. *Patterns used in Symbols are stored in the Swatches panel*

Begin with the first column on the left, and while the graph is selected, click the Burlap in the 3D and Materials panel to add it as one of the Properties; you will see it as a large circle on the graph with four square handles. This graphic will appear above your default material in the list. Refer to Figure 6-14.

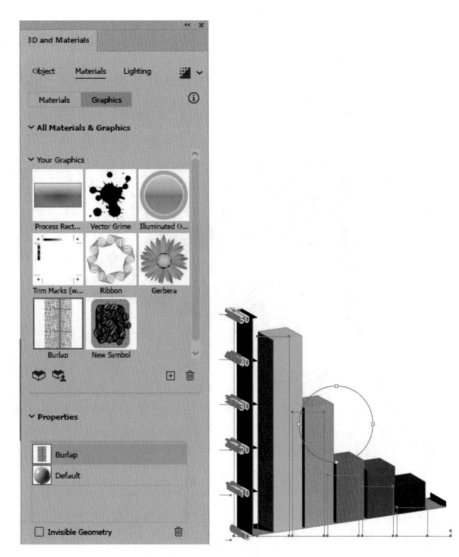

Figure 6-14. *3D and Materials panel in the Materials ➤Graphics tab and applying the first symbol to the selected graph*

Drag on the circle to move it and then scale it over the column by dragging on the handles so that the texture of that symbol covers the first column to about 276.3%. Do not rotate it. The arrow will turn to double arrows when near a bounding box handle, though you can also use the slider instead for a more accurate rotation. Rotation with handles may not show as a change in the panel. Refer to Figure 6-15.

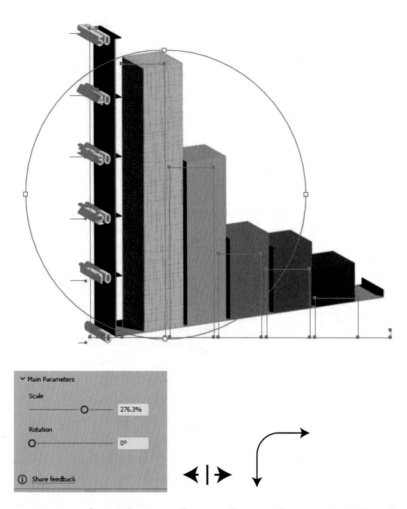

Figure 6-15. *Drag, scale, and rotate the graphic on the graph while selecting in the 3D and Materials panel Properties area or use the sliders in the Main Parameters*

Do not worry if it covers part of the top of the column as we will cover that with another symbol later. At this point, repeat those steps for the other four columns. Your scale size may vary for coverage. It's OK if your design does not look exactly like mine as this is just a texture. Refer to Figure 6-16.

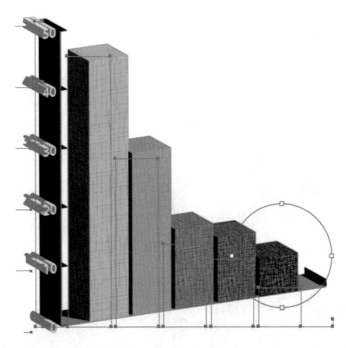

Figure 6-16. *Keep on adding more graphic burlap texture to the columns in the graph*

You should have a total of five burlap graphics in the properties. And at any point and time, if you want to adjust the scale of a specific texture, first select it in the Properties area and continue to scale it on the graph, and then select the next and make new adjustments as required. Refer to Figure 6-17.

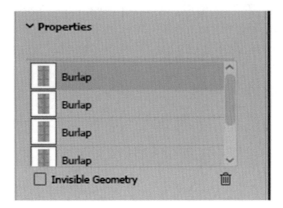

Figure 6-17. *3D and Materials panel Properties area, all newly added graphics appear in the list*

Likewise, if something does get out of order, you can drag the symbols up or down in the Properties list to keep organized. The topmost item is at the top of the list. Use Ctrl/CMD+Z to undo this if you make a mistake.

Now we need to add the new symbol of the coffee beans to the top of the boxes. Start with the column on the left. Select the graphic "New Symbol" to add it to the Properties list and add it to the Properties area of the 3D and Materials panel. Refer to Figure 6-18.

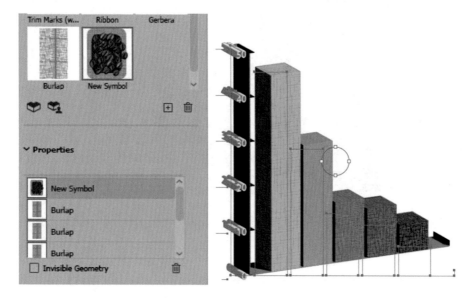

Figure 6-18. *3D and Materials panel Properties area, add another graphic so that it appears on the graph and in the Properties area*

Now drag that symbol to the top of the box and scale it to about 169.97%. If some of the pattern falls over the side, you can scale it again, but that is OK as we will cover that later. You do not need to rotate, but you can if you feel the coverage is not as you want it. Refer to Figure 6-19.

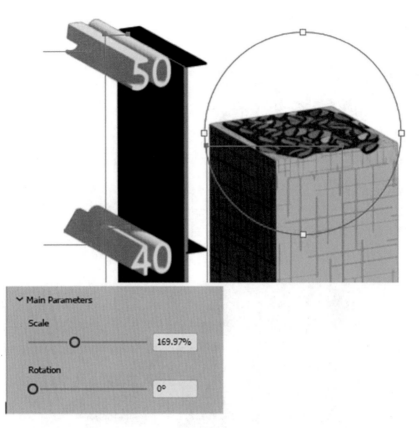

Figure 6-19. *3D and Materials panel Properties area, set the main parameters for the graph on the top of the column*

Continue to add the New Symbol to the top of the other boxes and scale as required. You will then have five new symbols in the properties. Use Ctrl/CMD++ and Ctrl/CMD +– when you need to zoom in and out to get a closer or distant look at where to move the symbols. Hold down your Hand Tool (spacebar) and drag it around on the artboard when you need to move around without disrupting the artwork. Refer to Figure 6-20.

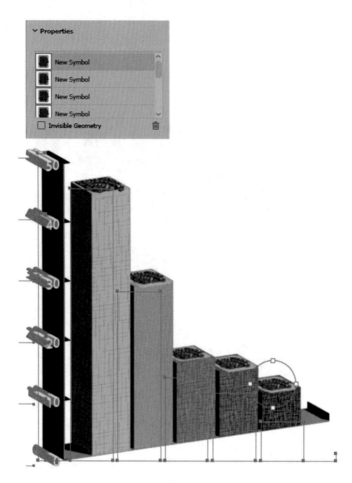

Figure 6-20. *3D and Materials panel Properties area, keep adding new symbols to the top of the columns*

File➤Save your work at this point.

On the graph itself, this is about how far you can take the design of the boxes with their Graphic Symbol covers. However, there is still more you can do to make each column appear boxlike. Refer to Figure 6-20.

You may want to do these next steps on their own layers if you are worried that you may move part of the graph by mistake. Then lock the layer that contains the graph before you continue with the project. Refer to Figure 6-21.

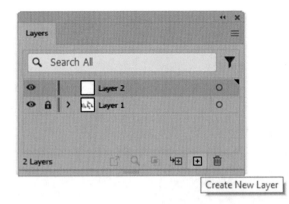

Figure 6-21. *Add a new layer using the Layers panel and lock Layer 1 so that you can continue to add more 3D items without moving the original graph*

Making the Wooden Planks

Use the Rectangle tool to make some wooden top and bottom planks for your graph on the new Layer 2. Drag one out just a little bit wider than the width column, but not too high, and make them brown color C=35 M=60 Y=80 K=25 with no stroke. Refer to Figure 6-22. Refer to 3D_Coffee_Graph_Final.ai for my exact plank sizes.

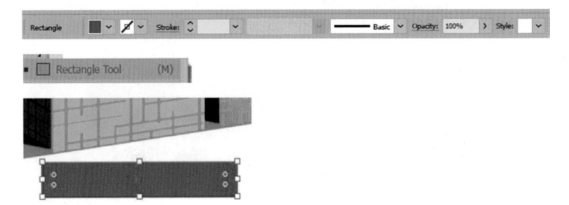

Figure 6-22. *Use the Rectangle tool and the Control panel to make wood-colored planks for the creation*

Again, use the 3D and Materials panel and set to the default Extrude which is the same as your graph settings for Depth, Bevel Off, and default Rotation of Off-Axis Front. Currently, the plank is too deep 50pt (0.6944 inches). Refer to Figure 6-23.

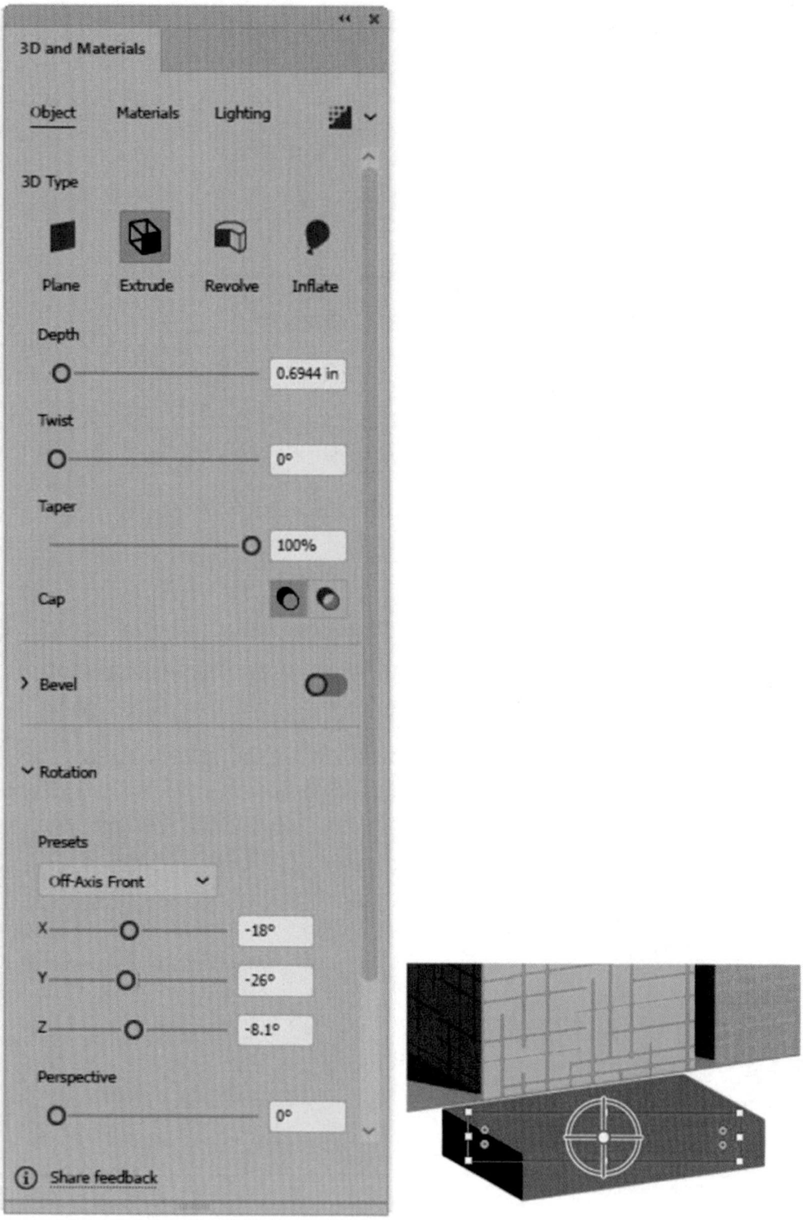

Figure 6-23. *3D and Materials panel set your rectangle to the default extrusion settings*

Set the depth very thin, such as 6.1941 pt (0.086 inches), and lay it against the base of the column to give a more wooded box appearance. Refer to Figure 6-24.

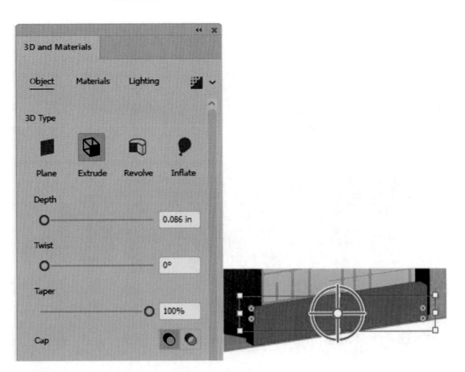

Figure 6-24. *3D and Materials panel set your rectangle's depth to a new setting*

Note   In this case, we are not adding additional Materials, or altering the Lighting or Shadow, but in your own project, you may want to experiment with this. Right now, we are keeping the design very simple.

To create additional planks at the same depth and rotation, Alt/Option+Drag more planks to cover the bases of the other columns as well. You may want to scale the width of them as they move farther into the distance. Use your Section tool to make your custom adjustments for the plank for each column. Refer to Figure 6-25.

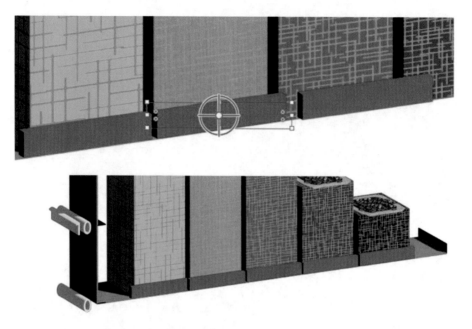

Figure 6-25. *Drag out and adjust more planks for the graph and scale them as required*

Note that as you put some planks in front of the others, some may appear out of order. Make sure, as you go along and select planks with your Selection tool, to use Object ➤Arrange ➤Send to Back or Send to Front so that the order is natural. Planks farther away in this case would be behind. Refer to Figure 6-26.

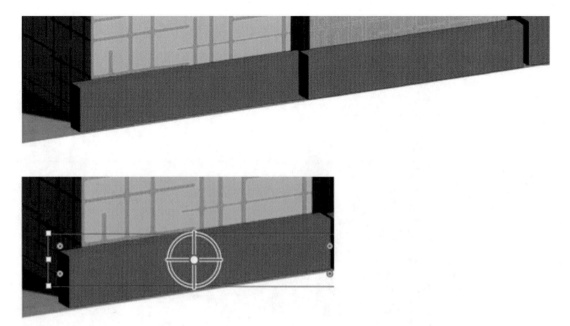

Figure 6-26. *Make sure the planks are in the correct order so that the closest are in the front*

Spend now some time to add Alt/Option+Drag more planks to the front, such as the tops of the boxes or ones in between to make it appear as if more boxes are stacked upon each other. It does not have to be uniform as some boxes will be bigger than others due to the height of the columns, but you do want them to appear as though they are slightly uniform from column to column. You may have to add more or less planks in spots to make it appear like the boxes are stacked upon one another. Refer to Figure 6-27.

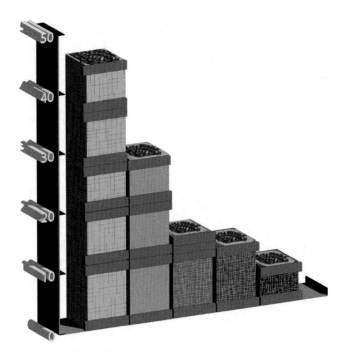

Figure 6-27. *Add more planks to make it appear like boxes are stacked on top of each other*

Next, you would need some planks on the left column box, so use Alt/Option+Drag and make a copy of one of the 3D extruded planks. Refer to Figure 6-28.

Figure 6-28. *Make a copy of a plank that you intend to rotate for the left side of the column*

In this case, a custom rotation was set. Using the symbol pattern on the side of your box may help you line up the boxes more accurately. Refer to Figure 6-29.

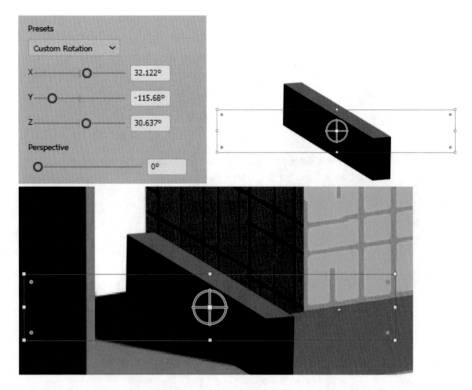

Figure 6-29. *3D and Materials panel rotate the plank and then drag to the new location on the graph*

Use Object➤Arrange ➤Send to Back so that the plank appears behind the other front plank. Refer to Figure 6-30.

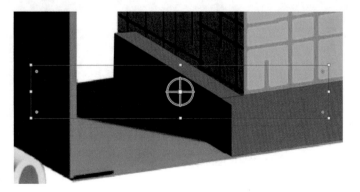

Figure 6-30. *Make sure that the plank is behind the other front plank in layer order*

You, may at this point, need to scale the plank so that it appears to go to the end of the box. Use your Selection tool to do that. However, after you scale, you may need to do a slight rotation on the X, Y, and Z axis to adjust for this. Refer to Figure 6-31.

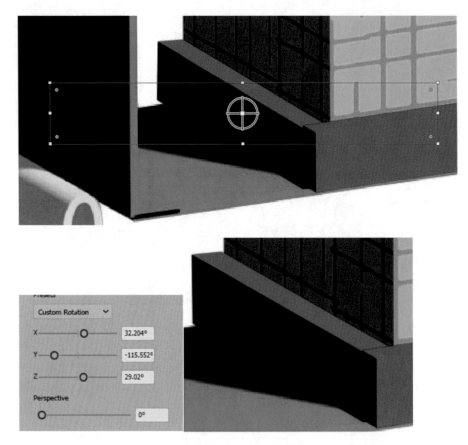

Figure 6-31. *Scale and rotate the plank further if it is not sitting as you want it to*

Don't worry if it is not perfect as it is supposed to look like wood. At this point, I used axes of X: 32.204°, Y: -115.552°, and Z: 29.02°.

Now continue to add Alt/Option+Drag more of the same planks to the left-hand side to make it appear like the planks go to the top of the column. And Object ➤Arrange➤ Send to Back as required. Refer to Figure 6-32.

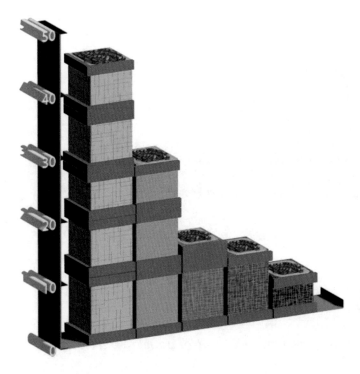

Figure 6-32. *Keep on adding planks to the left column so that it appears like completed boxes*

Make sure to zoom in with your zoom tool of Ctrl/CMD++ to get the planks to line up, and do not rush this process as you may need to move your planks up or down slightly until you are satisfied with the results.

Note that if the boxes were spaced farther apart, you could add more planks to the other left sides of the boxes. However, in this case, just use your Pen tool to make it appear as though you did add those planks to select locations. It does not have to be exact but just gives the appearance that the highlight of a plank is present in the spaces between the boxes. In this case, I used the swatch fill of C=35, M=60, Y=80, K=25. Refer to Figure 6-33.

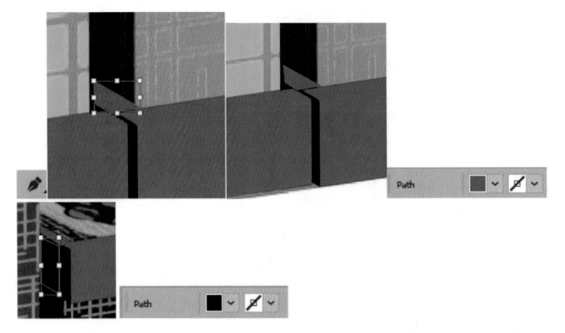

Figure 6-33. *Use the Pen tool and Control panel to make paths that appear like planks between the columns*

You may have to make several custom-shaped paths depending on how your planks fit. If required you can use Object ➤Arrange ➤Send to Back to move the custom shape to the back you need to overlap part of the front plank with your faux planks as well. In areas where darker shadows of the faux plank needs to appear on the upper left planks such as on the middle column and column on the far left, you can use the swatch color of C=50, M=70, Y=80, K=70. Refer to Figures 6-33 and 6-36.

Lastly, to finish off the plank look, make sure to use your Pen tool to add a path that appears as though there is a back and right plank as well.

However, for the top back and right planks of some of your boxes, you can use a 3D extrusion of your plank and put them on a layer behind your graph. Use your Layers panel to drag a copy of a plank onto a new layer. In this example "Layer 3". In the Layers panel, Alt/Option+Drag on the selected art target square to a new layer. Refer to Figure 6-34.

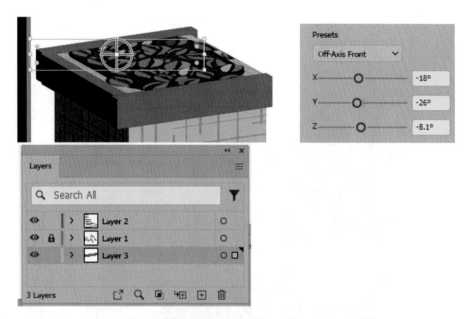

Figure 6-34. *Add another layer to the Layers panel so that you can add more planks behind and to the right of some of the columns*

You may need to scale or rotate some of your back or right-side 3D planks so that they fit. Take your time as you do this rotating on the X axis, but they don't need to be exact. Refer to Figure 6-35.

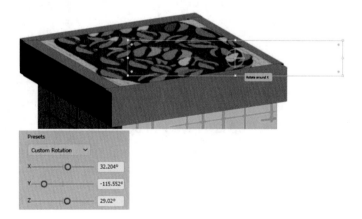

Figure 6-35. *Planks on the right may need further scaling and rotation to fit correctly*

When you have added additional planks or used your Pen tool and Control panel to add paths that appear as planks, the design so far should look something like this. Refer to Figure 6-36.

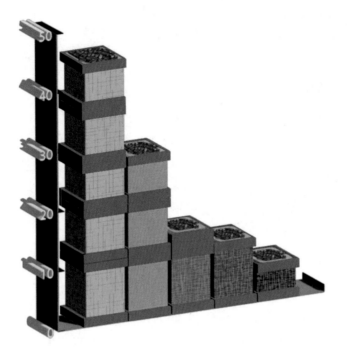

Figure 6-36. *Completed graph with all the planks added*

File ➤Save at this point and refer to my file 3D_Coffee_Graph_Final.ai if you need a reference.

Note   If some of your tick marks are slightly covered, you can, with your Pen tool, redraw those areas on the top layer with an open path and black fill. Refer to Figure 6-37.

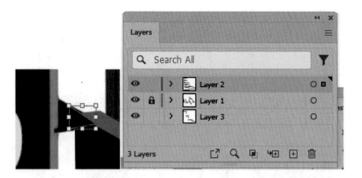

Figure 6-37. *Make some additional touch-ups to the tick marks with a new path if covered by a plank in a similar color*

Now I will show you how to alter your added text using the 3D plane in the 3D and Materials panel.

Adding Text

The next step is to add your text under each column as you displayed at the beginning of this project. Remember to refer to your original graph if you cannot remember the order that the text should be in. Refer to Figure 6-38.

Figure 6-38. *Refer to your older graph when you need to remember what the column category names were*

In this case, I used my Type tool on a new layer (Layer 4) to create all the surrounding text and added a bit more for the start of a legend as well as some text that I wanted to place above each column so that the reader knows the exact values as this can sometimes become a bit confusing if the focus is on a 3D design. Refer to Figure 6-39 and Figure 6-40.

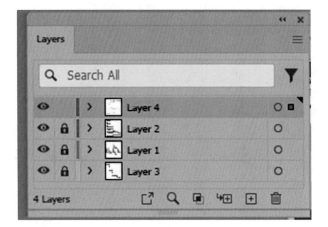

Figure 6-39. *Create a new top layer in the Layers panel for your type for the columns and the legend*

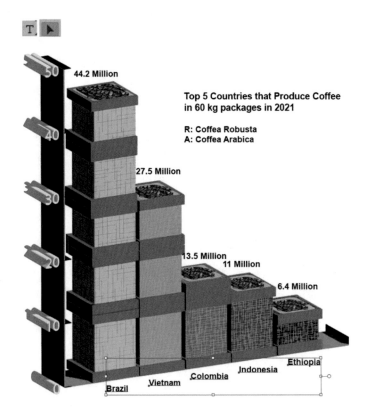

Figure 6-40. *Use the Type tool add text and select the type you plan to rotate using the Selection tool*

The text like this is OK. However, so that it matches with the 3D of the graph, Shift+click text for the graph that you would like to be part of a Plane setting and then click that icon in the 3D and Materials panel. And use the default rotation setting. Refer to Figure 6-41.

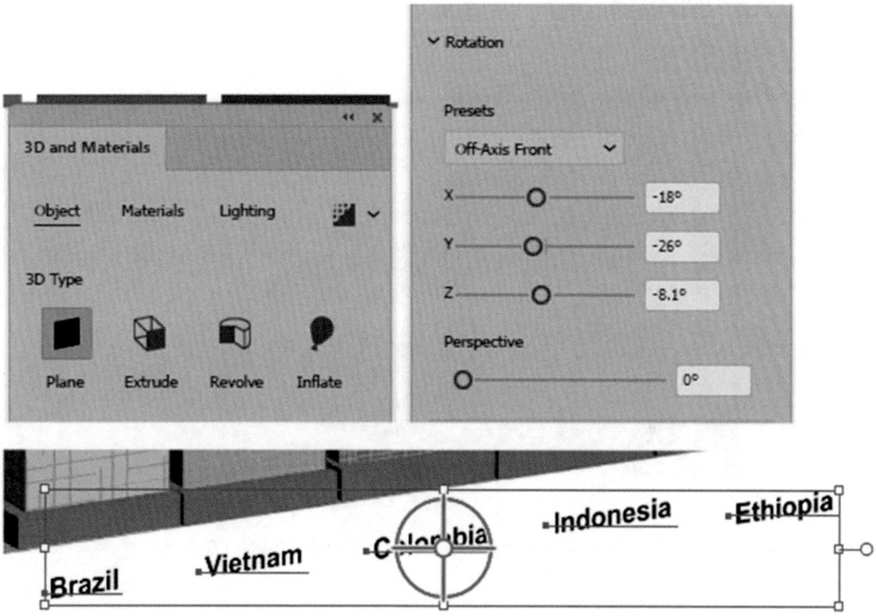

Figure 6-41. *3D and Materials panel with Plane settings and the type has a default rotation*

Continue to select other text and apply a similar rotation plane to it using the 3D and Materials panel. In this case, I did not rotate the legend. Remember to use your Selection tool afterward to move each line of text to the location you want it to be. File➤ Save your work at this point. Refer to Figure 6-42.

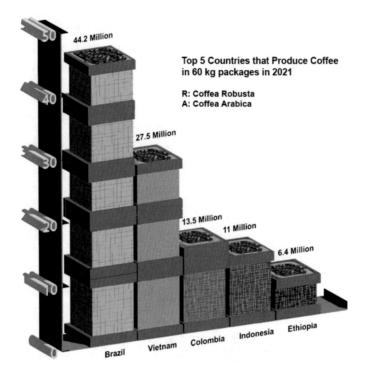

Figure 6-42. *Continue to rotate on the plane more text as required*

As you can see, there is a lot of work put into creating a custom graph design, so you should always plan it out and create your own mock-up before you begin.

Additionally, to add some further creative designs, you could enhance the legend and overlay a few more symbols on a new layer (Layer 5) and use the Selection tool to rotate to make it appear as though some of the boxes were stamped or wood burned. So, you can see that this project, when 3D is involved, can be as simple or complex as you want it to be. Note that as they become more complex, you would need a larger area to display your work. Remember to lock layers if you do not want to move an item by accident. Refer to Figure 6-43.

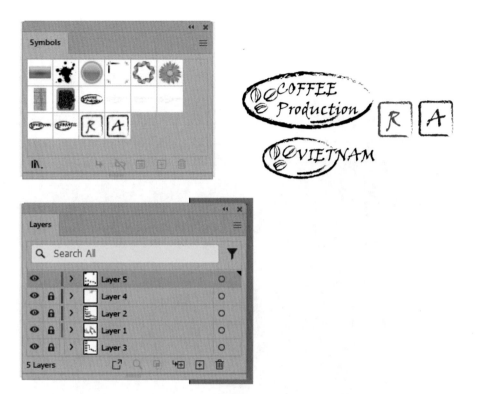

Figure 6-43. *Create more symbols and add them to your Symbols panel and create a new layer in the Layers panel to add them to*

Refer to the file 3D_Coffee_Graph_Final.ai to see the final result with its adjustments. Refer to Figure 6-44.

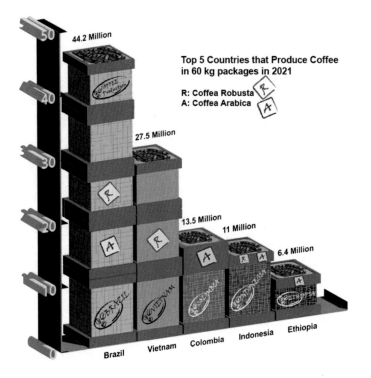

Figure 6-44. *Additional Symbols overlayed on the graph*

Optionally, you may choose to render your graphic afterward. However, if you are planning to just use it as part of a graphic design in Photoshop, you can always copy and paste the graphic into Photoshop and save it as a Smart Object layer and later flatten it for your production work. Refer to Figure 6-45 and the earlier section "Photoshop Tip for Infographic Use of 3D Files" from Chapter 5.

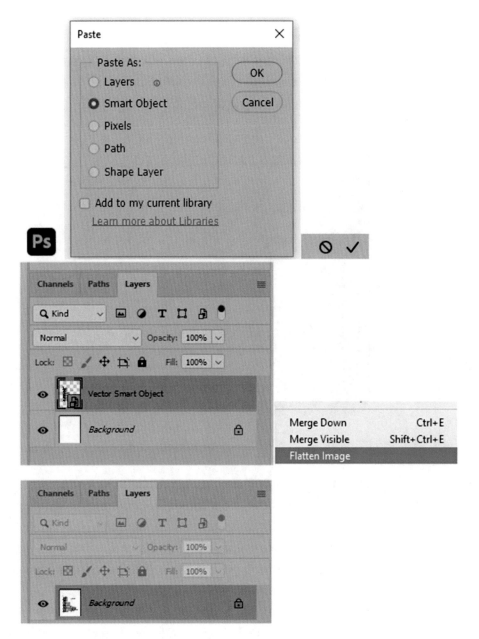

Figure 6-45. *In Photoshop, a graph copied as a Smart Object layer confirmed with the Options panel can later be flattened using the Layers panel menu so that you can use the graphic for other web or print projects*

For now, you could save this document in Photoshop as a .psd or .tif file. Later, in Volume 3, we will look at image file formats that can be used in an InDesign Layout. If for print, remember to convert the final document to Image ➤ Mode ➤ CMYK color.

Additional 3D Ideas

Reviewing what we have learned in these last six chapters and building on what we have seen so far, a column graph could be used to adapt the following:

Add a Drop Shadow effect behind a basic graph. Refer to Figure 6-46.

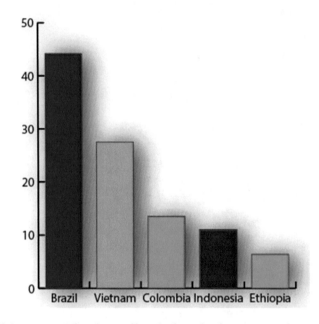

Figure 6-46. *Add a Drop Shadow effect behind a basic graph*

Try to create a similar graph like the coffee boxes but this time for finances, like a money stack extrusion, a column chart could be created. You would just need to update the color as well as the type of symbols that were used in the design. In this case, you would want to keep the graphic scale for the graphic in the Materials panel the same for all columns so that the stacked bills would appear uniform. Adding a graphic arrow that is extruded may add interest as well.

Note that for this graph, a slight rotation change was made so that the dollar bill graphic on the top was more visible and the depth was reduced. Refer to Figure 6-47.

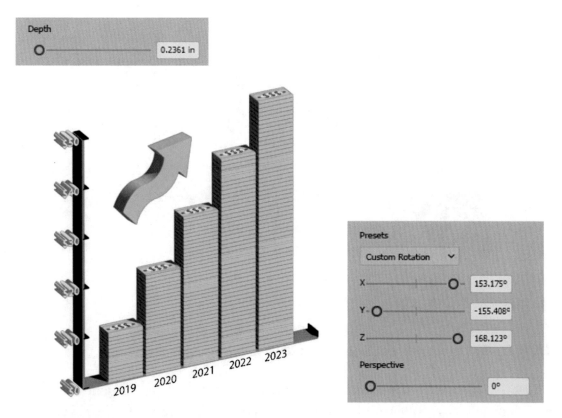

Figure 6-47. *Create a money or financial graph extrusion with custom materials, rotation, and depth settings*

Likewise, as mentioned, you could create a 3D extrusion of a pie graph as well. You could, before making the extrusion, move some of the wedges around so that they are separated if you need a more dynamic shape and then rotate as required. Materials and Graphic Symbols can be added as well. Refer to Figure 6-48.

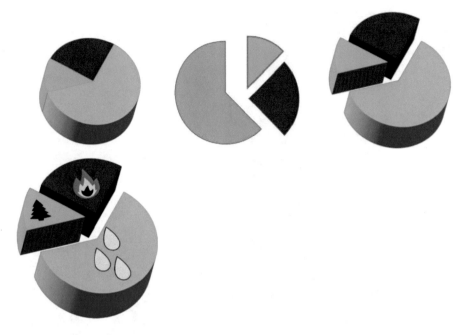

Figure 6-48. *Create an extrusion pie chart with wedges broken apart*

However, you could also enhance the basic graph shape with the Pen tool, add anchor point tool, and afterward, with 3D and Materials panel, revolve. To revolve, with the Direct Selection tool, select one column at a time and choose the 3D Type of Revolve. Refer to Figures 6-49 and 6-50.

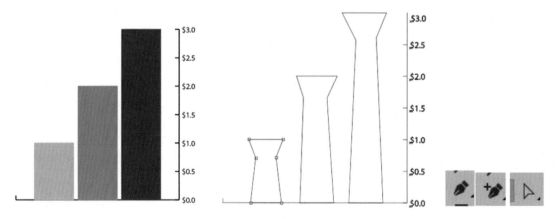

Figure 6-49. *Use a basic graph and your Pen and Direct Selection tool and add anchor point tool to alter the columns of a graph as seen here in Outline mode*

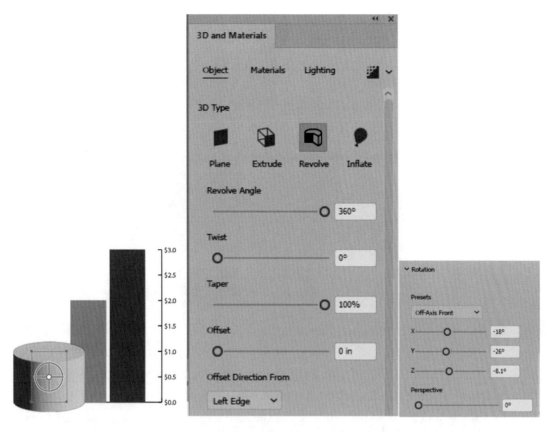

Figure 6-50. *Columns may need further adjustments after they have been selected, and an extrusion has been applied using the 3D and Materials panel*

Remember to use a copy of the original graph as your guide so that height remains intact. Note that the graph you are editing can start to ungroup and break apart from the data as you add more points or move selected columns or individual points on a path around.

Likewise, you could add extra gradient enhancements over the top to make a hole in the smoke/nuclear stack or add clouds for the smoke by overlaying additional paths, as seen earlier, as an adaptation in Chapter 3 for the 2D drawing. Refer to Figure 6-51 and Figure 6-52.

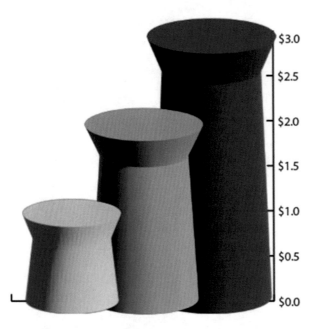

Figure 6-51. *Modified columns on the graph*

The columns in a chart could afterward be modified further to resemble cylindrical smoke stacks to represent pollution on the topic of fossil fuel or nuclear power. In this case, I kept the text and lines surrounding the stacks basic but did use a 3D plane for the numbers under the columns for the dates. Refer to Figure 6-52.

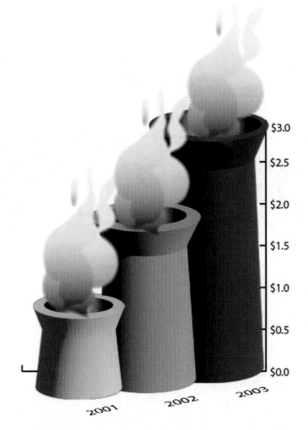

Figure 6-52. *3D Text added using the Plane settings and additional graphics added to make the columns appear more 3D-like*

I also moved and adjusted the placement of each stack using the Direct Selection tool to select a column and then nudging them up or down with the Arrow keys on my keyboard. Refer to Figure 6-52.

You would likely want to add other supplemental text around the graph for the legend to explain the value axis units further. Does it represent millions or billions?

For your own projects, consider how you could adapt 3D cylinders to resemble a test tube, medical bottles, or other beverage drinks which could overlay on the column chart to get the correct height settings.

At this point, you are likely pushing the limits of what can be done with the current graph in combination with the 3D and Materials panel to make more complex designs, like pyramid height or a more complex 3D structure. You would have to use the Pen tool or shape tool to draw a shape to overlay the graph and use Extrude to set a bevel. Refer to Figure 6-53.

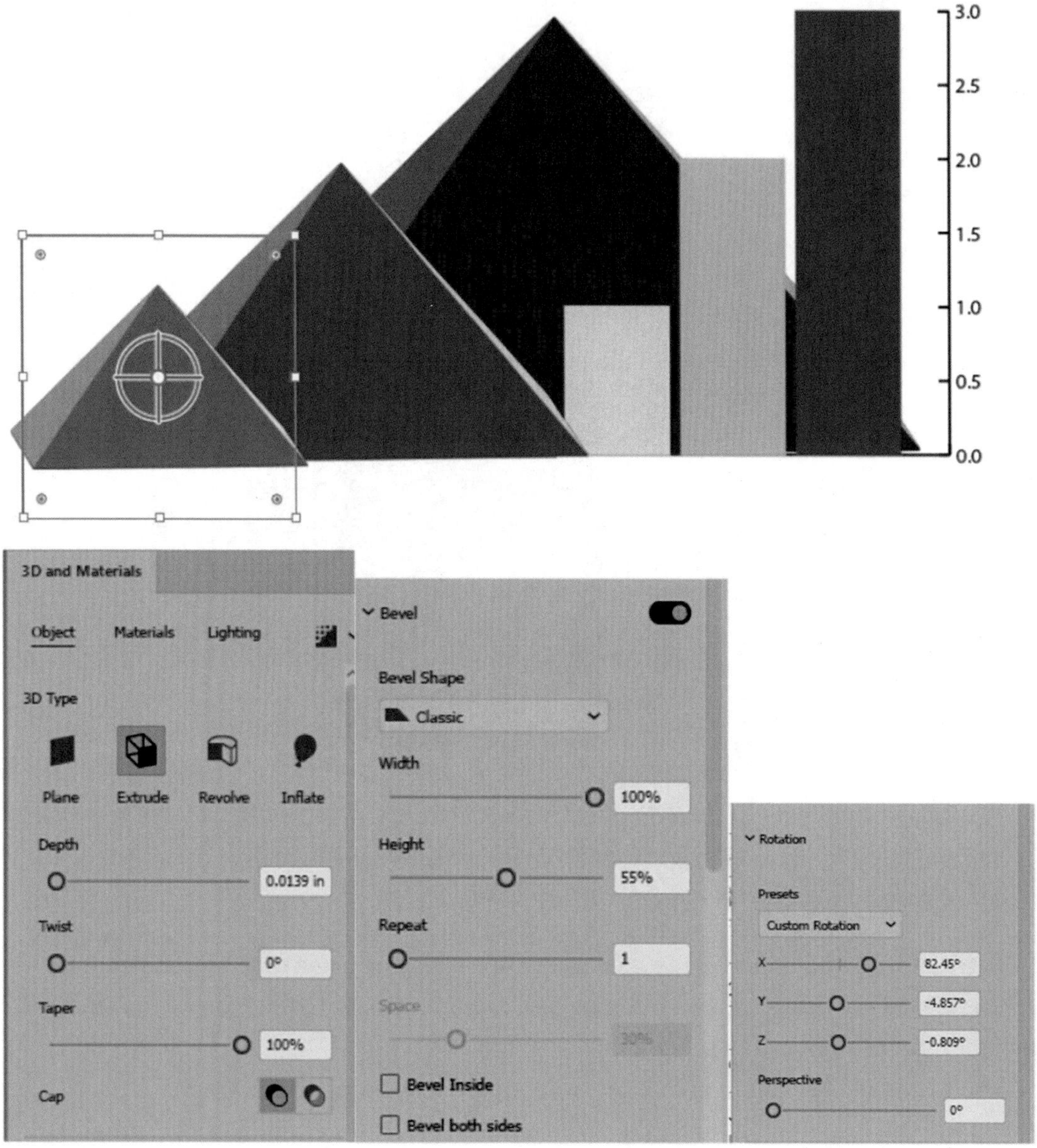

Figure 6-53. *Create your own graphics, modify them with the 3D and Materials, and overlay them over a basic graph to get the correct heights you require*

You can refer to these ideas in the file graphic_ideas2.ai.

Project Idea: Adapt Your Infographic with the Perspective Tools (Underground Soil Layers)

Keep in mind that if you are an advanced user, you may want to adapt parts of your graphic using the Perspective tools as well. Using the Perspective tools to describe soil layers underground for mining or gas and oil is easier if you can see part of the ground in a 3D-like wedge. The tools to use are the Selection tool as well as the Perspective Grid Tool (Shift+P), Perspective Selection tool (Shift+V), and your Plane switching widget. Refer to Figure 6-54.

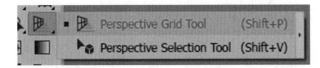

Figure 6-54. *Perspective Grid Tool, Perspective Selection tool, and Plane switching widget*

To show and hide the grid, use View ➤Perspective Grid➤ Show/Hide Grid; this submenu also has other grid viewing options. Refer to Figure 6-55.

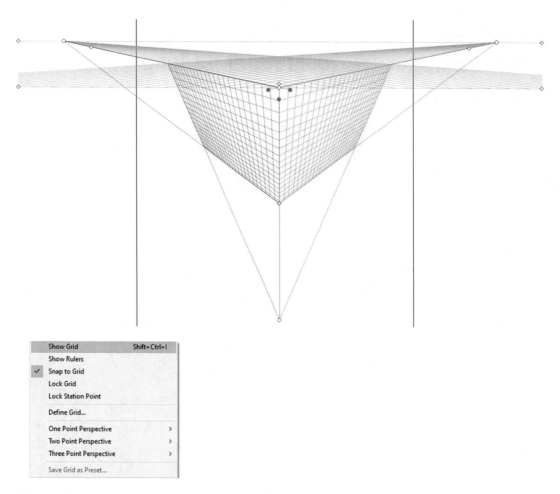

Figure 6-55. *Create your own custom Perspective Grid or use a default grid from the View➤Perspective grid menu*

While I will not be going into any detail on this complex topic, here are some pages that discuss this topic further should you want to try this in one of your own projects.

https://helpx.adobe.com/illustrator/using/perspective-drawing.html

https://helpx.adobe.com/illustrator/using/draw-and-modify-objects-perspective-grid.html

---

Note as you review these pages also refer to your Object➤ Perspective area as well.

If that topic is of interest to you, refer to my book mentioned at the beginning of the chapter.

You can use the Perspective Grid Tool to modify a custom three-point Perspective Grid by adjusting the various rulers and planes, and then you can add basic shapes or grouped paths using the Perspective Selection tool to drag, move, and scale the grouped soil paths, enhancing a landscape to give the appearance of soil layers stretching out under the horizon on the left and right grid planes. Refer to Figure 6-56.

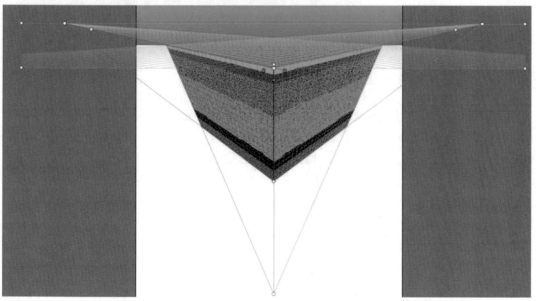

Figure 6-56. *Apply graphics to the grid*

While the grid is active, you can also draw on various planes with your shape tools as well, such as the Rectangle tool. These can be switched using the plane switching widget. Refer to Figure 6-56. I did that to create the upper green grass layer rectangle on the horizon plane. A pattern was also added to the grass using the Appearance panel as were the soil layers to give texture. You may want to add texture prior to creating the perspective. Refer to Figure 6-57.

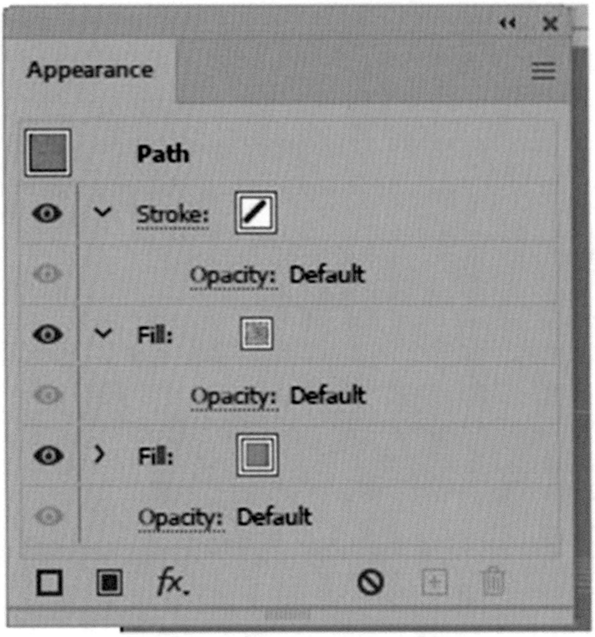

Figure 6-57. *Applied textures using the Appearance panel*

In addition, you can also add additional 3D enhancements such as a several 3D revolved half tree shapes as well as text. The text in this case was just placed on its own layer and rotated using the Selection tool as using the Perspective Selection tool to attach the text to the grid distorted the text too much. A line was also added down the center using the Line Segment tool to split the two planes so that it appeared more 3D-like. Refer to Figure 6-58 and Figure 6-59.

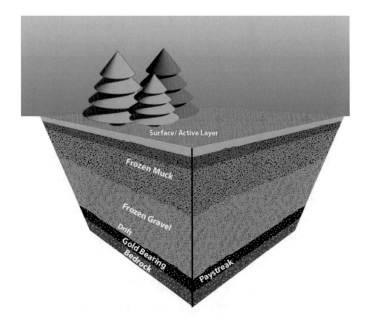

Figure 6-58. *Add text to the grid as well as overlay with 3D shapes created using paths*

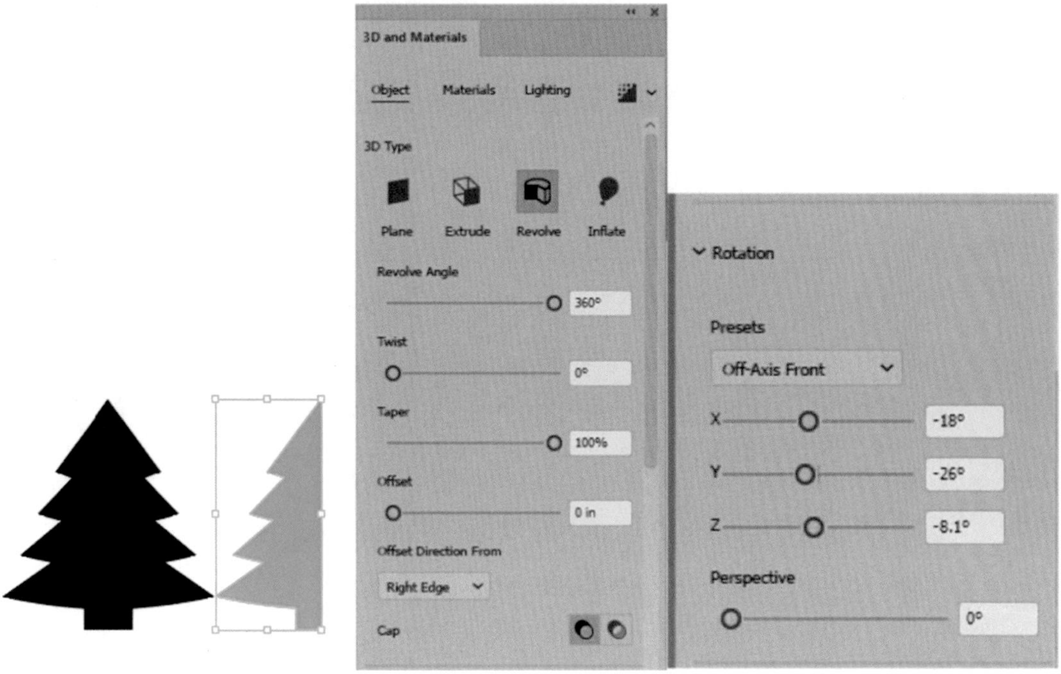

Figure 6-59. *3D shapes created using paths and the 3D and Materials panel*

You can review the file here in perspective_graphic.ai.

Make sure that you File➤Save any of your work at this point. You can File ➤Close any files you may have open and File ➤Exit any Adobe applications as this concludes our projects for this volume.

Summary

In this chapter, we looked at the 3D and Materials panel and learned how to add that effect to a graph to make it appear more 3D-like. We also looked briefly at the Perspective tools with their grid and how in combination with 3D items you could start to create an infographic landscape.

In Volume 3, we will look at how to add some basic interactivity to an infographic when it is placed on an HTML web page as well as look at how you can finalize your infographic project with your client and additional infographic ideas that could include working in Illustrator but also with other Adobe applications that are part of your Creative Cloud subscription.

Index

A

Altering graphs with symbols/designs, column/marker
add graph design to column, 128
  long-shaped symbol, Symbol libraries, 129
  Selection tool, 130
  symbols, 130
  Symbols panel to locate file, custom Symbols, 131
column design (*see* Column design, graph)
copied column path to no fill/stroke, 133
copy, smallest column, 132
create graph design
  add new design to graph design dialog box, 138
  former Rocket Symbol, 131
  graph design dialog box, 134
  Group Rocket pattern with the invisible rectangle, 132
  new design preview, Graph Design dialog box, 134
  rename new design, 135, 138
  sliding column design, 135–138
create transparent rectangle as backmost object, 132
graph design, 128
graph marker (*see* Graph marker)
recycle/extract graph design
  paste design, 160

store markers, create Artboard/Symbols panel, 159
Appearance panel, 187, 188, 199
Area graph, 37–39

B

Bar and column graphs, 281
Bar graph
  comparison of things, 29
  item colors, 29
  positive/negative number values, 29
  3D shape, 30
  Transpose row/column, 30, 31
  use case, 31
Bottom Axis
  prefix, 88
  scatter graphs, 86–88
Brick Offset, 120
Burlap, 293

C

Category Axis
  commit changes, 90, 91
  File ➤ Save, 91
  Graph Type Dialog box, 89
  Tick Marks
    Draw Number Tick Marks Between Labels, 90
    Draw #Tick Marks per Division, 90
    Length, 89

© Jennifer Harder 2024
J. Harder, *Creating Infographics with Adobe Illustrator: Volume 2*,
https://doi.org/10.1007/979-8-8688-0041-2

D

T, U

Transparency
      panel, 195, 198

V

Value Axis
   controls data numbers, 78

settings
   Add Labels, 82
   Tick Marks, 81, 82
   Tick Values, 79, 80

W, X, Y, Z

Wireframe rendering, 234

Printed in the United States
by Baker & Taylor Publisher Services